1914 – The Fail Watchtower Prophecy

INVESTIGATING
JEHOVAH'S WITNESSES

Why 1914 Is Important to Jehovah's Witnesses

Edward D. Andrews

INVESTIGATING JEHOVAH'S WITNESSES

Why 1914 Is Important to Jehovah's Witnesses

Edward D. Andrews

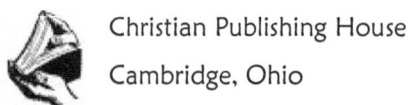

Christian Publishing House
Cambridge, Ohio

Copyright © 2017 Christian Publishing House

All rights reserved. Except for brief quotations in articles, other publications, book reviews, and blogs, no part of this book may be reproduced in any manner without prior written permission from the publishers. For information, write, support@christianpublishers.org

Unless otherwise indicated, Scripture quotations are from the Updated American Standard Version of the Holy Scriptures, 2016 edition (UASV).

INVESTIGATING JEHOVAH'S WITNESSES: Why 1914 Is Important to Jehovah's Witnesses

Authored by Edward D. Andrews

ISBN-13: **978-1-945757-51-8**

ISBN-10: **1-945757-51-5**

PREFACE This Writer's Intentions 5

INTRODUCTION Overview of Jehovah's Witnesses 7

CHAPTER 1 "The End of Gentile Times" (607 B.C.E. – 1914 C.E.) .15

CHAPTER 2 Then the End Will Come 51

CHAPTER 3 Correctly Understanding Bible Prophecy 68

CHAPTER 4 Correctly Understanding Signs of the End of the Age 76

CHAPTER 5 Correctly Understanding the Rapture.....................102

CHAPTER 6 Correctly Understand the Great Tribulation 117

CHAPTER 7 Correctly Understanding Armageddon 128

CHAPTER 8 Correctly Understanding the Resurrection Hope 136

CHAPTER 9 Correctly Understanding the Millennium 145

CHAPTER 10 Correctly Understanding the Final Judgment 167

CHAPTER 11 Correctly Understanding What Happens to the Unevangelized 170

CHAPTER 12 Correctly Understanding the Book of Life and Whose Names Are Written in the Book of Life?.. 171

    Bibliography...172

PREFACE This Writer's Intentions

I am a former Jehovah's Witness, who was a Bible student in the extreme and has remained so, even after my departure. Since leaving the Jehovah's Witnesses, I have gone on to get an extensive education. I have associates of Applied Science in criminal justice at Zane State, a Bachelor of Science in Religion at Liberty Baptist Theological Seminary, Masters of Arts in Biblical Studies at Temple-Baptist Seminary, and an M.Div. in Theology from Liberty Baptist Theological Seminary. I am working toward my Ph.D. in Biblical Studies. I am currently the CEO and President of Christian Publishing House, the parent company of Bible Translation Magazine and Christian Way of Life Magazine. I have authored sixteen books and coauthored, updated, and expanded three books, as well as dozens of articles.

The intention of this book is to investigate the biblical chronology behind Jehovah's Witnesses most controversial doctrinal position that Jesus began to rule invisibly from heaven in October 1914. This biblical chronology of the Witnesses hinges upon their belief that the destruction of Jerusalem by the Babylonians, which they say occurred in 607 B.C.E.[1] The Witnesses conclude that Chapter 4 of the book of Daniel prophesied a 2,520 year period that began in 607 B.C.E. and ended in 1914 C.E. They state, "Clearly, the 'seven times' and 'the appointed times of the nations' refer to the same time period."[2] (Lu 21:24) It is their position that when the Babylonians conquered Jerusalem, the Davidic line of kings was interrupted, God's throne was "trampled on by the nations" until 1914, at which time Jesus began to rule invisibly from heaven.

In chapter 1 we will take their chronology from the back of their 1984 New World Translation Reference Bible.[3] We will take the points one-by-one, seeing where they get things right, and where the interpretation breaks down.

Chronology

A. 1914 (C.E.) ends Gentile Times

- Line of Kingdom rulers interrupted, 607 B.C.E. Eze 21:25-27
- "Seven times" to pass until rule restored. Da 4:32, 16, 17

---

[1] *What Does the Bible Really Teach?*, page 216, Watchtower Bible & Tract Society. It should be noted that secular historians date the event of Jerusalem's destruction to the year of 587 B.C.E.
[2] Watchtower 06 7/15 pp. 6-7 God's Kingdom--Superior in Every Way
[3] New World Translation Reference edition 6-6A Bible Topics for Discussion ***

- Seven = 2 × 3 ½ times, or 2 × 1,260 days. Re 12:6, 14; 11:2, 3
- A day for a year. [Makes 2,520 years] Eze 4:6; Nu 14:34
- To run until Kingdom's establishment. Lu 21:24; Da 7:13, 14

In chapter 2 we will take the time to talk about this craze of Christianity, which also has been overly focusing on such terms as the "end times" or "the last days." While none of us can know the precise time of Jesus' return, how should we view the time that is remaining?

In Chapter 3 we will give the reader a correct understanding of Bible prophecy. **In Chapter 4** we will give the reader a correct understanding of the signs of the end of the age. **In Chapter 5** we will give the reader a correct understanding of the rapture. **In Chapter 6** we will give the reader a correct understanding of the great tribulation. **In Chapter 7** we will give the reader a correct understanding of Armageddon. **In Chapter 8** we will give the reader a correct understanding of the Resurrection. **In Chapter 9** we will give the reader a correct understanding of the millennium. **In Chapter 10** we will give the reader a correct understanding of the final judgment. **In Chapter 11** we will give the reader a correct understanding of what will happen to the unevangelized. **In Chapter 12** we will give the reader a correct understanding of what the book of life is, who have their name written in the book of life, and can their name be erased (removed) from the book of life.

INTRODUCTION Overview of Jehovah's Witnesses

Before beginning this section, I again will mention that I am a former Jehovah's Witness. I am not a disgruntled former Jehovah's Witness, and I do not hold any malice toward the Jehovah's Witnesses. In order to be fair to the Witnesses, I am going to introduce you to them by way of their own literature. The numbers below under Fast Facts are the current correct numbers. Any others below are from the 1990 Jehovah's Witness publication, *Mankind's Search for God*.[4] Below I am not going to indent the quoted material; you will recognize my interjections in this introduction because they will come at the end of each section, and will be within bold square brackets **[ ]**.

Fast Facts -- Worldwide

- **239** - Lands where Jehovah's Witnesses preach
- **595** - Languages in which we publish Bibles and Bible-based literature
- **111,719** - Congregations
- **8,340,000** – Jehovah's Witnesses who teach the Bible
- **19,000,000** - People who attend our meetings or conventions
- **179,000,000** - Bibles published by Jehovah's Witnesses in **116** languages
- **20,000,000,000** - Pieces of Bible-based literature published by Jehovah's Witnesses over the past ten years[5]

A Young Man in Search of God

In 1870, a zealous young man, Charles Taze Russell (1852-1916), began to ask many questions about Christendom's traditional teachings. As a youth, he worked in his father's haberdashery in the bustling industrial city of Allegheny (now part of Pittsburgh), Pennsylvania, U.S.A. His religious background was Presbyterian and Congregational. However, he was perturbed by such teachings as predestination and eternal torment in hellfire. What were his reasons for doubting these basic doctrines of some of Christendom's religions? He wrote: "A God that would use his

---

[4] Watchtower Bible and Tract Society; Unknown edition (1990)
5 http://www.jw.org/en/jehovahs-witnesses/

power to create human beings whom he foreknew and predestinated should be eternally tormented, could be neither wise, just nor loving. His standard would be lower than that of many men." Jeremiah 7:31; 19:5; 32:35; 1 John 4:8, 9.

While still in his late teens, Russell started a weekly Bible study group with other young men. They began to analyze the Bible's teachings on other subjects, such as immortality of the soul as well as Christ's ransom sacrifice and his second coming. In 1877, at the age of 25, Russell sold his share in his father's prospering business and began a full-time preaching career.

In 1878 Russell had a major disagreement with one of his collaborators, who had rejected the teaching that Christ's death could be an atonement for sinners. In his rebuttal, Russell wrote: "Christ accomplished various good things for us in his death and resurrection. He was our substitute in death; he died the just *for* the unjust—*all* were unjust. Jesus Christ by the grace of God tasted death for *every man*. . . . He became the author of eternal salvation unto all them that obey him." He continued: "To redeem is to buy back. What did Christ buy back for all men? Life. We lost it by the disobedience of the first Adam. The second Adam [Christ] bought it back with his own life."—Mark 10:45; Romans 5:7, 8; 1 John 2:2; 4:9, 10.

Always a staunch advocate of the ransom doctrine, Russell severed all ties with this former collaborator. In July 1879, Russell started to publish *Zion's Watch Tower and Herald of Christ's Presence*, known worldwide today as *The Watchtower—Announcing Jehovah's Kingdom*. In 1881 he, in association with other dedicated Christians, established a nonprofit Bible society. It was called Zion's Watch Tower Tract Society, known today as the Watch Tower Bible and Tract Society of Pennsylvania, the legal agency that acts in behalf of Jehovah's Witnesses. From the very beginning, Russell insisted that there would be no collections taken at congregation meetings nor contributions solicited through the Watch Tower publications. The people who joined Russell in deep Bible study became known simply as the Bible Students.

[This is straightforward history of the beginnings of the Jehovah's Witnesses.]

A Return to Bible Truth

As a result of their Bible study, Russell and his associates came to reject Christendom's teachings of a mysterious "Most Holy Trinity," an inherently immortal human soul, and eternal torment in hellfire. They also rejected the need for a separate seminary-trained clergy class. They wanted to return to the humble origins of Christianity, with spiritually qualified elders to lead the congregations without thought of a salary or remuneration. 1 Timothy 3:1-7; Titus 1:5-9.

In their investigation of God's Word, those Bible Students were keenly interested in the prophecies of the Christian Greek Scriptures related to "the end of the world" and to Christ's "coming." (Matthew 24:3, *KJ*) By turning to the Greek text, they discovered that Christ's "coming" was, in fact, a *"pa·rou·si'a,"* or *invisible presence.*[6] Therefore, Christ had given his disciples information about the evidence of his invisible presence in the time of the end, not a future visible coming. Along with this study, those Bible students had a keen desire to understand the Bible's chronology in relation to Christ's presence. Without understanding all the details, Russell and his associates realized that 1914 would be a crucial date in human history. Matthew 24:3-22; Luke 21:7-33, *Int.*

Russell knew that a great preaching work had to be done. He was conscious of the words of Jesus recorded by Matthew: "And this good news of the kingdom will be preached in all the inhabited earth for a witness to all the nations; and then the end will come." (Matthew 24:14; Mark 13:10) There was a sense of urgency to the activity of those Bible Students prior to 1914. They believed that their preaching activity would culminate in that year, and therefore they felt they should expend every effort to help others to know "this good news of the kingdom." Eventually, C. T. Russell's Bible sermons were being published in thousands of newspapers around the world.

[Aside from their disagreeing with the doctrinal positions of Christianity, this is the correct history.]

Tests and Changes

In 1916, at the age of 64, Charles Taze Russell died suddenly in the course of a preaching tour across the United States. Now what would happen to the Bible Students? Would they fold up as if they were followers of a mere man? How would they face the tests of World War I (1914-18), in which slaughter the United States would soon be involved?

The reaction of most of the Bible Students was typified by the words of W. E. Van Amburgh, an official of the Watch Tower Society: "This great worldwide work is not the work of one person. It is far too great for that. It is God's work and it changes not. God has used many servants in the past and He will doubtless use many in the future. Our consecration

---

[6] See further discussion of the meaning of the word *parousia* on pages 115 – 116.

is not to a man, or to a man's work, but *to do the will of God*, as He shall reveal it unto us through His Word and providential leadings. God is still at the helm." 1 Corinthians 3:3-9.

In January 1917, Joseph F. Rutherford, a lawyer and keen student of the Bible, was elected as the second president of the Watch Tower Society. He had a dynamic personality and could not be intimidated. He knew that God's Kingdom had to be preached. Mark 13:10.

[Again, the historical facts are true, but they did leave out that Rutherford, the second president of the Watchtower Bible & Tract Society, has been reported that he was an alcoholic, earning him the nickname "Booze Joe."]

Renewed Zeal and a New Name

The Watch Tower Society organized conventions in the United States in 1919 and in 1922. After the persecution of World War I in the United States, it was almost like another Pentecost for the few thousand Bible Students at that time. (Acts 2:1-4) Instead of yielding to fear of man, they took up with even more vigor the Bible call to go out and preach to the nations. In 1919 the Watch Tower Society produced a companion magazine to the *Watch Tower* called *The Golden Age*, known worldwide today as *Awake!* This has served as a powerful instrument to awaken people to the significance of the times in which we live and to build confidence in the Creator's promise of a peaceful new world.

During the 1920's and 1930's, the Bible Students gave more and more emphasis to the early Christian method of preaching—from house to house. (Acts 20:20) Each believer had the responsibility to witness to as many people as possible regarding Christ's Kingdom rule. They came to see clearly from the Bible that the great issue before mankind was that of universal sovereignty and that Jehovah God's crushing Satan and all his ruinous works on earth would settle this. (Romans 16:20; Revelation 11:17, 18) In the context of this issue, it was appreciated that the salvation of man was secondary to the vindication of God as the rightful Sovereign. Therefore, there would have to be on earth faithful witnesses willing to testify to God's purposes and supremacy. How was this need satisfied? Job 1:6-12; John 8:44; 1 John 5:19, 20.

In July 1931, the Bible Students held a convention in Columbus, Ohio, during which the thousands present adopted a resolution. In it they joyfully embraced "the name which the mouth of the Lord God has named," and they declared: "We desire to be known as and called by the name, to wit, 'Jehovah's witnesses.'" Ever since that date, Jehovah's Witnesses have become known worldwide not only for their distinctive beliefs but also for their zealous house-to-house and street ministry. Isaiah 43:10-12; Matthew 28:19, 20; Acts 1:8.

In 1935 the Witnesses came to a clearer understanding regarding the heavenly Kingdom class, who will reign with Christ, and their subjects on the earth. They already knew that the number of anointed Christians called to rule with Christ from the heavens would be only 144,000. So, what would be the hope for the rest of mankind? A government needs subjects to justify its existence. This heavenly government, the Kingdom, would also have millions of obedient subjects here on earth. These would be the "great crowd, which no man was able to number, out of all nations and tribes and peoples and tongues," who cry out: "Salvation we owe to our God [Jehovah], who is seated on the throne, and to the Lamb [Christ Jesus]." Revelation 7:4, 9, 10; 14:1-3; Romans 8:16, 17.

This understanding about the great crowd helped Jehovah's Witnesses to see that they had before them a tremendous challenge, to find and teach all those millions who were searching for the true God and who would form the "great crowd." It would involve an international educational campaign. It would require trained speakers and ministers. Schools would be needed. All of this was envisioned by the next president of the Watch Tower Society.

[Again, the history is correct, while their doctrinal positions are contrary to orthodox teachings of Christianity.]

Worldwide Search for Seekers of God

In 1931 there were under 50,000 Witnesses in fewer than 50 lands. The events of the 1930's and 1940's did not make their preaching any easier. This period saw the rise of Fascism and Nazism and the outbreak of World War II. In 1942 J. F. Rutherford died. The Watch Tower Society would need vigorous leadership in order to give further impetus to the preaching of Jehovah's Witnesses.

In 1942, at the age of 36, Nathan H. Knorr was chosen to be the third president of the Watch Tower Society. He was an energetic organizer with clear insight into the need to promote the preaching of the good news in all the world as fast as possible, even though the nations were still embroiled in World War II. As a result, he immediately put into effect a plan for a school to train missionaries, called the Watchtower Bible School of Gilead. The first hundred students, all full-time ministers, were enrolled in January 1943. They studied the Bible and related ministerial subjects intensively for nearly six months before being sent out to their assignments, mainly in foreign countries. Up to 1990, 89 classes have graduated, and thousands of ministers have gone out from Gilead to serve around the world.

In 1943 there were only 126,329 Witnesses preaching in 54 countries. In spite of atrocious opposition from Nazism, Fascism, Communism, and Catholic Action as well as from the so-called democracies during World War II, by 1946 Jehovah's Witnesses had reached a peak of over 176,000 Kingdom preachers. Forty-four years later, there were nearly four million active in over 200 lands, islands, and territories. Without a doubt, their clear identification by name and action has served to make them known worldwide. But other factors have been involved that have greatly influenced their effectiveness. Zechariah 4:6.

[More history, but it should be noted that the Jehovah's Witnesses have always taken the preaching and teaching work of Matthew 28:19-20 very serious.]

A Bible Education Organization

Jehovah's Witnesses hold weekly Bible study meetings in their Kingdom Halls that serve over 60,000 congregations throughout the earth. These meetings are not based on ritual or on emotion but on the gaining of accurate knowledge of God, his Word, and his purposes. Therefore, Jehovah's Witnesses come together three times a week to increase their understanding of the Bible and to learn how to preach and teach its message to others. Romans 12:1, 2; Philippians 1:9-11; Hebrews 10:24, 25.

For example, a midweek meeting includes the Theocratic Ministry School, in which members of the congregation may be enrolled. This school, presided over by a qualified Christian elder, serves to train men, women, and children in the art of teaching and self-expression in accordance with Bible principles. The apostle Paul stated: "Let your utterance be always with graciousness, seasoned with salt, so as to know how you ought to give an answer to each one." In their Christian meetings, the Witnesses also learn how to express the Kingdom message "with a mild temper and deep respect." Colossians 4:6; 1 Peter 3:15.

On a different day, the Witnesses also meet for a 45-minute Bible discourse followed by a one-hour congregation consideration (by means of questions and answers) of a Bible theme related to Christian teaching or conduct. Members of the congregation are free to participate. Every year the Witnesses also attend three larger meetings, assemblies and conventions of one to four days, where thousands usually gather to listen to Bible discourses. As a result of these and other free meetings, each Witness deepens his or her knowledge of God's promises for this earth and for mankind in addition to acquiring an excellent education in Christian morals. Each one is drawn closer to the true God, Jehovah, by following the teachings and example of Christ Jesus. John 6:44, 65; 17:3; 1 Peter 1:15, 16.

[More history, as well as their taking the need for each member to be a teacher of God's Word more serious than most.]

How Are the Witnesses Organized?

Logically, if Jehovah's Witnesses hold meetings and are organized to preach, they must have someone to take the lead. However, they do not have a paid clergy class nor do they have any charismatic leader on a pedestal. (Matthew 23:10) Jesus said: "You received free, give free." (Matthew 10:8; Acts 8:18-21) In each congregation, there are spiritually qualified elders and ministerial servants, many of whom have secular employment and care for a family, who voluntarily take the lead in teaching and directing the congregation. This is precisely the model set by first-century Christians. Acts 20:17; Philippians 1:1; 1 Timothy 3:1-10, 12, 13.

How are these elders and ministerial servants appointed? Their appointments are made under the supervision of a governing body of anointed elders from various lands whose function is parallel to that of the body of apostles and elders in Jerusalem who took the lead in the early Christian congregation. As we saw in Chapter 11, no one apostle had the primacy over the others. They came to their decisions as a body, and these were respected by the congregations scattered throughout the ancient Roman world. Acts 15:4-6, 22, 23, 30, 31.

The same arrangement functions for the Governing Body of Jehovah's Witnesses today. They hold weekly meetings at their world headquarters in Brooklyn, New York, and instructions are then sent from there to the Branch Committees around the world that superintend the ministerial activity in each country. By following the example of the earliest Christians, Jehovah's Witnesses have been able to cover vast portions of the earth with the preaching of the good news of God's Kingdom. That work continues on a global scale. Matthew 10:23; 1 Corinthians 15:58.

[One thing that is not disputed is the fact that the Witnesses are and have always been very organized in everything they do.]

Flocking to the True God

During the 20th century, Jehovah's Witnesses have prospered throughout the earth. This has even been true in lands where they have been under ban or proscription. These bans were imposed mainly by regimes that failed to understand the neutral position of Jehovah's Witnesses regarding the political and nationalistic allegiances of this world. (See box, page 347.) Yet, in such lands, tens of thousands of people have turned to God's Kingdom as the only true hope for peace and security for mankind. In most nations a tremendous witness has been given, and now there are millions of active Witnesses everywhere.

With their Christian love and their hope of "a new heaven and a new earth," Jehovah's Witnesses are looking to the near future for world-stirring events that must soon put an end to all injustice, corruption, and unrighteousness on this earth. For that reason they will continue to visit their neighbors in a sincere effort to bring honesthearted ones nearer to the true God, Jehovah. Revelation 21:1-4; Mark 13:10; Romans 10:11-15.[7]

[The numbers herein, the effectiveness of the Witnesses, with so many from other Christian denominations flocking to them, it should be time for a wake-up call.]

---

[7] *Mankind's Search for God* chap. 15 pp. 350-365 A Return to the True God

CHAPTER 1 "The End of Gentile Times" (607 B.C.E. - 1914 C.E.)

Proof-Texting is using isolated quotations from Scripture(s) to establish a doctrinal position. The Jehovah's Witnesses do this to establish what they call the End of the Gentile Times. Below is from the back of the New World Translation Reference Bible, published by the Watchtower Bible and Tract Society. We will be using the Revised, 2013 New World Translation.

6. Chronology[8]

A. 1914 (C.E.) ends Gentile Times

Line of Kingdom rulers interrupted, 607 B.C.E. Eze 21:25-27

"Seven times" to pass until rule restored. Da 4:32, 16, 17

Seven = 2 × 3 ½ times, or 2 × 1,260 days. Re 12:6, 14; 11:2, 3

A day for a year. [Makes 2,520 years] Eze 4:6; Nu 14:34

To run until Kingdom's establishment. Lu 21:24; Da 7:13, 14

Note that the Jehovah's Witnesses jump from one text to the next, throughout the Bible, to establish 1914, as the year that Jesus started ruling invisibly from heaven. Many times, the quotes that they pull from all over the Bible do not really reflect what the authors of those Bible books meant to convey. Within correct biblical interpretation, the interpreter knows that any verse in the Bible has its own context. What is context? Context is the words, phrases, or the other verses that come before and after a particular word or passage in the Bible, which help to explain what the author meant by the words that he used. Now, proof-texting is only wrong, if you pull the verses out of their context, and apply them to a doctrinal position, which is giving them a meaning that the author did not intend. In Romans chapter 9, the Apostle Paul quotes eleven times from other parts of the Bible.[9] However, Paul is not using the verses that he pulls from different books of the Old Testament out of context. They are being used as examples of Israelite history, as it relates to the sovereignty of God: the example of Esau and Jacob, the example of Pharaoh, the example from Hosea, and the example from Isaiah. The concluding two points of Paul were, (1) **"Through faith, the Gentiles have found**

---

[8] td 6-7A Bible Topics for Discussion in Reference Bible (New World Translation)

[9] The quotations are found in Romans chapter 9, verses 7 (Genesis 21:12), 9 (Genesis 18:14), 12 (Genesis 25:23), 13 (Malachi 1:2, 3), 15 (Exodus 33:19), 17 (Exodus 9:16), 25 (Hosea 2:23), 26 (Hosea 1:10), 27, 28 (Isaiah 10:22, 23), 29 (Isaiah 1:9), and 33 (Isaiah 28:16).

Nelson H. Barbour

righteousness without even seeking it (9:30)." (2) "**Through the law Israel has not found righteousness even after seeking it** (9:31–33)."[10]

What many Christians do not realize is, the modern day Jehovah's Witnesses got their start back in 1870, with Charles Taze Russell (founder), having Bible studies with former Adventists, who had left the Adventist movement, because of what would become known as the "Great Disappointment." William Miller (a former Baptist minister) was the founder of the Adventist movement, so they have been referred to as the Millerites. **Nelson H. Barbour**, a Millerite Adventist gave the doctrinal teaching that chronologically pointed to 1914 as the beginning of the 'Last Days.' However, the Witnesses known as the International Bible Students in those days were not prophesying that Jesus was going to begin his invisible rulership from heaven in 1914, the start of the Last Days; they were proclaiming,

> Russell believed that Christ had returned invisibly in 1874, and that he had been ruling from the heavens since that date. He predicted that a period known as the "Gentile Times" would end in 1914, and that Christ would take power of Earth's affairs at that time. He interpreted the outbreak of World War I as the beginning of Armageddon, which he viewed to be both a gradual deterioration of civilized society, and a climactic multi-national attack on a restored Israel accompanied by worldwide anarchy.[11]

The religion's doctrines surrounding 1914 are the legacy of a series of emphatic claims regarding the years 1799,[12] 1874,[13] 1878,[14] 1914,[15] 1918[16] and 1925[17] made in

---

[10] http://biblia.com/books/outlnbbl/Ro9.6-29

[11] http://en.wikipedia.org/wiki/Charles_Taze_Russell#Theology_and_teachings

[12] *The Watchtower*, March 1, 1922, page 73, "The indisputable facts, therefore, show that the 'time of the end' began in 1799; that the Lord's second presence began in 1874."

[13] IBID

[14] "Our Faith" (PDF). The Herald of the Morning: 52. September 1875.

[15] *The Watchtower*, July 15, 1894, p. 1677: "We see no reason for changing the figures—nor could we change them if we would. They are, we believe, God's dates, not ours. But bear in mind that the end of 1914 is not the date for the beginning, but for the end of the time of trouble."

[16] September 1, 1916 *The Watchtower*, pages 264-265

the Watch Tower Society's publications between 1879 and 1924. Claims about the significance of those years, including the presence of Jesus Christ, the beginning of the "last days", the destruction of worldly governments and the earthly resurrection of Jewish patriarchs, were successively abandoned.[18] In 1922 the society's principal journal, *The Watch Tower*, described its chronology as "no stronger than its weakest link", but also claimed the chronological relationships to be "of divine origin and divinely corroborated...in a class by itself, absolutely and unqualifiedly correct"[19] and "indisputable facts", while repudiation of Russell's teachings was described as "equivalent to a repudiation of the Lord."[20]

Here is the irony; the Watchtower ran an article about setting dates and the "Great Disappointment" of William Miller's 1844 date, titled **The "Investigative Judgment" A Bible-Based Doctrine?**[21] Here is how that article begins,

OCTOBER 22, 1844, was a day of great anticipation for some 50,000 people on the East Coast of the United States. Their spiritual leader, William Miller, had said that Jesus Christ would return on that very day. The Millerites, as they were called, waited in their meeting places until darkness fell. Then the next day dawned, but the Lord had not come. Disillusioned,

---

[17] *Millions Now Living Will Never Die*, 1920, page 97, "Based upon the argument heretofore set forth, then, that the old order of things, the old world, is ending and is therefore passing away, and that the new order is coming in, and that 1925 shall mark the resurrection of the faithful worthies of old and the beginning of reconstruction, it is reasonable to conclude that millions of people now on the earth will be still on the earth in 1925. Then, based upon the promises set forth in the divine Word, we must reach the positive and indisputable conclusion that millions now living will never die."

[18] Holden, Andrew (2002). *Jehovah's Witnesses: Portrait of a Contemporary Religious Movement*. Routledge. p. 1

[19] "The Strong Cable of Chronology", *Watch Tower*, July 15, 1922, page 217, "The chronology of present truth is, to begin with, a string of dates... Thus far it is a chain, and no stronger than its weakest link. There exist, however, well established relationships among the dates of present-truth chronology. These internal connections of the dates impart a much greater strength than can be found in other [secular, archeological] chronologies. Some of them are of so remarkable a character as clearly to indicate that this chronology is not of man, but of God. Being of divine origin and divinely corroborated, present-truth chronology stands in a class by itself, absolutely and unqualifiedly correct."

[20] *The Watchtower*, May 1, 1922, page 132, "To abandon or repudiate the Lord's chosen instrument means to abandon or repudiate the Lord himself, upon the principle that he who rejects the servant sent by the Master thereby rejects the Master. ... Brother Russell was the Lord's servant. Then to repudiate him and his work is equivalent to a repudiation of the Lord, upon the principle heretofore announced."

[21] *Watchtower Magazine* 1997 7/15 p. 25 The "Investigative Judgment" A Bible-Based Doctrine?

they returned home and thereafter recalled that day as the "Great Disappointment."

What the Millerites did was repackage their 1844 doctrine into a new name, the "Investigative Judgment." In other words, Jesus did not return as they thought he would be in 1844, but it was an invisible return, to investigate the lives of the dead and then the living, to see if they were fit for heaven, this being the Investigative Judgment. The Watchtower above then states, "However, some respected scholars in the Seventh-Day Adventist (SDA) Church have been wondering if the 'investigative judgment' is a Bible-based doctrine. Why are they having second thoughts about it? If you were a Seventh-Day Adventist, this question would concern you." Well, this should be of interest to all Jehovah's Witnesses that are fond of their 1914 doctrinal position as well. Not only because the Witnesses copied the playbook of the Adventists "Great Disappointment" by simply altering the 1914 doctrine, as opposed to abandoning it. Moreover, the Watchtower mentioned above article goes on to debunk this Investigative Judgment" by noting that the Seventh Day Adventists got their new doctrinal position by proof-texting.

Note what the Watchtower says next "One SDA scholar says that this reasoning is based on the "proof-text" method. A person finds "a certain word like sanctuary in Dan. 8:14, the same word in Lev. 16, the same word in Heb. 7, 8, 9" and holds 'that they are all talking about the same thing.'" Really, the Watchtower is bringing up the context and proof-texting. A heading in the Watchtower actually asks, "What Does the Context Reveal?" Then, the Watchtower goes on to write,

> Now consider the context. Adventists hold that Daniel 8:14 is "a contextual island," having nothing to do with the preceding verses. But do you get that impression when you read Daniel 8:9-14 in the accompanying box entitled "Daniel 8:14 in Context"? Verse 9 identifies an aggressor, a small horn. Verses 10-12 reveal that this aggressor will attack the sanctuary. Verse 13 asks, 'How long will this aggression continue?' And verse 14 answers: "Until two thousand three hundred evenings and mornings; and the holy place will certainly be brought into its right condition." Clearly, verse 13 raises a question that is answered in verse 14. Theologian Desmond Ford says: "To detach Dan. 8:14 from this cry ["How long?" verse 13] is to be exegetically at sea without an anchor."
>
> Why do Adventists detach verse 14 from the context? To avoid an awkward conclusion. The context ascribes the defilement of the sanctuary, mentioned in verse 14, to the activities of the little horn. However, the "investigative

judgment" doctrine attributes the defilement of the sanctuary to the activities of Christ. He is said to transfer the sins of believers to the heavenly sanctuary. So, what happens if Adventists accept both the doctrine and the context? Dr. Raymond F. Cottrell, a Seventh-Day Adventist and former associate editor of the *SDA Bible Commentary*, writes: "To pretend to ourselves that the SDA interpretation reads Daniel 8:14 in context then would thus be to identify the little horn as Christ." Dr. Cottrell honestly admits: "We can't have both context and the Adventist interpretation." With regard to the "investigative judgment," therefore, the Adventist Church had to make a choice—accept the doctrine or the context of Daniel 8:14. Unfortunately, it embraced the former and dropped the latter. No wonder, says Dr. Cottrell, that informed Bible students blame Adventists for "reading *into* Scripture" what cannot "be drawn *from* Scripture"!

After demonstrating that Daniel 8:44 was being used out of its context, the Watchtower goes on to show the mistake of proof-texting by drawing on other verses because they have similar terminology. Hebrews 9 and Leviticus 16, does not work because what Paul penned in Hebrews 9 had nothing to do with what Daniel wrote at 8:14. Moreover, the SDA trying to tie Leviticus 16 into Daniel 8:14, because of the King James' rendering of 'cleansed sanctuary' of Daniel 8:44 does not work. Because "cleansed" in the King James Version "is a mistranslation of a form of the Hebrew verb *tsadhaq* (meaning 'to be righteous') used at Daniel 8:14." What follows is the most important statement in the whole Watchtower article, which brings us back to the 1914 chronology of the Witnesses.

> **We would encourage Adventists to examine** the doctrine of "investigative judgment" to see whether its pillars are **based solidly on the Bible** or are founded on the unstable sands of tradition. The apostle Paul wisely urged: "Make sure of all things; hold fast to what is fine."--1 Thessalonians 5:21. (Bold mne)

The Witnesses would encourage the Seventh Day Adventists **to examine** the doctrine of the investigative judgment, to make sure that **it is based solidly on the Bible**. Really? We can only imagine what would happen to any Jehovah's Witnesses if he or she ever dared to investigate the 1914 doctrine. Elders, who would visit them, would counsel them to stop. Moreover, if they refused, the Congregation elders would form a committee of three elders, who would then continue to tell them to set aside their investigation. If they still refused, they would be disfellowshiped (expelled). If they, as the Watchtower suggested, talked to others, encouraging them to investigate 1914, they would be labeled an apostate. In other words, only those outside of the Jehovah's Witnesses should investigate their doctrinal position(s), to ascertain whether they are "based solidly on the Bible or are founded on the unstable sands of tradition." The Watchtower would argue that they have no need to investigate because they have the truth. Well, that truth has been changed numerous times. Let us now investigate their proof-texting, to see if the verses are being used out of their context, or if they have the meaning that the Jehovah's Witnesses attribute to them, in order to get their support for 1914. In order to **not** be criticized by the Witnesses, we will use their translation, the New World Translation, along with the English Standard Version and the New American Standard Bible.

Gentile Times or Appointed Times of the Nations
SEVEN TIMES

607 .... ◄B.C.E. | C.E.► 1914

What we have here is a period of time (2,520 years), which runs from October 607 B.C.E. to October 1914 C.E.

This is referred to in the Bible at Luke 21:24 as "the appointed times of the nations" (NWT), "the times of the Gentiles" (ESV), and "the times of the Gentiles" (NASB), according to the doctrinal position of the Governing Body of Jehovah's Witnesses.[22] The Governing Body believes that this "appointed times of the nations was set in place by God, so his Witnesses would know when Jesus started ruling as king of the heavenly kingdom. The "Gentile Times" begins when God's people, the Israelites were removed, and the "nations" began to rule (607 B.C.E.), ending when Christ was enthroned in heaven in 1914 C.E.

The last Jewish king to sit on God's throne here on earth was in 607 B.C.E., and Zedekiah was removed from that throne in that very year when the Gentile nation Babylon destroyed Jerusalem. "When Judah's king was deposed, the royal turban and the crown were removed."[23]

---

[22] The Governing Body of Jehovah's Witnesses, also known as the "faithful slave" is the ones, who determine the beliefs of the Jehovah's Witnesses. This is based on Matthew 24:45, which is yet another example of using a verse out of context, and will appear in a future article.
[23] *Watchtower Magazine* 88 9/15 pp. 19-20 par. 16 Jehovah Unsheathes His Sword!

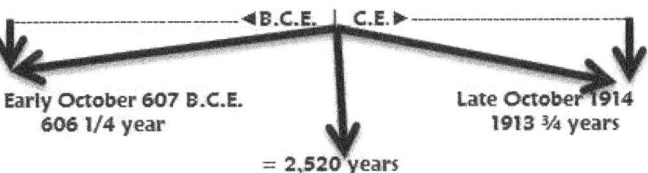

A. 1914 (C.E.) ends Gentile Times[24]

- **Line of Kingdom rulers interrupted, 607 B.C.E. Eze 21:25-27**

This verse is used to establish the beginning of the "Gentile Times" that began in 607 B.C.E., with the dethronement of the last Jewish king Zedekiah, when the gentile nation Babylon destroyed Jerusalem and ended in 1914 C.E. with the enthronement of Jesus Christ. We will talk on this more below, but verse 27 of Ezekiel 21 says in the ESV says, "A ruin, ruin, ruin I will make it [dethronement of Zedekiah and destruction of Jerusalem]. This also shall not be, until he comes [Jesus Christ], the one to whom judgment belongs, and I will give it to him [Jesus Christ]." How long until he, Jesus comes to set up his throne?

- **"Seven times" to pass until rule restored. Da 4:32, 16, 17**

The Jehovah's Witnesses jump from Ezekiel over to Daniel to establish the length of time that is to pass for the "Gentile Times." Here the Faithful Slave uses the dream of Nebuchadnezzar of Babylon, to signify the Gentile Times, as it was this Gentile nation, who dethroned the Jewish king, who sat on God's throne here on earth. This is known as the "seven times." Daniel 4:16 in the NWT says, "and let seven times pass over it." The ESV says, "Let seven periods of time pass over him." The NASB says, "Let seven periods of time pass over him." How long are this "seven times," or "seven periods of times"?

- **Seven = 2 × 3 ½ times, or 2 × 1,260 days. Re 12:6, 14; 11:2, 3**

The faithful slave jumps to the book of Revelation, using these verses to establish the length of the "seven times." These verses in Revelation, if combined, say that a time and times and half a time (3.5 times), is 1,260 days. Thus, they conclude that, since 3.5 times is 1,260 days, they just need to double the 1,260, because 3.5 times plus 3.5 times is 7 times. Thus, the 1,260 days × 2 would equal 2,520 days. Their commentary on

---

[24] We have added bullets to separate their points that make up their chronological argument. We will also interject points in between each of the bullets.

Daniel says, "Evidently, Nebuchadnezzar's "seven times" involved seven years. In prophecy, a year averages 360 days or 12 months of 30 days each. (Compare Revelation 12:6, 14.) So the king's "seven times," or seven years, were 360 days multiplied by 7, or 2,520 days."[25] Well, how to they get the 2,520 to be 2, 520 years?

- **A day for a year. [Makes 2,520 years] Eze 4:6; Nu 14:34**

The Jehovah's Witnesses Bible Encyclopedia, *Insight on the Scriptures*, says, "'Seven times,' according to this count, would equal 2,520 days. That a specific number of days may be used in the Bible record to represent prophetically an equivalent number of years can be seen by reading the accounts at Numbers 14:34 and Ezekiel 4:6. Only by applying the formula there expressed of "a day for a year" to the 'seven times' of this prophecy can the vision of Daniel chapter 4 have significant fulfillment beyond the day of now extinct Nebuchadnezzar, as the evidence thus far presented gives reason to expect. They, therefore, represent 2,520 years."[26] These 2,520 years are to run until God's Kingdom is established through his King Jesus Christ.

- **To run until Kingdom's establishment. Lu 21:24; Da 7:13, 14**

What we have here is a period of time (2,520 years), which runs from October 607 B.C.E. to October 1914 C.E. This is referred to in the Bible at Luke 21:24) as "the appointed times of the nations" (NWT), "the times of the Gentiles" (ESV), and "the times of the Gentiles" (NASB), according to the doctrinal position of the Governing Body of Jehovah's Witnesses. Now, it is true that Daniel 7:13-14 is referring to Jesus, as the Son of Man being "given dominion and glory and a kingdom."

Investigation of the Texts Used to Support the Gentile Times

We will investigate the texts that were mentioned above, but delve a little deeper, so as to see if they are being used out of context. First, we will give the reader the texts in a table of the New World Translation, the English Standard Version and the New American Standard Bible side-by-side. Then, we will give a full quotation from the Watchtower Bible & Tract Societies literature. We will follow this with the quotes of the New World Translation alone, with square brackets, embedding their interpretation within the text. Then, will follow with our commentary on

---

[25] *Pay Attention to Daniel's Prophecy* chap. 6 p. 96 par. 26 Unraveling the Mystery of the Great Tree

[26] *Insight on the Scriptures*, Vol. 1 p. 135 Appointed Times of the Nations

the same verses, and then, we will move on to the next text, following the same pattern. Note that we will remove any em dashes that they use in their literatures, because it does not load well for eBooks.

Line of Kingdom Rulers Interrupted, 607 B.C.E.[27]

Ezekiel 21:25-27 New World Translation (NWT)	Ezekiel 21:25-27 English Standard Version (ESV)	Ezekiel 21:25-27 New American Standard Bible (NASB)
25 "But your day has come, O fatally wounded, wicked chieftain of Israel, the time of your final punishment. 26 This is what the Sovereign Lord Jehovah says: 'Remove the turban, and take off the crown. This will not remain the same. Raise up the low one, and bring low the high one. 27 A ruin, a ruin, a ruin I will make it. And it will not belong to anyone until the one who has the legal right comes, and I will give it to him.'	25 And you, O profane wicked one, prince of Israel, whose day has come, the time of your final punishment, 26 thus says the Lord God: Remove the turban and take off the crown. Things shall not remain as they are. Exalt that which is low, and bring low that which is exalted. 27 A ruin, ruin, ruin I will make it. This also shall not be, until he comes, the one to whom judgment belongs, and I will give it to him.	25 And you, O slain, wicked one, the prince of Israel, whose day has come, in the time of the punishment of the end,' 26 thus says the Lord God, 'Remove the turban and take off the crown; this *will* no longer *be* the same. Exalt that which is low and abase that which is high. 27 A ruin, a ruin, a ruin, I will make it. This also will be no more until He comes whose right it is, and I will give it *to Him*.'

By rebelling, Zedekiah wounded himself in a deadly way. (*Read Ezekiel 21:25-27.*) When Judah's king was deposed, the royal turban and the crown were removed. (2 Kings 25:1-7) The "high" kingdom of Judah was 'brought low' by being destroyed in 607 B.C.E. Thus the "low" Gentile kingdoms were

---

[27] Specifically, The 1984 Reference Bible edition, **6A Bible Topics for Discussion**

"put on high," leaving them in control of the earth without interference by a typical kingdom of God. (Deuteronomy 28:13, 15, 36, 43, 44) So began "the appointed times of the nations," the Gentile Times, that ended in 1914 when God conferred kingship upon Jesus Christ, 'the one having the legal right' to it. (Luke 21:20-24; Psalm 110:1, 2; Daniel 4:15-28; 7:13, 14) With Jesus on a heavenly throne, Gentile nations cannot trample upon what ancient Jerusalem symbolized, the Kingdom of David's legal heir. Hebrews 12:22.[28]

Ezekiel 21:25-27 New World Translation (NWT)

25 "But your day has come [Zedekiah, last king of Judah], O fatally wounded, wicked chieftain of Israel, the time of your final punishment [607 B.C.E.].[29] **26** This is what the Sovereign Lord Jehovah says: 'Remove the turban, and take off the crown [Judah's king was deposed, as Jehovah's human king on his earthly throne]. This will not remain the same [as Jerusalem had been the throne of Jehovah's earthly king for 900 years, and would be no more]. Raise up the low one [the Gentile nations, starting with Babylon were raised up by destroying the high one, Jerusalem], and bring low the high one [by Jerusalem, the high one, being destroyed in 607 B.C.E., made the low one]. **27** A ruin, a ruin, a ruin I will make it [Jerusalem]. And it will not belong to anyone until the one who has the legal right comes, and I will give it to him.' [Jesus Christ enthroned in heaven in 1914]

It is true that the Israelites were being punished for their continuous open rebellion against Jehovah, their God, by way of removing Zedekiah and having Babylon destroy Jerusalem and Judah. However, is it true that the Gentile nations were being placed on high, to rule until Christ? Before answering our question, let us quote verse 24 for the context of why Israel was being destroyed.

Ezekiel 21:24 New World Translation (NWT)

24 "Therefore this is what the Sovereign Lord Jehovah says: 'You have caused your own guilt to be remembered by exposing your transgressions and causing your sins to be seen in all your actions. Now that you have been remembered, you will be taken by force.'

---

[28] **Watchtower 88 9/15 pp. 19-20 par. 16 Jehovah Unsheathes His Sword!**

[29] The chronology of the Jehovah's Witnesses is different than that of evangelical Christianity. They have Jerusalem being destroyed in 607 B.C.E., while evangelical Christianity has it being destroyed in 587 B.C.E. We do not have the space to discuss the difference in dates.

Now, let us quote two well-known and respected commentaries, to see if the Watchtower's faithful and discreet slave[30] has it correct. The first, Holman Old Testament Commentary, will offer the background of who is being discussed, looking at our verses (25-27), but those that lie before our verses as well; then, the New American Commentary will offer the same in gist.

Holman Old Testament Commentary

21:18-27. In this section the sword motif continues, but now the agent of the Lord who wields the sword is identified as the **king of Babylon**, King Nebuchadnezzar. Once again Ezekiel is to carry out a physical sign, this time to depict the choice of routes the king of Babylon will take in his military march. Ezekiel was to construct a fork in the road to depict the decision the king must make in the direction of his military campaign. One direction for the sword would lead **against Rabbah of the Ammonites** and the other **against Judah and fortified Jerusalem**. The reason Judah is mentioned along with Rabbah may be because these two peoples together conspired against Babylonia in 589/588 B.C. (Jer. 27:3). Nebuchadnezzar had thus set out to punish these rebellious states.

In order to come to his decision, the king of Babylon would consult various means of divination; he would **cast lots**

---

[30] We turn to the Watchtower in the article, "Who Is the Faithful and Discreet Slave?" Shortly before his death, Jesus had a private conversation with four of his disciples—Peter, James, John, and Andrew. As Jesus was foretelling the sign of his presence in the last days, he raised a vital question: "Who really is the faithful and discreet slave whom his master appointed over his domestics, to give them their food at the proper time?" (Matthew 24:3, 45; Mark 13:3, 4) Jesus was assuring his disciples that as their "master," he would appoint those who would provide a steady supply of spiritual food for his followers during the time of the end. Who would make up this slave?
It is a small group of anointed followers of Jesus. The "slave" is closely identified with the Governing Body of Jehovah's Witnesses. It dispenses timely spiritual food to fellow worshippers of Jehovah. We are dependent on this faithful slave to keep giving us our "measure of food supplies at the proper time." Luke 12:42.
It manages the household of God. (1 Timothy 3:15) Jesus gave the slave the weighty responsibility of managing the work of the earthly part of Jehovah's organization—looking after its material assets, directing the preaching activity, and teaching us through our congregations. Thus, to provide us with what we need when we need it, "the faithful and discreet slave" is distributing spiritual food by means of the publications we use in our ministry, as well as through the programs that are presented at our meetings and assemblies. The slave is *faithful* to Bible truths and to its commission to preach the good news, and it is *discreet* about how it wisely cares for Christ's interests on earth. (Acts 10:42) Jehovah is blessing its work with increase and abundant spiritual provisions. Isaiah 60:22; 65:13.

https://www.jw.org/en/publications/books/jehovahs-will/faithful-discreet-slave/

with arrows, consult his idols, and **examine the liver**. These were common pagan practices, but nowhere else in Scripture are they clustered together as they are in this passage. These pagan practices were expressly forbidden to the Israelites (Deut. 18:10; 2 Kgs. 17:17). God would use these pagan means to accomplish his purposes. He would orchestrate the divination devices in such a way that the choice for the king of Babylonia would be to march against his people in Judah and Jerusalem.

When the king arrived at his destination, he would **set up battering rams, command to slaughter, sound the battle cry, build a ramp, and erect siege works**. Believing God's promise rendered Jerusalem inviolable to judgment, the Israelites would initially think this judgment could not take place until God used this situation to remind them of their guilt. The siege would eventually lead to the captivity of the city. The Israelites are identified as those who had **sworn allegiance** to the king in reference to the treaty agreement that had been established between Judah and Babylonia (2 Chr. 36:13; Ezek. 17:12-18).

God's message to his people in all these events is that the people of the holy city will be **taken captive** as they finally realize their guilt and their rebellion. God has an additional message for the royal prince. Because this day of captivity will come, the royal prince should remove the symbols of royalty, **the turban** and **the** crown. The turban typically occurs in reference to the headgear of the high priest (Exod. 28:4), but it also seems to be used as a setting for the crown (Exod. 39:31; Lev. 8:9).

The office of kingship will suffer dramatically until it is restored to the one **to whom it rightfully belongs**, a reference to the Messiah who had qualities of both a king and a prince (Gen. 49:10; Heb. 5-7). Thus Judah's loss of a reigning king would last until the time the rightful king (the Messiah) would appear (Jer. 23:5-6; Zech. 6:12-15; Matt. 21:1-11). The ruler who was to be stripped of his royalty was undoubtedly King Zedekiah. It seems that it was too late for Israel to repent.[31]

The New American Commentary

"Therefore" introduces the fundamental reason for Judah's exile: "open rebellion" against God. The "profane and wicked

---

[31] Rooker, Mark; Anders, Max (2006-01-01). *Holman Old Testament Commentary - Ezekiel* (Kindle Locations 3416-3440). B&H Publishing. Kindle Edition.

prince of Israel" is a reference to Zedekiah (v. 25); he would lose his crown, and the kingdom of Judah would end (v. 26). The crown would be held in reserve until "he comes to whom it rightfully belongs" (v. 27). This messianic prophecy echoes the words of Gen 49:10, which depicts the Messiah as a future King (see also Ps 2:6; Jer 23:5–6; Ezek 37:24; Zech 6:12–15). Zedekiah would be dethroned and humiliated (vv. 25–27), and his kingdom, including Jerusalem, would be a ruin (v. 27).[32]

We see that, in essence, the Jehovah's Witnesses have interpreted this text correctly; the Israelites were being punished for their continuous open rebellion against Their God, Jehovah, by way of removing Zedekiah and having Babylon destroy Jerusalem and Judah. As to whether the Gentile nations were being raised on high, while God's chosen people were being laid low, it does seem to fit the context. As we do know that, the dethroned King of Jerusalem, Jehovah's heavenly throne here on earth was to be out of commission, in ruin "until He comes whose right it is, and I will give it *to Him*" (NASB), namely, the Messiah, Jesus Christ. However, was this prophetically referring to the time when Jesus came in the first-century C.E., or his second coming, still in the future?

When it says that Jehovah's king to his people was to be in ruin **"until [the Messiah] comes, the one whose right it is, and I will give it to [Jesus Christ],"** it has similar language to Genesis 49:10, as was stated above.

Genesis 49:10 New American Standard Bible (NASB)

[10] "The scepter shall not depart from Judah,
Nor the ruler's staff from between his feet,
Until Shiloh [meaning "He whose it Is"[33]] comes,
And to him *shall be* the obedience of the peoples.

That is to say, the "scepter" [symbolizing authority] and the "staff" [denoting rulership] would not be restored until "he whose it is" comes, who is of the line of Judah, i.e., the Messiah, Jesus Christ. After Zedekiah was removed, there was no one who could claim such, until,

Zechariah 9:9 New American Standard Bible (NASB)	**Matthew 21:4-7, 10-10** English Standard Version (ESV)
[9] Rejoice greatly, O daughter of Zion!	[4] This took place to fulfill what

---

[32] Lamar Eugene Cooper, *Ezekiel*, vol. 17, The New American Commentary (Nashville: Broadman & Holman Publishers, 1994), 214–215.
[33] Robert L. Thomas, *New American Standard Hebrew-Aramaic and Greek Dictionaries: Updated Edition* (Anaheim: Foundation Publications, Inc., 1998).

Shout *in triumph*, O daughter of Jerusalem! Behold, your king is coming to you; He is just and endowed with salvation, Humble, and mounted on a donkey, Even on a colt, the foal of a donkey.	was spoken by the prophet, saying, **5** "Say to the daughter of Zion, 'Behold, your king is coming to you, humble, and mounted on a donkey, on a colt, the foal of a beast of burden.'" **6** The disciples went and did as Jesus had directed them. **7** They brought the donkey and the colt and put on them their cloaks, and he sat on them. **10** And when he entered Jerusalem, the whole city was stirred up, saying, "Who is this?" **11** And the crowds said, "This is the prophet Jesus, from Nazareth of Galilee."

"Seven times" to Pass Until Rule Restored

The Jehovah's Witnesses jump from Ezekiel over to Daniel to establish the length of time that is to pass for the "Gentile Times." Here the Faithful Slave of the Jehovah's Witnesses uses the dream of Nebuchadnezzar of Babylon, to signify the Gentile Times, as it was this Gentile nation, who dethroned the Jewish king, who sat on God's throne here on earth. The texts lie below; after that, we will take a deeper look what they say about these texts, and whether that is what Daniel truly meant.

Daniel 4:32	**Daniel 4:32**	**Daniel 4:32**
New World Translation (NWT)	English Standard Version (ESV)	New American Standard Bible (NASB)
32 and from mankind you are being driven away. With the beasts of the field your dwelling will be, and you will be given vegetation to eat just like bulls, and seven times will pass over	**32** and you shall be driven from among men, and your dwelling shall be with the beasts of the field. And you shall be made to eat grass like an ox, and	**32** and you will be driven away from mankind, and your dwelling place *will be* with the beasts of the field. You will be given grass to eat like cattle, and seven

you, until you know that the Most High is Ruler in the kingdom of mankind and that he grants it to whomever he wants.'"

Daniel 4:15-17

New World Translation (NWT)

¹⁵ But leave the stump with its roots in the ground, with a banding of iron and of copper, among the grass of the field. Let it be wet with the dew of the heavens, and let its portion be with the beasts among the vegetation of the earth. ¹⁶ Let its heart be changed from that of a human, and let it be given the heart of a beast, and let seven times pass over it. ¹⁷This is by the decree of watchers, and the request is by the word of the holy ones, so that people living may know that the Most High is Ruler in the kingdom of mankind and that he gives it to whomever he wants, and he sets up over it even the lowliest of men."

seven periods of time shall pass over you, until you know that the Most High rules the kingdom of men and gives it to whom he will."

Daniel 4:15-17

English Standard Version (ESV)

¹⁵ But leave the stump of its roots in the earth, bound with a band of iron and bronze, amid the tender grass of the field. Let him be wet with the dew of heaven. Let his portion be with the beasts in the grass of the earth. ¹⁶ Let his mind be changed from a man's, and let a beast's mind be given to him; and let seven periods of time pass over him.¹⁷ The sentence is by the decree of the watchers, the decision by the word of the holy ones, to the end that the living may know that the Most High rules the kingdom of men and gives it to whom he will and sets over it the lowliest of men.'

periods of time will pass over you until you recognize that the Most High is ruler over the realm of mankind and bestows it on whomever He wishes.'

Daniel 4:15-17

New American Standard Bible (NASB)

¹⁵ "Yet leave the stump with its roots in the ground,
But with a band of iron and bronze *around it*
In the new grass of the field;
And let him be drenched with the dew of heaven,
And let him share with the beasts in the grass of the earth.
¹⁶ "Let his mind be changed from *that of* a man
And let a beast's mind be given to him,
And let seven periods of time pass over him.
¹⁷ "This sentence is by the decree of the *angelic* watchers
And the decision is a command of the holy ones,
In order that the

living may know That the Most High is ruler over the realm of mankind, And bestows it on whom He wishes And sets over it the lowliest of men."

The Babylonians had their own religious concept of good and evil spirit creatures. But who was this "watcher," or sentinel, from heaven? Called "a holy one," he was a righteous angel representing God. (Compare Psalm 103:20, 21.) Imagine the questions that must have plagued Nebuchadnezzar! Why chop this tree down? What good is the rootstock restrained from growth by bands of iron and of copper? Indeed, what purpose is served by a mere stump?

Nebuchadnezzar must have been completely mystified as he heard the watcher's further words ... The rootstock of a tree does not have a human heart beating inside it. For that matter, how can the heart of a beast be given to a tree's rootstock? What are the "seven times"? And how does all of this relate to rulership in "the kingdom of mankind"? Surely Nebuchadnezzar wanted to know.

Upon hearing the dream, Daniel was momentarily astonished, then fearful. Urged by Nebuchadnezzar to explain it, the prophet said: "O my lord, may the dream apply to those hating you, and its interpretation to your adversaries. The tree that you beheld, that grew great and became strong . . . , it is you, O king, because you have grown great and become strong, and your grandeur has grown great and reached to the heavens, and your rulership to the extremity of the earth." (Daniel 4:18-22) In the Scriptures, trees can symbolize individuals, rulers, and kingdoms. (Psalm 1:3; Jeremiah 17:7, 8; Ezekiel, chapter 31) Like the immense tree of his dream, Nebuchadnezzar had "grown great and become strong" as the head of a world power. But "rulership to the extremity of the earth," involving the whole kingdom of mankind, is represented by the great tree. It therefore symbolizes Jehovah's universal sovereignty, particularly in its relationship to the earth. Daniel 4:17.

During Nebuchadnezzar's madness, "his very hair grew long just like eagles' feathers and his nails like birds' claws." (Daniel 4:33) This took longer than seven days or seven weeks.

Various translations read "seven times," and alternatives are "appointed (definite) times" or "time periods." (Daniel 4:16, 23, 25, 32) A variant of the Old Greek (Septuagint) reads "seven years." The "seven times" were treated as "seven years" by the first-century Jewish historian Josephus. (Antiquities of the Jews, Book 10, Chapter 10, paragraph 6) And certain Hebrew scholars have viewed these "times" as "years." "Seven years" is the rendering in An American Translation, Today's English Version, and the translation by James Moffatt.

Evidently, Nebuchadnezzar's "seven times" involved seven years. In prophecy, a year averages 360 days, or 12 months of 30 days each. (Compare Revelation 12:6, 14.) So the king's "seven times," or seven years, were 360 days multiplied by 7, or 2,520 days. But what about the major fulfillment of his dream? The prophetic "seven times" lasted much longer than 2,520 days. This was indicated by Jesus' words: "Jerusalem will be trampled on by the nations, until the appointed times of the nations are fulfilled." (Luke 21:24) That 'trampling' began in 607 B.C.E. when Jerusalem was destroyed and the typical kingdom of God ceased to function in Judah. When would the trampling end? At "the times of restoration of all things," when divine sovereignty would again be manifested toward the earth through symbolic Jerusalem, the Kingdom of God. Acts 3:21.[34]

The Jehovah's Witnesses have the historical setting correct. Their position is stated in the phrase, "'seven times' to pass until rule restored." Nebuchadnezzar was haughty and excessively abusive to God's people. Therefore, God chose to remove Nebuchadnezzar for seven times, or seven years by turning Nebuchadnezzar mad, known today as *lycanthropy*, where the person is mentally transformed into believing they are a wolf-like creature. The seven years or seven times did pass for Nebuchadnezzar before his rule was restored. This, the Jehovah's Witnesses say is the initial fulfillment of the prophetic dream.

However, the Jehovah's Witnesses mean more by this, as we see by the "tree in the midst of the earth [Dan 4:10-12], and its height was great. The tree grew and became strong, and its top reached to heaven, and it was visible to the end of the whole earth." (ESV) For the Witnesses, this tree's size being earth wide leads them to believe that it has to represent more than Nebuchadnezzar being cut down from power for seven times, i.e., seven years. Therefore they say, "'**rulership to the extremity of the earth**,' involving the whole kingdom of mankind, is

---

[34] *Pay Attention to Daniel's Prophecy* chap. 6 pp. 84-87, 95-96 pars. 6-10, 25-26 Unraveling the Mystery of the Great Tree ***

represented by the great tree. It, therefore, symbolizes Jehovah's universal sovereignty, particularly in its relationship to the earth." (Dan 4:17) In other words, they are saying that God's rulership (universal sovereignty) on this earth was being cut down and banded for seven times, namely, seven years of 360 days each, totally 2,520 days. The only problem with this is that Daniel Interprets Nebuchadnezzar's dream for us. Daniel says,

Daniel 4:21-22	Daniel 4:21-22
New World Translation (NWT)	English Standard Version (ESV)
[20] "'The tree that you saw that grew great and became strong, whose top reached the heavens and was visible to all the earth, [21] which had beautiful foliage, abundant fruit, and food for all, beneath which the beasts of the field would dwell and on whose branches the birds of the heavens would reside, [22] it is you, O king, because you have grown great and become strong, and your grandeur has grown and reached to the heavens, and your rulership to the ends of the earth	[20] The tree you saw, which grew and became strong, so that its top reached to heaven, and it was visible to the end of the whole earth, [21] whose leaves were beautiful and its fruit abundant, and in which was food for all, under which beasts of the field found shade, and in whose branches the birds of the heavens lived—[22] it is you, O king, who have grown and become strong. Your greatness has grown and reaches to heaven, and your dominion to the ends of the earth.

Even though, we know that the Witness have the historical setting correct, they have gone beyond Scripture, into the realms of eisegesis, reading their interpretation into the Scriptures. They are doing the very thing they accused the Seventh Day Adventists of, failing "to examine the doctrine ... to see whether its pillars are based solidly on the Bible or are founded on the unstable sands of tradition." Saying that the "apostle Paul wisely urged: "Make sure of all things; hold fast to what is fine.'" Clearly, they are adding the allegorical interpretation of making the tree in Nebuchadnezzar's dream stand for the "sovereignty of God," when God's own Prophet, inspired by Holy Spirit specifically tells us that the tree stood for Nebuchadnezzar, is as Daniel said, **"The tree that you saw that grew great and became strong ... it is you, O king."** (NWT, 2013) Now, the "sovereignty of God" was involved, but not that it was being cut down. What was going to be done to Nebuchadnezzar was "In order that the living may know that the Most High is ruler over the realm of mankind." (Dan 4:17, NASB) The Scriptures show that **(1)** God chose a people, the Israelites, **(2)** they abandoned and rebelled against him for a thousand years, **(3)** God used the world power of Babylon to overthrow his own people and take them captive. **(4)** The Babylonians began to think too much of themselves, especially Nebuchadnezzar, they began to acts wickedly toward humanity as well as the Israelites; God's chosen people, to excess. **(5)** So, again, God punished Nebuchadnezzar, "in order that the living may know that the Most High is ruler over the realm of mankind." (Dan 4:17, NASB) However, look at the Witness literature below, as they go beyond Scripture,

> As represented by the great tree, Nebuchadnezzar symbolized world rulership. But remember, the tree stands for rulership and sovereignty far grander than that of Babylon's king. It symbolizes the universal sovereignty of Jehovah, "the King of the heavens," especially with respect to the earth. Before Jerusalem's destruction by the Babylonians, the kingdom centered in that city with David and his heirs sitting on "Jehovah's throne" represented God's sovereignty with reference to the earth. (1 Chronicles 29:23) God himself had such sovereignty chopped down and banded in 607 B.C.E. when he used Nebuchadnezzar to destroy Jerusalem. Exercise of divine sovereignty toward the earth by a kingdom in the line of David was restrained for seven times. How long were these seven times? When did they begin, and what marked their end?[35]

The Jehovah's Witnesses are trying to tie two different historical events together. True, God's human king on earth was through the Davidic rulership and was brought to an end by the destruction of Jerusalem, because no other king sat on that throne after Zedekiah. However, this is coming from the historical books of Samuel, Kings, and Chronicles, not the book of Daniel chapter 4. Daniel in chapter 4 is dealing with,

- Nebuchadnezzar stating what the Most High God has done for him
- Nebuchadnezzar has a dream and then searches for an interpreter
- The dream was a vision of a great tree
- Daniel then interprets the dream for Nebuchadnezzar

---

[35] *Daniel's Prophecy*, **chap. 6 pp. 94-95 par. 24 Unraveling the Mystery of the Great Tree**

- Nebuchadnezzar then goes through the humiliation of being a wolf-like creature for seven times
- God had thus judged Nebuchadnezzar for his excessive pride and ambition
- This judgment demonstrated to the king of the world power on earth, as well as mankind, that the Most High God was sovereign
- Nebuchadnezzar, after his recovery, then praises and extols the King of the heavens

Even though their interpretation fails at this point, by their trying to combine two different historical events into one vision of a great tree by Nebuchadnezzar, even though God's own prophet interpreted that tree to symbolize Nebuchadnezzar himself, let us move on to the next leap the Jehovah's Witnesses have to make.

The Witnesses have to make the historical setting that they have correct into more if they are going to have that seven times, which they have misappropriated from, seven years for Nebuchadnezzar, to be 2,520 years of the restraining of Davidic rulership on earth. They need to leave this context of seven times in Daniel and go elsewhere to another context. There would be no problem with this; if they had not fiddled with the interpretation of Daniel, to fit their own preconceived interpretation. However, before doing that let us look at two other commentaries so that we know the Witnesses at least have the historical setting correct.

The Homan Old Testament Commentary

> **4:15–16.** Only the stump and the roots remained, and whatever protruded above ground would be **bound with iron and bronze** just to sit there lifeless **in the grass of the field**. A metal band around tree stumps hardly preserves anything, so some scholars consider this (particularly in context of the words **grass** and **field**) to refer to the bondage of Nebuchadnezzar in his insanity.
>
> Indeed, all of a sudden the neuter pronouns turn masculine, and the tree becomes a man! Of no dead stump would anyone ever say, **let his mind be changed from that of a man and let him be given the mind of an animal**, a statement surely calculated to increase the terror of this ancient king. The word for **mind** describes the inner self, often called heart throughout the Bible. It includes emotions and morality, the decisions of one's will, and the way one behaves. The intelligent and reasonable king, highly sophisticated for his time,

would plunge into insanity and behave like an animal **among the plants of the earth**.

This judgment would be imposed **till seven times pass by for him**. The word for **times** is *iddanin*, which appears again in verses 23, 25, and 32 of this chapter. Virtually every serious commentator understands the meaning to be years rather than some indefinite amount of time. Seven is the Hebrew number of fulfillment or completion. To be sure, the word can refer to seasons, and we will have to deal with the designation again in our study.

4:17. We have already observed that if we had to select a key verse for the Book of Daniel, we could probably do no better than 4:17. The central message of the book (apart from its distinctive prophecies) focuses right here, and it comes from the mouth of Nebuchadnezzar, relating the message of the angel who declared the destruction of the tree. But now we learn that this decision comes from multiple **messengers, the holy ones declare the verdict**.

Furthermore, we understand that this judgment upon the great tree which represents the great king has a distinct purpose: **so that the living may know that the Most High is sovereign over the kingdoms of men and gives them to anyone he wishes and sets over them the lowliest of men**. We see this theme often throughout Scripture (Ps. 24:1; Isa. 40:15; Acts 17:24,26; Rom. 13:1). Nebuchadnezzar had been selected to serve as God's vice regent on earth and had fouled his office by slaughtering thousands of people, including the Jews. Now it is time for punishment, another theme common to Scripture (Amos 1:3–13).

God controls human kingdoms, and he may choose to select humble rather than proud leaders. Nebuchadnezzar had propelled himself into the latter category. This was not a revolutionary thought in the seventh century B.C.; we find it as early as Job 5:11: "The lowly he sets on high, and those who mourn are lifted to safety." Have a look at this key verse through the creative heart and pen of Eugene Peterson: "The angels announce this decree, the holy watchman bring this sentence, so that everyone living will know that the High God rules human kingdoms. He arranges kingdom affairs however he wishes, and makes leaders out of losers" (The Message).[36]

We can see from the Holman Old Testament Commentary that the Jehovah's Witnesses have the historical setting of these verses correct. Again, Jerusalem had pushed Jehovah God to the end of his patience with them, by their almost 1,000 years of rebellion and false worship that was so bad, some Jewish leaders had sacrificed their own sons to the false god Molech. Therefore, Jehovah chose to use the world power at that time, Babylon, to punish the Jewish leaders, by destroying Jerusalem, removing the last Davidic King, Zedekiah, who sat on the throne, and taking the people captive for seventy years into Babylonia. However, Babylon went beyond the pale with its wicked treatment of humanity, including God's chosen people, excessive pride, and ambition, so Nebuchadnezzar losing his mind for seven years was Babylon's initial punishment. Now, let us consider another trusted commentary.

The New American Commentary

4:14–15a [11–12a] The angel commanded that the tree be cut down and stripped of its branches, leaves, and fruit (v. 14). When this is done, the animals and birds are forced to flee its protection and are no longer able to be satisfied by its produce. Yet the tree is not to be completely destroyed. Its stump and roots are left standing in the middle of the grassy field, suggesting the possibility that the tree may grow again (v. 15). The stump is to be "bound with iron and bronze," which means that a strong band or fence was to be placed around the stump of the tree in order to protect it from destruction. Verses 23 and 26 demonstrate that this metal band is symbolic of the preservation of Nebuchadnezzar's life and kingdom.[37]

4:15b–16 [12b–13] Now the description changes from a tree to that symbolized by the tree, a man. This man was to live outdoors with the animals of the field ("among the plants ["herbage, grass" eaten by the grazing animals] of the earth"), where he would be exposed to the elements of nature ("drenched with the dew").

"His mind" (lit., "heart" [*lĕbab*], used here as the seat of reason [cf. Jer 5:21; Hos 7:11]) will "be changed"[38] from that of

---

[36] Anders, Max; Gangel, Kenneth (2002-01-02). Holman Old Testament Commentary - Daniel (p. 97-99). B&H Publishing. Kindle Edition.
[37] See Montgomery (*Daniel*, 233) and Young (*Daniel*, 104) for a discussion of other views concerning this metal "band."
[38] "A verb used in Akkadian for mental derangement" (A. Jeffery, "The Book of Daniel," *IB* [Nashville: Abingdon, 1956], 411).

a man to that of an animal (v. 16). This individual would actually believe himself to be an animal, a psychological phenomenon known as lycanthropy. "Lycanthropy" (lit. wolf-man) originally referred to the delusion of believing oneself to be a wolf like creature (the primitive werewolf superstition was inspired by this malady) but today has come to be a general designation regardless of the type of animal involved.[39] P. Keck reports that studies "suggest that lycanthropy, though unusual, is very much alive in the twentieth century."[40] Persons involved in Keck's studies believed themselves to be a wide assortment of animals—wolves, gerbils, dogs, birds, cats, rabbits, tigers, and an unidentified creature. In 1946 R. K. Harrison observed a patient in a British mental institution with an illness virtually identical to that described in the Book of Daniel. The patient wandered about the grounds of the institution eating grass as if he were a cow. His drink consisted of water. Harrison stated that "the only physical abnormality noted consisted of a lengthening of the hair and a coarse, thickened condition of the fingernails."[41]

Nebuchadnezzar's illness would continue until "seven times pass by for him." Most scholars, ancient and modern,[42] have interpreted the "seven times" as seven years (cf. 7:25), although there are those who take the phrase to denote merely a period of time, the length of which is unspecified.[43] Yet the word "time" would be expected to designate some definite and well-known period such as days, weeks, months, or years. Since seven days, weeks, or even months seem to be too short a duration for the illness, it is reasonable to suppose that the time was seven years. As Wood explains, the idea is that "the full

---

[39] P. Keck, and colleagues, "Lycanthropy: Alive and Well in the Twentieth Century," *Psychological Medicine* 18 (1988): 113–20. For a brief introduction to the subject see the article by T. A. Fahy, "Lycanthropy: A Review," *Journal of the Royal Society of Medicine* 82 (1989): 37ff. Other helpful studies include P. G. Coll, and colleagues, "Lycanthropy Lives On," *British Journal of Psychiatry* 147 (1985): 201–2; H. A. Rosenstock and K. R. Vincent, "A Case of Lycanthropy," *American Journal of Psychiatry* 134:10 (1977): 1147–49. See also Montgomery, *Daniel*, 220; Lacocque, *Daniel*, 80 (who cites King George III of England and Otto of Bavaria as victims of this malady).
[40] Keck, "Lycanthropy," 119.
[41] R. K. Harrison, *Introduction to the Old Testament* (Grand Rapids: Eerdmans, 1979), 1116–17.
[42] E.g., the LXX; the rabbis; Josephus, *Antiquities* 10.10.6; Jerome, *Daniel*, 46; Driver, *Daniel*, 51; Lacocque, *Daniel*, 80; Archer, "Daniel," 61.
[43] E.g., Anderson, *Signs and Wonders*, 44; Baldwin, *Daniel*, 112; Young, *Daniel*, 105; C. F. Keil, *Biblical Commentary on the Book of Daniel* (Grand Rapids: Eerdmans, 1973), 152–53; Leupold, *Daniel*, 185. Young and Keil probably were influenced in their interpretation by a reluctance to accept "seven years" as the meaning in 7:25 and 12:7.

cycle of seasons, with all the changes in types of weather involved, would pass over the king seven times."[44]

4:17 [14] "The decision is announced by messengers" may also be translated, "The decision is by decree of the messengers"; and the parallel phrase, "The holy ones declare the verdict" may be rendered, "A declaration [decision] of the holy ones is the verdict." The NIV's translation would signify that the angels ("messengers" and "holy ones") merely announced the heavenly decision, but the alternate renderings indicate that they somehow may have been involved in the decree. Of course, this is God's decision (as the second part of the verse makes clear), and the holy angels would naturally concur with the divine decrees. Further, the saints will take part in the final judgment (cf. 1 Cor 6:3).

Heaven's decision to judge this man with insanity was made in order that all "the living may know that the Most High is sovereign over the kingdoms of men." Montgomery rightly calls this "one of the immortal sentences of the Hebrew Scriptures!"[45] God gives these kingdoms "to anyone he wishes." As a further rebuke to Nebuchadnezzar's pride and to that of all the kings of the earth, God points out that at times he even allows the "lowliest of men" to reign. Montgomery adds that this is "a truism in the facts of history." Therefore a king should not be filled with pride, for it is not by his ability but by God's permissive will that he reigns. Archer rightly points out, however, that one criterion that affects God's choice of kings is "the moral condition of the people to be ruled over."[46]

4:20–22 [17–19] Daniel then interpreted the dream. He explained that the great tree represented Nebuchadnezzar and his vast kingdom, which had afforded prosperity ("abundant fruit" and "food") and protection ("shelter") to the peoples of the earth. In the Old Testament the tree figure is employed elsewhere to speak of man in his pride (cf. Isa 2:12–13; 10:34; Ezek 31:3–17).

4:31–32 [28–29] While the boastful words were still coming out of the king's mouth, a voice from heaven pronounced judgment upon him. Evidently this was an audible announcement (at least to the king). The voice, probably of an angel, declared that heaven had "decreed" his judgment. It was

---

[44] Wood, *Daniel*, 111.
[45] IBID
[46] Archer, "Daniel," 61.

as good as done. Nebuchadnezzar would live with the wild animals and eat grass like the cattle for seven years ("seven times") until he finally repented of his pride and gave glory to God.[47]

Here again, we see that the Jehovah's Witnesses have the historical setting correct, but have overstepped by taking Daniel's interpretation of Nebuchadnezzar's dream of the great tree, and adding on another interpretation that is not support by the text in Daniel Chapter 4. Even though we know they have overstepped at this point, let us go on to how they get the "seven times" to equal 2,520 years.

Seven = 2 × 3 ½ Times, or 2 × 1,260 Days

Revelation 12:6	Revelation 12:6	Revelation 12:6
New World Translation (NWT)	English Standard Version (ESV)	New American Standard Bible (NASB)
⁶ And the woman fled into the wilderness, where she has a place prepared by God and where they would feed her for 1,260 days.	⁶ and the woman fled into the wilderness, where she has a place prepared by God, in which she is to be nourished for 1,260 days.	⁶ Then the woman fled into the wilderness where she *had a place prepared by God, so that there she would be nourished for one thousand two hundred and sixty days.
Revelation 12:14	**Revelation 12:14**	**Revelation 12:14**
New World Translation (NWT)	English Standard Version (ESV)	New American Standard Bible (NASB)
¹⁴ But the two wings of the great eagle were given to the woman, so that she might fly into the wilderness to her place, where she is to be fed for a time and times and half a time away from the face of the serpent.	¹⁴ But the woman was given the two wings of the great eagle so that she might fly from the serpent into the wilderness, to the place where she is to be nourished for a time, and times, and	¹⁴ But the two wings of the great eagle were given to the woman, so that she could fly into the wilderness to her place, where she *was
Revelation 11:2-3		

---

[47] Stephen R. Miller, *Daniel*, vol. 18, The New American Commentary (Nashville: Broadman & Holman Publishers, 1994), 133–135, 141–142.

New World Translation (NWT)	Revelation 11:2-3 English Standard Version (ESV)	Revelation 11:2-3 New American Standard Bible (NASB)
² But as for the courtyard that is outside the temple sanctuary, leave it out and do not measure it, because it has been given to the nations, and they will trample the holy city underfoot for 42 months. ³ I will cause my two witnesses to prophesy for 1,260 days dressed in sackcloth."	² but do not measure the court outside the temple; leave that out, for it is given over to the nations, and they will trample the holy city for forty-two months. ³ And I will grant authority to my two witnesses, and they will prophesy for 1,260 days, clothed in sackcloth."	nourished for a time and times and half a time, from the presence of the serpent. ² Leave out the court which is outside the temple and do not measure it, for it has been given to the nations; and they will tread underfoot the holy city for forty-two months. ³ And I will grant *authority* to my two witnesses, and they will prophesy for twelve hundred and sixty days, clothed in sackcloth."

The Jehovah's Witnesses jumped us to revelation because of the similar terminology. We are looking at the seven times in Daniel, so of course, we want to know how long the seven times are. They already agreed that the seven times was seven years for Nebuchadnezzar, as the initial fulfillment. However, they need more. Look at the quote below,

> Evidently, Nebuchadnezzar's "seven times" involved seven years. In prophecy, a year averages 360 days or 12 months of 30 days each. (Compare Revelation 12:6, 14.) So the king's "seven times," or seven years, were 360 days multiplied by 7, or 2,520 days. But what about the major fulfillment of his dream? The prophetic "seven times" lasted much longer than 2,520 days ... If we were to count 2,520 literal days from Jerusalem's destruction in 607 B.C.E., that would bring us only to 600 B.C.E., a year having no Scriptural significance ... Since

the "seven times" are prophetic, we must apply to the 2,520 days the Scriptural rule: "A day for a year."[48]

In the above paragraph, you see they go to Revelation, because the 1,260 days is 3.5 years and is also referred to as "a time, and times, and half a time." In other words, their 1,260 days is 3.5 times. Well, they need to know about seven times, which would be twice the 3.5, namely. 7 times would then be 2,520 days, as you just double 1,260 days. However, we need to hold the press. Why it is all sounding so good. They want to use the 3.5 times (1,260 days) of a whole other context, to clarify their seven times of Daniel chapter 4. Nevertheless, this is not the only problem. They are going to use other verses to give you their "Scriptural rule: "'a day for a year.'" In other words, they are going to get the seven times to be 2.520 days, and then tell you the rule of "a day for a year," meaning 2,520 years. Is this "based solidly on the Bible or are founded on the unstable sands of tradition"? That is what they claimed was wrong with the Seventh Day Adventist interpretation of Daniel 8:44. **"You can't have your cake and eat it (too)"** is a popular English idiomatic proverb or figure of speech," which means "one cannot or should not have or want more than one deserves or can handle, or that one cannot or should not try to have two incompatible things."[49] We are interested in the latter point of trying to have two incompatible things. They want to have their rule of "a day for a year," so as to arrive at 2,520 years and go to Revelation to get their desired outcome. However, how long is the 1.260 days in Revelation? Is it going to follow the rule of "a day for a year," meaning 1,260 years? No, the Jehovah's Witnesses skip that rule when interpreting the Book of Revelation. See the quote from their commentary on Revelation below,

> How long did this respite for the seed of God's woman last? Revelation 12:6 says 1,260 days. Revelation 12:14 calls the period a time, times, and half a time; in other words, three and a half times. In fact, both expressions stand for three and a half years ...[50]

Notice here that they say the days are a literal three and a half years. Yes, they do not use the Scriptural rule "a day for a year" here. Why? They interpret this reference to days literally, because it fits into their interpretation of this section of Revelation.

---

[48] ***Daniel's Prophecy*, chap. 6 pp. 95-96 pars. 26-28 Unraveling the Mystery of the Great Tree**

[49] http://en.wikipedia.org/wiki/You_can't_have_your_cake_and_eat_it

[50] ***Revelation—Its Grand Climax at Hand!* chap. 27 p. 184 par. 26 God's Kingdom Is Born!**

Another question that comes to mind, 'why did they have to leave the book of Daniel to talk about "prophetic times" as they call them, as Daniel 7:25 and 12:7 have the exact same wording as Revelation.

Daniel 7:25	**Daniel 12:7**
New World Translation (NWT) 25 He will speak words against the Most High, and he will continually harass the holy ones of the Supreme One. He will intend to change times and law, and they will be given into his hand for a time, times, and half a time.* * That is, three and a half times.	New World Translation (NWT) 7 Then I heard the man clothed in linen, who was up above the waters of the stream, as he raised his right hand and his left hand to the heavens and swore by the One who is alive forever: "It will be for an appointed time, appointed times, and half a time.* As soon as the dashing to pieces of the power of the holy people comes to an end, all these things will come to their finish." * That is, three and a half times.

I wonder if the above three and a half times are treated like the seven times, "a day for a year." Here is a quote from their Daniel's Prophecy book, which proves quite interesting.

> Since Nebuchadnezzar's "seven times" of madness amounted to seven years, the three and a half times are three and a half years. (Daniel 4:16, 25) *An American Translation* reads: "They shall be handed over to him for a year, two years, and half a year." James Moffatt's version says: "For three years and half a year." The same period is mentioned at Revelation 11:2-7, which states that God's witnesses would preach dressed in sackcloth for 42 months, or 1,260 days, and then be killed.[51]

Notice that they actually use the Nebuchadnezzar dream of the image of the great tree, to justify having this three and a half times interpreted literally as three and a half years. As we just saw, the Witnesses had worked so hard to give us the final fulfillment of making those seven times (2,520 days) be viewed as 2,520 years. Now they are using the initial fulfillment, which they claim applies to Nebuchadnezzar's literal seven years of madness. It is awful convenient having to fulfillments

---

[51] *Daniel's Prophecy*, chap. 9 p. 142 par. 28 Who Will Rule the World?

applied to one dream vision so that it can be used in two completely different ways. We are back to "**you can't have your cake and eat it (too)**." What about Daniel 12:7? The Daniel's Prophecy book says,

> Both prophecies in Daniel (7:25 and 12:7) refer to 'a time, times, and half a time.' Scholars generally recognize this to mean three and a half times. Revelation refers to the same period as 42 months, or 1,260 days. (Revelation 11:2, 3) This confirms that the three and a half times in Daniel refer to three and a half years of 360 days each.[52]

Here again, they are not consistent with their Scriptural rule, "a day for a year." In fact, we have yet to look at the Scriptural support that they use to come up with such a rule. In Ezekiel 4:6 below, you will see "In this third symbolic act, Ezekiel was commanded to lie on his left side for 390 days, bearing the sinful years of the house of Israel, and on his right side for 40 days, representing the sinful years of the house of Judah."[53] Yes, everyone agrees, this symbolic drama is "a day for each year." However, does it seem reasonable to take this formula (a day for each year), which is spelled out specifically here in Ezekiel, and make it a Scriptural rule that is applied where it fits one's doctrinal position, but ignore it in others that does not fit one's doctrinal position?

Ezekiel 4:6 New World Translation (NWT)	Ezekiel 4:6 English Standard Version (ESV)	Ezekiel 4:6 New American Standard Bible (NASB)
6 And you must complete them. "Then for a second time you will lie down, on your right side, and you will carry the guilt of the house of Judah for 40 days. A day for a year, a day for a year, is what I have given you.	**6** And when you have completed these, you shall lie down a second time, but on your right side, and bear the punishment of the house of Judah. Forty days I assign you, a day for each year.	**6** When you have completed these, you shall lie down a second time, *but* on your right side and bear the iniquity of the house of Judah; I have assigned it to you for forty days, a day for each year.
Numbers 14:34 New World Translation (NWT)	**Numbers 14:34** English Standard Version (ESV)	**Numbers 14:34** New American
34 According to the	**34** According to the	

---

[52] **Daniel's Prophecy, chap. 17 p. 295 par. 17 Identifying True Worshipers in the Time of the End**

[53] Rooker, Mark; Anders, Max (2006-01-01). Holman Old Testament Commentary - Ezekiel (Kindle Locations 1381-1383). B&H Publishing. Kindle Edition.

number of the days that you spied out the land, 40 days, a day for a year, a day for a year, you will answer for your errors 40 years, for you will know what it means to oppose me.	number of the days in which you spied out the land, forty days, a year for each day, you shall bear your iniquity forty years, and you shall know my displeasure.'	Standard Bible (NASB) 34 According to the number of days which you spied out the land, forty days, for every day you shall bear your guilt a year, *even* forty years, and you will know My opposition.

Again, does it seem reasonable to take this formula (a day for each year), which is spelled out specifically here in Numbers, and make it a Scriptural rule that is applied where it fits one's doctrinal position, but ignores it in others that do not fit one's doctrinal position? Regardless, let us move on to the final heading that deals with "the appointed times of the nations," and how that fits herein.

To Run Until Kingdom's Establishment

Luke 21:24 New World Translation (NWT)	Luke 21:24 English Standard Version (ESV)	Luke 21:24 New American Standard Bible (NASB)
24 And they will fall by the edge of the sword and be led captive into all the nations; and Jerusalem will be trampled on by the nations until the appointed times of the nations are fulfilled.	24 They will fall by the edge of the sword and be led captive among all nations, and Jerusalem will be trampled underfoot by the Gentiles until the times of the Gentiles are fulfilled.	24 and they will fall by the edge of the sword, and will be led captive into all the nations, and Jerusalem will be trampled underfoot by the Gentiles until the times of the Gentiles are fulfilled.

What we have here is a period of time (2520 years), which runs from October 607 B.C.E. to October 1914 C.E. According to the Jehovah's Witnesses, this is referred to in the Bible at Luke 21:24 as "the appointed times of the nations" (NWT), "the times of the Gentiles" (ESV), and "the times of the Gentiles" (NASB), according to the doctrinal position of the Governing Body of Jehovah's Witnesses. It might be best if we let the Jehovah's Witnesses' literature give us a review of how they got here. As you will see below, we are going to use those same "seven times" of Nebuchadnezzar's dream of the great tree, yet once more, by tying it to the "appointed times of the nations."

A key to understanding when Kingdom rule begins is found in the words of Jesus. "Jerusalem will be trampled on by the nations," he said, "until the appointed times of the nations are fulfilled." (Luke 21:24) Jerusalem was the only city in all the earth that was directly associated with God's name. (1 Kings 11:36; Matthew 5:35) It was the capital of a God-approved earthly kingdom. That city was to be trampled on by the nations in that the rule by God over his people was to be interrupted by worldly governments. When would this begin?

The last king to sit on Jehovah's throne in Jerusalem was told: "Remove the turban, and lift off the crown. . . . It will certainly become no one's until he comes who has the legal right, and I must give it to him." (Ezekiel 21:25-27) The crown was to be lifted off the head of that king, and God's rulership over His people was to be interrupted. This happened in 607 B.C.E. when the Babylonians destroyed Jerusalem. During "the appointed times" that were to follow, God would not have a government on the earth to represent his rulership. Only at the end of those times would Jehovah give the power to rule to the one "who has the legal right"—Jesus Christ. How long would that period be?

A prophecy in the Bible book of Daniel states: "Chop the tree down, and ruin it. However, leave its rootstock itself in the earth, but with a banding of iron and of copper . . . until seven times themselves pass over it." (Daniel 4:23) As we will see, the "seven times" mentioned here are equal in length to "the appointed times of the nations."

In the Bible, individuals, rulers, and kingdoms are at times represented by trees. (Psalm 1:3; Jeremiah 17:7, 8; Ezekiel, chapter 31) The symbolic tree "was visible to the extremity of the whole earth." (Daniel 4:11) Thus, the rulership represented by the tree that was to be chopped down and banded extended "to the extremity of the earth," involving the whole kingdom of mankind. (Daniel 4:17, 20, 22) The tree therefore represents the supreme rulership of God, particularly in its relationship to the earth. This rulership was expressed for a time through the kingdom that Jehovah set up over the nation of Israel. The symbolic tree was cut down, and bands of iron and copper were placed upon the stump in order to prevent its growth. This indicated that God's representative rulership on earth was to cease its operation, as happened in 607 B.C.E. --but not indefinitely. The tree would remain banded until "seven times" had passed. At the end of that period, Jehovah would give rulership to the legal heir, Jesus Christ. Clearly, the "seven times" and "the appointed times of the nations" refer to the same time period. [The Watchtower says clearly, but it is not so clear after the above investigation. Brackets mine]

The Bible helps us to determine the length of the "seven times." It equates 1,260 days with "a time [one time] and times [two times, plural] and half a time"—a total of three and a half "times." (Revelation 12:6, 14) This means that twice that number, or seven times, is 2,520 days. (Brackets theirs)

When we count 2,520 literal days from 607 B.C.E., we come to 600 B.C.E. However, the seven times lasted much longer than that. They were still in progress when Jesus spoke of "the appointed times of the nations." The seven times, therefore, are prophetic. Hence, we must apply the Scriptural rule: "A day for a year." (Numbers 14:34; Ezekiel 4:6) In that case, the seven times of earth's domination by worldly powers without divine interference amount to 2,520 years. Counting 2,520 years from 607 B.C.E. brings us to 1914 C.E. That is the year when "the appointed times of the nations," or seven times, ended. This means that Jesus Christ began to rule as King of God's Kingdom in 1914.[54]

The Destruction of Jerusalem Begins the Times of the Gentiles

The witnesses are correct again about the historical setting of Luke 21:24.

Luke 21:24 English Standard Version (ESV)

[24] They will fall by the edge of the sword and be led captive among all nations, and Jerusalem will be trampled underfoot by the Gentiles, until the times of the Gentiles are fulfilled.

Jesus prophesied, "**they** [the Jewish people] **will fall by the edge of the sword.** The Jewish historian Josephus, who lived during that time,

---

[54] **Watchtower 06 7/15 pp. 6-7 God's Kingdom—Superior in Every Way**

wrote that General Titus came with the Roman army in 70 C.E., and he destroyed the city, killing over 1,000,000,000 Jews.[55]

Jesus went on to say that the Jewish people would "**be led captive among all nations**." This is true as well; as Joseph informs us that 97,000 were taken captive.[56]

Jesus goes on to prophesy that "**Jerusalem will be trampled underfoot by the Gentiles**." The Roman attack came under General Gallus in 66 C.E proved very effective, and he could have destroyed Jerusalem, but instead, pulled back, leaving the job incomplete for what seems like no reason. This left a window of opportunity for any Christians in Jerusalem to comprehend that this is what Jesus was talking about, and flee. Because unknown to them at the time. General Titus would be back with the Roman army in 70 C.E., and he would destroy the city.

The Witnesses are correct about one aspect of their interpretation of Luke 21:24.

Jesus went on to prophesy that the Gentiles would stay dominant "**until the times of the Gentiles are fulfilled**." What did Jesus mean? He meant that from the time of the destruction of Jerusalem, until "that" time, the times of the Gentiles would take place.[57] The Witnesses have the aspect that the Gentile nations would be ruling over the earth until Jesus' return.

The Witnesses go wrong when they write, "clearly, the '**seven times**' [of Nebuchadnezzar's dream of a great tree, which stood for Babylon] and '**the appointed times of the nations**' [the times of the Gentiles] refer to the same time period." What Jesus was explicitly referring to, as his start time of the times of the nations, was the destruction of Jerusalem in 70 C.E. forward. The Witnesses are highjacking Jesus' words and retroactively applying them to 600 years before he uttered them. "He has set up a time for the Gentiles to reign over the city. Everything will follow his plan. That way you will know early on that God's Word is true as it paints the signs of the end for you."[58]

---

[55] Cf. Wars 6.5.1 (6.271–73); 6.9.3 (6.420).
[56] Wars 6.9.3 (6.420); 7.5.3 (7.118); 7.5.5 (7.138); 7.5.6 (7.154).
[57] See Acts 13:46-48; 18:5-6; 28:25-28; cf. also Mark 13:10; Rom 9:30-33; 11:11-16.
[58] Trent C. Butler, *Luke*, vol. 3, Holman New Testament Commentary (Nashville, TN: Broadman & Holman Publishers, 2000), 353.

The Son of Man Is Given Dominion

Daniel 7:13-14 is used along with Luke 21:24 as texts to support the last leg of this journey, the Gentile times were to run until Kingdom's establishment in 1914. How do the Witnesses explicitly interpret these two verses in Daniel chapter 7? Please read the verses first; then, we will quote the Witness literature once more.

Daniel 7:13-14 New World Translation (NWT)	Daniel 7:13-14 English Standard Version (ESV)	Daniel 7:13--14 New American Standard Bible (NASB)
13 "I kept watching in the visions of the night, and look! with the clouds of the heavens, someone like a son of man was coming; and he gained access to the Ancient of Days, and they brought him up close before that One. **14** And to him there were given rulership, honor, and a kingdom, that the peoples, nations, and language groups should all serve him. His rulership is an everlasting rulership that will not pass away, and his kingdom will not be destroyed.	**13** "I saw in the night visions, and behold, with the clouds of heaven there came one like a son of man, and he came to the Ancient of Days and was presented before him. **14** And to him was given dominion and glory and a kingdom, that all peoples, nations, and languages should serve him; his dominion is an everlasting dominion, which shall not pass away, and his kingdom one that shall not be destroyed.	**13** "I kept looking in the night visions, And behold, with the clouds of heaven One like a Son of Man was coming, And He came up to the Ancient of Days And was presented before Him. **14** "And to Him was given dominion, Glory and a kingdom, That all the peoples, nations and *men of every* language Might serve Him. His dominion is an everlasting dominion Which will not pass away; And His kingdom is one Which will not be destroyed.

The Watchtower writes,

When mediating the new covenant, Jesus made an additional covenant with his followers, saying: "I make a covenant with you, just as my Father has made a covenant with me, for a kingdom." (Luke 22:29) This Kingdom covenant put things in place for the fulfillment of a remarkable vision, recorded at Daniel 7:13, 14, 22, 27. Daniel saw "someone like a son of man" being given kingly authority by "the Ancient of Days," Jehovah God. Then Daniel saw that "the holy ones took possession of the kingdom itself." Jesus is the one "like a son of man" who, in 1914, received the heavenly Kingdom from Jehovah God. His spirit-anointed disciples are "the holy ones" who share with him in that Kingdom. (1 Thessalonians 2:12)[59]

The Daniel's Prophecy Book by the Watchtower writes,

"I kept on beholding in the visions of the night, and, see there!" exclaimed Daniel. "With the clouds of the heavens someone like a son of man happened to be coming; and to the Ancient of Days he gained access, and they brought him up close even before that One." (Daniel 7:13) When on earth, Jesus Christ called himself "the Son of man," indicating his kinship to mankind. (Matthew 16:13; 25:31) To the Sanhedrin, or Jewish high court, Jesus said: "You will see the Son of man sitting at the right hand of power and coming on the clouds of heaven." (Matthew 26:64) So in Daniel's vision, the one coming, invisible to human eyes, and gaining access to Jehovah God was the resurrected, glorified Jesus Christ. When did this occur?

With Jesus Christ, God has made a covenant for a Kingdom, just as he had made one with King David. (2 Samuel 7:11-16; Luke 22:28-30) When "the appointed times of the nations" ended in 1914 C.E., Jesus Christ, as David's royal heir, could rightfully receive Kingdom rule. Daniel's prophetic record reads: "To him there were given rulership and dignity and kingdom, that the peoples, national groups and languages should all serve even him. His rulership is an indefinitely lasting rulership that will not pass away, and his kingdom one that will not be brought to ruin." (Daniel 7:14) Thus the Messianic Kingdom was established in heaven in 1914.[60]

In some sense, the Jehovah's Witnesses have Daniel 7:13-14 correct. The son of man is Jesus Christ, and it is referring to the time when Jesus would begin ruling. We again are told that Jesus began to rule in 1914. They are not using this verse to support the date, just that he would begin to rule and that Jesus is the son of man spoke of in Daniel Chapter 7. Other sources below make the same observation.

"One like a son of man" has been interpreted in three primary ways—as an angel (Michael), a personification of the people of God (Israel), and the Messiah. The NT apostles (see

---

[59] Watchtower 98 2/1 p. 17 par. 18 Greater Blessings Through the New Covenant
[60] Daniel's Prophecy, chap. 9 pp. 145-146 pars. 36-37 Who Will Rule the World?

Jn 12:34) and Christ Himself (Mk 14:61–62) confirm the latter view, specifically that the "son of man" is Jesus of Nazareth. Early post-biblical Jewish literature (e.g., 1 Enoch 46:1; 48:10; 4 Ezra 13) also reflects the messianic view. That the "son of man" of verse 13 was considered a divine personage is affirmed by the high priest's charge of blasphemy (Mk 14:64) when Jesus identified Himself as the One "coming with the clouds of heaven" (Mk 14:62). Jesus' use of this title for Himself is one of the strongest evidences that He claimed to be the Messiah. "Son of man" is especially common in eschatological passages (see, e.g., Mt 16:27, 28; 19:28; 24:30; 25:31), and the phrase "a son of man coming with the clouds of heaven" is an allusion to the second advent of Christ, as Mt 24:30 makes clear.[61]

This verse emphasizes the universal—**all peoples, nations and men of every language worshiped him**—and everlasting—**His dominion is an everlasting dominion that will not pass away**—rule of the Son of Man. Jesus probably had this verse in mind when he told his disciples, "All authority in heaven and on earth has been given to me" (Matt 28:18).[62]

The final analysis is that this chronology breaks down several times throughout because the Witnesses have not followed the same advice they gave the Seventh Days Adventist,

We would encourage Adventists to examine the doctrine of "investigative judgment" to see whether its pillars are based solidly on the Bible or are founded on the unstable sands of tradition. The apostle Paul wisely urged: "Make sure of all things; hold fast to what is fine."-- 1 Thessalonians 5:21.[63]

---

[61] Ted Cabal et al., *The Apologetics Study Bible: Real Questions, Straight Answers, Stronger Faith* (Nashville, TN: Holman Bible Publishers, 2007), 1282.
[62] Mark Mangano, *Esther & Daniel*, The College Press NIV Commentary (Joplin, MO: College Press Pub., 2001), 249.
[63] Watchtower 97 7/15 p. 29 The "Investigative Judgment"—A Bible-Based Doctrine?

CHAPTER 2 Then the End Will Come

From Abraham to Us

Matthew 23:37 English Standard Version (ESV)

³⁷ "O Jerusalem, Jerusalem, the city that kills the prophets and stones those who are sent to it! How often would I have gathered your children together as a hen gathers her brood under her wings, and you were not willing!

The nation of Israel came about because God had chosen Abraham after the flood of Noah, due to Abraham's great faith. God had made promises to Abraham because, in a test of his faithfulness, he was willing to sacrifice his only son. And the angel of Jehovah called to Abraham from heaven,

Genesis 22:16-18 English Standard Version (ESV)

¹⁶ and said, "By myself I have sworn, declares the Lord, because you have done this and have not withheld your son, your only son, ¹⁷ I will surely bless you, and I will surely multiply your offspring as the stars of heaven and as the sand that is on the seashore. And your offspring shall possess the gate of his enemies, ¹⁸ and in your (seed) offspring shall all the nations of the earth be blessed, because you have obeyed my voice."

These promises came true, as Isaac, the son of Abraham, had two sons, Esau and Jacob. Jacob was chosen by God, to carry this promise through him and his offspring, and his name was changed to Israel (meaning "he strives against God") after he wrestled with the angel (Gen. 32:28). Jacob/Israel had twelve sons, who became the twelve tribes of Israel, i.e., the nation of Israel. The nation of Israel was taken into slavery for 215 years in the land of Egypt before Moses was used by God to rescue them.

The nation of Israel was rebellious and troublesome from the very beginning. So much so that they could not even enter into the Promised Land, and was made to wonder in the wilderness for 40 years. Once in the Promise Land, the nation of Israel rebelled off and on, as well as entering into and out of extreme false worship. In addition, they killed prophets sent by God for about 1,500 years, or until God's last act of mercy upon them, the arrival of the Messiah for his three and a half year ministry, wherein he tried to bring them the kingdom. The proverbial straw that broke the camel's back was the result of this last effort, as they killed the Son of God as well.

Matthew 21:43 English Standard Version (ESV)	**Matthew 23:38-39** English Standard Version (ESV)
[43] Therefore I tell you, the kingdom of God will be taken away from you and given to a people producing its fruits.	[38] See, your house is left to you desolate. [39] For I tell you, you will not see me again, until you say, 'Blessed is he who comes in the name of the Lord.'"

Because of their rejection of the Son of God, the Kingdom of God was taken from them, in that they were no longer God's chosen people. Some may ask, 'what about Genesis 13:15, where God promised Abraham, "for all the land that you see I will give to you and to your offspring **forever**." Then, Genesis 17:7,' in which God promises Abraham, "And I will establish my covenant between me and you and your offspring after you throughout their generations for an **everlasting covenant**, to be God to you and to your offspring after you." What about the promise at Genesis 22:18, which we quoted above, "your (seed) offspring shall all the nations of the earth be blessed, because you have obeyed my voice."

The covenant with Abraham covered the following throughout its initial implementation with Abraham and its expansion with Isaac and Jacob (Genesis 13:14-17; 15:18; 17:2-8, 19; 22:15-18):

- Through Abraham the promised seed (offspring) of Genesis 3:15 would come;
- This seed (offspring) would possess the gate of his enemies;
- Abraham's seed (offspring) through Isaac would be countless to humans then;
- Abraham's name would be made great;
- The Promise Land would be given to Abraham and his offspring forever;
- All families of the earth would bless themselves by means of the seed (offspring).

Let us use Genesis 13:15 as our example of dealing with the term "forever" (Heb., *olam*), where God promised Abraham, "for all the land that you see I will give to you and to your offspring **forever**." The Hebrew behind forever is a combination of the preposition *ad* (as far as, even to, until, while) and the noun *olam* (forever, ever, everlasting, evermore, perpetual, old, ancient, world)

First, all words have a range of meaning, but not all of those meanings are captured in each use of the word. The context enables a translator/interpreter to determine which of the senses apply in a text. Before going on, "It should be noted that there is no general word for time in Hebrew, neither are there special terms for the past, present, future, and eternity. The word *[olam]* should be compared, with special attention given to the nineteen times when these words are used together."[64]

There are times when *olam* is used in the context, where it is literally referring to something that is forever, "the throne of David shall be established before Jehovah forever *(olam)*." (1 Ki 2:45) Nevertheless, the Hebrew expression *olam in and of itself* does not mean "forever."

> Jenni holds that its basic meaning "most distant times" can refer to either the remote past or to the future or to both as due to the fact that it does not occur independently (as a subject or as an object) but only in connection with prepositions indicating direction (*min* "since," *'ad* "until," *lĕ* "up to") or as an adverbial accusative of direction or finally as the modifying genitive in the construct relationship. In the latter instance *'ōlām* can express by itself the whole range of meanings denoted by all the prepositions "since, until, to the most distant time"; i.e. it assumes the meaning "(unlimited, incalculable) continuance, eternity." (THAT II,[65] p. 230) J. Barr (Biblical Words for Time (1969), p. 73) says, "We might therefore best state the "basic meaning" as a kind of range between 'remotest time' and 'perpetuity'".[66]

Exodus 31:16 English Standard Version (ESV)	Exodus 31:16 Lexham English Bible (LEB)	Exodus 31:16 New American Standard Bible (NASB)
¹⁶ Therefore the people of Israel shall keep the Sabbath, observing the Sabbath throughout their generations, as **a covenant forever**	¹⁶ The *Israelites* will pay attention to the Sabbath *in order* to fulfill the Sabbath throughout their generations *as* a **lasting [olam]**	¹⁶ So the sons of Israel shall observe the sabbath, to celebrate the sabbath throughout their

---

[64] Carl Schultz, "1565 עֵדָה," ed. R. Laird Harris, Gleason L. Archer Jr., and Bruce K. Waltke, *Theological Wordbook of the Old Testament* (Chicago: Moody Press, 1999), 645.
[65] THAT E. Jenni u. C. Westermann, *Theologisches handbuch zum Alten Testament*
[66] Allan A. Macrae, "1631 עלם," ed. R. Laird Harris, Gleason L. Archer Jr., and Bruce K. Waltke, *Theological Wordbook of the Old Testament* (Chicago: Moody Press, 1999), 672–673.

[olam].	covenant.	generations as **a perpetual [olam] covenant.**'

From the above Exodus 3:16 reference to the Sabbath, we can see that translations are taking *olam* differently because some are aware that the Mosaic Law covenant did not last forever. Therefore, *olam* can refer to something that lasts for an indefinitely period of time. Indefinite in that we do not know when it will end.

Romans 10:4	Galatians 5:18
New American Standard Bible (NASB)	New American Standard Bible (NASB)
⁴ For Christ is the **end of the law** for righteousness to everyone who believes.	¹⁸ But if you are led by the Spirit, you are **not under the Law**.

As you can see, by the ransom sacrifice of Christ Jesus (Matt 20:28), he ended the Mosaic Law, meaning Christians were/are no longer under the Law, so they need not obey the Sabbath regulations. If they were under the Mosaic Law, they would have to take every Saturday off from work, they would have to take every seventh year off from work, and anyone disobeying would be stoned to death.

Colossians 2:16	Hebrews 9:15
New American Standard Bible (NASB)	New American Standard Bible (NASB)
¹⁶ Therefore no one is to act as your judge in regard to food or drink or in respect to a festival or a new moon or **a Sabbath day**	¹⁵ For this reason He is the mediator of **a new covenant**, so that, since a death has taken place for the redemption of the transgressions that were *committed* under **the first covenant**, those who have been called may receive the promise of the eternal inheritance.

Another example of *olam* not referring to something that is everlasting, eternal, forever, is the Aaronic priesthood, which also ended with the arrival of Jesus Christ.

Exodus 40:15	Hebrews 7:20-24	Hebrews 10:1
English Standard Version (ESV)	English Standard Version (ESV)	English Standard Version (ESV)
¹⁵ and anoint them, as you anointed their father, that they may serve me as priests. And their anointing shall admit them to a perpetual **[olam]** priesthood throughout their generations."	²⁰ And it was not without an oath. For those who formerly became priests were made such without an oath, ²¹ but this one was made a priest with an oath by the one who said to him: "The Lord has sworn and will not change his mind, 'You are a priest forever.'" ²² This makes Jesus the guarantor of a better covenant. ²³ The former priests were many in number, because they were prevented by death from continuing in office, ²⁴ but he holds his priesthood permanently, because he continues forever.	**10** For since the law has but a shadow of the good things to come instead of the true form of these realities, it can never, by the same sacrifices that are continually offered every year, make perfect those who draw near.

Through Abraham, the promised seed of Genesis 3:15 did come, by way of Jesus Christ. The Israelites were countless, at the time they fully occupied the Promise Land, in human perception at that time. There is little doubt that the name of Abraham became great, as the Jewish people lay claim to him, the Christians lay claim to him, and even Islam lays claim to him. The Promise Land was given to Abraham and his offspring for 'lasting times' or to "most distant times." The Jewish people may very well inhabit the Promise Land forever, but from the late 16th century B.C.E. up unto the time Christ destroys God's enemies (1 Cor. 15:23-26), this is definitely lasting times. All families of the earth have certainly been blessed by means of the seed of Abraham (Jesus Christ), which will go on forever, literally.

Therefore, while the Israelites (Jewish people), are no longer God's chosen people specifically, they to have an opportunity to enter into or under the Kingdom of God, by their acceptance of Jesus Christ.

Jesus Foretells Destruction of the Temple and Disciples Ask a Question

Matthew 24:1-3 English Standard Version (ESV)

¹ Jesus left the temple and was going away, when his disciples came to point out to him the buildings of the temple. ² But he answered them, "You see all these, do you not? Truly, I say to you, there will not be left here one stone upon another that will not be thrown down." ³ As he sat on the Mount of Olives, the disciples came to him privately, saying, "Tell us, when will these things be, and what will be the sign of your coming and of the end of the age?"

Here in verse three, we have Jesus and the disciples taking a seat on the Mount of Olives, looking down on the temple below. The temple compound was the ninth wonder of the ancient world. Jesus had just told the disciples that this marvel was going to be so devastated in a coming destruction, "there will not be left here one stone upon another that will not be thrown down." Looking down, the disciples asked Jesus what they thought to be but one question, not knowing the answer that Jesus would give, showed it to be three separate questions. Of course, the initial question **(1)** was their wondering when the destruction that Jesus spoke of was coming. There second portion of that question was **(2)** what will be the sign of your coming. The third portion of the question was **(3)** the end of the age.⁶⁷ Herein, we will focus on questions **(2)** and **(3)**. In short, **(1)** the destruction of Jerusalem took place in 70 C.E., just 37-years after the death, resurrection, and ascension of Christ.

> They ask these questions about the destruction of Jerusalem and the temple, his own second coming (... [*parousia*], presence, common in the papyri for the visit of the emperor), and the end of the world. Did they think that they were all to take place simultaneously? There is no way to answer. At any rate Jesus treats all three in this great eschatological discourse, the most difficult problem in the Synoptic Gospels. ... It is sufficient for our purpose to think of Jesus as using the destruction of the temple and of Jerusalem which did happen in that generation in a.d. 70, as also a symbol of his own second coming and of the end of the world (... [*sunteleias tou aiōnos*]) or consummation of the age. In a painting the artist by skilful perspective may give on the same surface the inside of a room, the fields outside the window, and the sky far beyond. Certainly in this discourse Jesus blends in apocalyptic language the background of his death on the cross, the coming destruction of Jerusalem, his own second coming and the end of the world. He now touches one, now the other. It is not easy for us to separate clearly the various items.⁶⁸

In "what will be the sign of your **coming**," the Greek word behind "coming" (*parousia*) needs a little more in-depth explaining.

> *Parousia* ... lit., "a presence," *para*, "with," and *ousia*, "being" (from *eimi*, "to be"), denotes both an "arrival" and a consequent "presence with." For instance, in a papyrus letter a lady speaks of the necessity of her parousia in a place in order to attend to matters relating to her property there. Paul speaks of his *parousia* in Philippi, Phil. 2:12 (in contrast to his *apousia*, "his absence"; see absence). Other words denote "the arrival" (see *eisodos* and *eleusis*, above). *Parousia* is used to describe the

---

⁶⁷ Whether one sees this as two questions or three questions is not that big of a difference. If it is two questions; then, the coming/presence of Christ and the end of the age are being treated as one event. However, if there are three; then, the coming/presence of Christ and the end of the age are being treated as two events. Either way, you have Christ's coming/presence and the end of the age. If the Greek word *parousia* carries the sense of both the arrival of Christ and his presence for a time before the end of the age, as explained by *Vine's Expository Dictionary*, this seems to better support it being a three part question. How long that interval is between the arrival, the presence and the conclusion, no one can truly know.

⁶⁸ A.T. Robertson, *Word Pictures in the New Testament* (Nashville, TN: Broadman Press, 1933), Mt 24:3.

presence of Christ with His disciples on the Mount of Transfiguration, 2 Pet. 1:16. When used of the return of Christ, at the rapture of the church, it signifies, not merely His momentary "coming" for His saints, but His presence with them from that moment until His revelation and manifestation to the world. In some passages the word gives prominence to the beginning of that period, the course of the period being implied, 1 Cor. 15:23; 1 Thess. 4:15; 5:23; 2 Thess. 2:1; Jas. 5:7-8; 2 Pet. 3:4. In some, the course is prominent, Matt. 24:3, 37; 1 Thess. 3:13; 1 John 2:28; in others the conclusion of the period, Matt. 24:27; 2 Thess. 2:8.[69]

"What will be the sign of your coming" As we can see from the context of Matthew 24 and Vine's *Expository Dictionary*, parousia, describes not only the arrival of Christ, but his presence as well. This does not give us the sense of a coming and some swift departure. Rather, the presence aspect is a period of time that we cannot know the exact length of, so it does no good even to speculate by adding adjectives, like a "lengthy" or "short" presence.

"the end of the age" What is meant by the Greek word *aion*, which is translated "age." It refers to a certain period of time, an epoch, or age.

> *aion* (αἰών, 165), "an age, era" (to be connected with *aei*, "ever," rather than with *ao*, "to breathe"), signifies a period of indefinite duration, or time viewed in relation to what takes place in the period.[70]

What period of time is being referred to here? If we look at God's use of Moses to help in the Exodus of his people from Egypt, and Moses penning of the Mosaic Law, we would say that from the Exodus to the sacrifice ransom death of Christ was an "age" (period of time or epoch) where the Israelite nation was the only way to God. Then, Jesus entered humanity into another age by his ransom sacrifice, which runs up unto his second coming/presence and the end of this age of Christianity.

Jesus answers this two or three-part question throughout the rest of Matthew 24 and chapter 25. Matthew gives us Jesus' presentation of the events that lead to Jesus coming and presence, to set up his kingdom to

---

[69] The reader should be aware that the Greek word parousia does mean presence, the word is derived from para (with) and ousia (being). However, it does not denote the idea of invisible as the Jehovah Witnesses attest to. See W. E. Vine, Merrill F. Unger, and William White Jr., *Vine's Complete Expository Dictionary of Old and New Testament Words* (Nashville, TN: T. Nelson, 1996), 111.

[70] W. E. Vine, Merrill F. Unger, and William White Jr., *Vine's Complete Expository Dictionary of Old and New Testament Words* (Nashville, TN: T. Nelson, 1996), 19.

rule **over** the earth for a thousand years. Most will be shocked by my saying "over" the earth, as almost all translations render Revelation 5:10 as "and you have made them a kingdom and priests to our God, and they shall reign **on** the earth."

epí [2093] is in the genitive and can range from: "on, upon; over; at, by; before, in the presence of; when, under, at the time of;"[71] Below you are going to find a list of the genitive epi within Revelation that has a similar construction.

If we are to establish that some translations are choosing a rendering because it suits their doctrine, we must compare how they render the same thing elsewhere. I do believe that the English is a problem in trying to say, "They shall reign **on** the earth." First, because this is not a location issue: i.e., "where." The genitive *epi* is dealing not with where, but with authority over, which is expressed by having it over ... not on ...

Please also take special note that the context of all of these epi genitives that follow the active indicative verb and then are followed by the genitive definite article and noun are dealing with authority.

> The verb "to reign" is properly used of kings and queens, and here implies complete power over the world and its inhabitants. So another way of expressing this is "and they shall rule over the world and its inhabitants" or "they shall have power over ...."[72]

Revelation 5:9-10 has a high level of theological content. It either says that Jesus and his co-rulers are going to over the earth, or on the earth. It is theological bias to have several cases of similar context and the same grammatical construction, rendering the verses the same every time, yet to then render one verse contrary to the others, simply because it aligns with one's theology. Please see Revelation 2:26; 6:8; 9:11; 11:6; 13:7; 14:18; 16:9; 17:18, and then look at Revelation **5:10**. Nowhere in Scripture does it say that Jesus is going to rule over the earth.

Signs of the End of the Age

Matthew 24:4 New American Standard Bible (NASB)

⁴ And Jesus answered and said to them, "See to it that no one misleads you.

---

[71] William D. Mounce, Mounce's Complete Expository Dictionary of Old & New Testament Words (Grand Rapids, MI: Zondervan, 2006), 1150.
[72] Bratcher, Robert G.; Hatton, Howard: A Handbook on the Revelation to John. New York: United Bible Societies, 1993 (UBS Handbook Series; Helps for Translators), S. 105

Jesus' disciples, like any other Jew of the day, would have seen the destruction of Jerusalem in 70 C.E., the first century Jewish historian, Josephus, tells us 1,100,000 Jews were killed in the destruction of Jerusalem, with another 97,000 taken captive. (War VI. 9.3)[73] Therefore, here in advance (33 C.E.), Jesus wanted his disciples to be on the watch, to not be misled, as though the destruction of Jerusalem (66-70 C.E.) also meant "the end of the age."

Matthew 24:5 English Standard Version (ESV)

5 For many will come in my name, saying, 'I am the Christ,' and they will lead many astray.

Yes, this would be one of the ways that many coming in Jesus' name would have led the disciples astray, claiming to be the Christ (Hebrew *Messiah*), namely the "anointed one." Therefore, it would not be Christians alone, who would be filling this role as false christs/messiahs/anointed ones.

> "From Josephus it appears that in the first century before the destruction of the Temple [in 70 C.E.] a number of Messiahs arose promising relief from the Roman yoke, and finding ready followers ... Thus about 44, Josephus reports, a certain impostor, Theudas, who claimed to be a prophet, appeared and urged the people to follow him with their belongings to the Jordan, which he would divide for them. According to Acts v. 36 (which seems to refer to a different date), he secured about 400 followers. Cuspius Fadus sent a troop of horsemen after him and his band, slew many of them, and took captive others, together with their leader, beheading the latter ... Another, an Egyptian, is said to have gathered together 30,000 adherents, whom he summoned to the Mount of Olives, opposite Jerusalem, promising that at his command the walls of Jerusalem would fall down, and that he and his followers would enter and possess themselves of the city. But Felix, the procurator (c. 55-60), met the throng with his soldiery. The prophet escaped, but those with him were killed or taken, and the multitude dispersed. Another, whom Josephus styles an impostor, promised the people "deliverance and freedom from their miseries" if they would follow him to the wilderness. Both leader and followers were killed by the troops of Festus, the procurator (60-62; "Ant." xx. 8, § 10). Even when Jerusalem was already in process of destruction by the Romans, a prophet, according to Josephus suborned by the defenders to keep the

---

[73] Flavius Josephus and William Whiston, *The Works of Josephus: Complete and Unabridged* (Peabody: Hendrickson, 1987).

people from deserting announced that God commanded them to come to the Temple, there to receive miraculous signs of their deliverance. Those who came met death in the flames.

Unlike these Messiahs, who expected their people's deliverance to be achieved through divine intervention, Menahem, the son of Judas the Galilean and grandson of Hezekiah, the leader of the Zealots, who had troubled Herod, was a warrior. When the war broke out he attacked Masada with his band, armed his followers with the weapons stored there, and proceeded to Jerusalem, where he captured the fortress Antonia, overpowering the troops of Agrippa II. Emboldened by his success, he behaved as a king, and claimed the leadership of all the troops. Thereby he aroused the enmity of Eleazar, another Zealot leader, and met death as a result of a conspiracy against him (ib. ii. 17, § 9). He is probably identical with the Menahem b. Hezekiah mentioned in Sanh. 98b, and called, with reference to Lam. i. 17, "the comforter ["menaḥem"] that should relieve" (comp. Hamburger, "R. B. T." Supplement, iii. 80). With the destruction of the Temple the appearance of Messiahs ceased for a time. Sixty years later a politico-Messianic movement of large proportions took place with Bar Kokba at its head. This leader of the revolt against Rome was hailed as Messiah-king by Akiba, who referred to him. *The Jewish Encyclopedia* lists 28 false Messiahs between the years 132 C.E. and 1744 C.E.[74]

Matthew 24:6 English Standard Version (ESV)

⁶ And you will hear of wars and rumors of wars. See that you are not alarmed, for this must take place, but the end is not yet.

There have been religious leaders that have been misled by the two Great Wars of the 20th century, World War I and II, associating each of them with the "end of the age." The First Jewish–Roman War (66–73 C.E.),[75] at times called The Great Revolt, could have misled the disciples into thinking that the end was imminent. Therefore, Jesus tells them that they should not be alarmed, and that the end is not yet. This counsel of Jesus has had to be applied from First Jewish–Roman War to the two Great Wars of the 20th century, every time a war came along, which seems to be an end all for humanity. Nevertheless, this one sign alone is

---

[74] Vol. X, pp. 252-255.
[75] The Second Jewish–Roman War (132–135 C.E.) Simon Bar Kokba, who claimed to be the long awaited Messiah, led a revolt against Roman Emperor Hadrian (76-139), for setting up a shrine to Jupiter (supreme Roman god), on the temple site in Jerusalem, as well as outlawing circumcision and instruction of the Law in public.

not enough to signal the end, because imperfect humans are prone to war.

Matthew 24:7 English Standard Version (ESV)

⁷ For nation will rise against nation, and kingdom against kingdom, and there will be famines and earthquakes in various places.

Here Jesus expounds on his previous comments about war because the conflicts of humankind have been so pervasive that there was a need for a reference book, *Dictionary of Wars* by George C. Kohn. Therefore, while we should take note of current events, wars, rumors of wars and even kingdom against kingdom is not enough alone to suppose that the end is here. Therefore, Jesus adds yet another two signs, famines and earthquakes. These two have been a part of humankind's history. Of course, the impact is going to be far greater with seven billion living people on earth, as opposed to a hundred million in 100 C.E. Nevertheless, these are just the beginning.

Matthew 24:8 English Standard Version (ESV)

⁸ All these are but the beginning of the birth pains.

Wars, rumors of wars, kingdoms again kingdom, famines, and earthquakes are just the beginning of the things to come. However, they are not the goal post that the end is imminent. Such tragedies being merely a "beginning of the birth pains," the end was "not yet." Men likely cannot appreciate this verse, because the woman only knows the pain of giving birth to a child. It is the most natural thing in her life and yet the most painful. Therefore, consider that what comes after this metaphorical concept is going to be far more painful for humankind. These pains will grow in severity until the birth of the end of the age, and the return of Jesus. Nevertheless, like any other birth that has finally reached the end, the joy of a newborn child makes one forget the prior pains. This is true after the tribulation, the joys from the Kingdom will outweigh the previous pains.

Matthew 24:9 English Standard Version (ESV)

⁹ "Then they will deliver you up to tribulation and put you to death, and you will be hated by all nations for my name's sake.

Verse 9 of the new section, 9-12, begins with "then" (Greek *tote*), which brings the reader into another section of signs, offering us more of the lines in the fingerprint, the full picture that we are at the time of to the end. "Then" can have the meaning coming *after*, or *at the same time*, or it could mean simply, *therefore*. It would seem that "then" is best understood as meaning 'at the same time,' because these signs, as well as those that we covered in 4-7, and those coming in verse 10 are of a composite sign. Meaning, you are looking for a time when they are all happening and on a worldwide scale.

Who are "they" that deliver Christians up to tribulation? It would be those Christians of verse 5, who were led astray, abandoning the Christian faith. The last 30 years, this has truly seen the abandonment of Christianity, as well as much tribulation for those that have remained faithful. What I am primarily referring to is liberal Christianity (80 percent of Christianity), who has abandoned the biblical truth, for the lie so that they can maintain a good relationship with the world, and progressivism. Christianity has never been more hated than it is today. Sadly, conservative Christians have been deeply opposed and persecuted by liberal Christianity, atheists, not to mention Islam and other religions.

Verse 9 says they will deliver you over (ESV), or hand you over (HCSB), to tribulation. If one is handed over, he must first be seized and then delivered to those, who are seeking to do him harm, even death. Why are the Christians hated so? Former Christians and liberal Christians hate the stand that conservative Christians take by truly living by God's Word, in a world that is anything but. Radical Islam is simply trying to impose themselves on everyone who stands in their way of dominating the world. Thus, being handed over is a result of one's true faith in Jesus Christ.

Matthew 24:10 English Standard Version (ESV)

[10] And then many will fall away and betray one another and hate one another.

While early Christianity suffered horrible deaths through being martyred for simply being a Christian, the hatred today is just as vile by those that slaughter Christians around the world. Nevertheless, persecution through social media, news media, and by way of lawsuits, and protests in the streets, has become the new form of persecution in the Western world. Many have fallen away from Jesus, becoming apostates toward their former brothers and sisters, loathing their very existence.

Matthew 24:11 English Standard Version (ESV)

[11] And many false prophets will arise and lead many astray.

What is a prophet? The primary meaning is one who proclaims the word of God, a spokesperson for God. Therefore, a false prophet would be a spokesperson giving the impression that he is a spokesman for God, but really he is far from it. These ones are very subtle and deceptive in their ability to present themselves as a person representing God. Some modern day examples would be, Jim Bakker, Kenneth Copeland, Benny Hinn, T.D. Jakes, Joyce Meyer, Juanita Bynum, Creflo Dollar, Eddie Long,

Pat Robertson, and Joel Olsteen. Of course, these are just some of the televangelists, who are false prophets, with tens of millions of followers. Other false prophet religious leaders have tens of millions of followers as well. Then, there are charismatic Christian denominations that numbered over 500 million followers. These ones claim gifts of God (faith healing, speaking in tongues, etc.), which clearly are anything but. The true Christians are falling away in great numbers, being led astray by these false prophets, and those who have not, need to remain awake!

Matthew 24:12 English Standard Version (ESV)

[12] And because lawlessness will be increased, the love of many will grow cold.

The world we live in is overflowing with murders, rapes, armed robberies, and assaults, not to mention the wars. It has grown so pervasive that many have grown callused to seeing the newspapers, websites and television news filled with one heinous crime, one after another. In looking at just one city in the United States, in 2012, 532 people were murdered in the city of Chicago, with a population of 2.7 million. However, in San Pedro Sula of the country Honduras, 1,143 people were murdered with only a population of 719,447. Statistics from the United Nations reported 250,000 cases of rape or attempted rape annually. However, it must be kept in mind that because of the savagery of the times, in "many parts of the world, rape is very rarely reported, due to the extreme social stigma cast on women who have been raped, or the fear of being disowned by their families, or subjected to violence, including honor killings."[76]

Verse 12 says that the love of "the love of many will **grow cold**," and indeed it has. There are atrocious crimes against individuals, groups, nations, which would cripple the mind of anyone living decades ago. However, because of seeing it every day, all day long, the world has grown hardened to the lawlessness that exists around them. Christians carry the hope of salvation in their heart, which Jesus addresses next.

Matthew 24:13 English Standard Version (ESV)

[13] But the one who endures to the end will be saved.

What are we to endure? We are to endure while we maintain our walk with God through false Christs who will lead many astray, the wars, and the natural disasters. We are to endure while we maintain our walk with God through the loss of many of our spiritual brothers and sisters who fall away, the betrayal of former Christians, and the hatred of humankind who is alienated from God. We are to endure while we

---

[76] http://en.wikipedia.org/wiki/Rape_statistics

maintain our walk with God through false prophets that have arisen and lead many astray, the increase of the lawlessness in this world, and the love of humanity growing colder. Yes, each of us, who survives to the end of the Christian era, to the return of Christ, will be saved from Jesus' destruction of the wicked. However, we are not to simply sit around; we have work to accomplish that is the last sign of the end of the age.

Matthew 24:14 English Standard Version (ESV)

¹⁴ And this gospel of the kingdom will be proclaimed throughout the whole world as a testimony to all nations, and then the end will come.

This is the last of the signs that Jesus gave that should concern us, as it is directly related to the end of the age, and the return of Christ, namely **'the gospel of the kingdom being proclaimed throughout the whole world.'** Jesus makes it very clear what he meant by "the whole world," by then saying "all nations" (Gk., *ethnos*). What Jesus meant here was more directed toward all races, not so much the "nations" that we know the world to be divided into today. Therefore, Jesus speaking of the whole world was a reference to "**a body of persons united by kinship, culture, and common traditions, *nation, people*.**"[77] Today, while for the most part, nations are made up of different races, the world is also becoming a melting pot.

In the phrase "**testimony** to all nations," we find the Greek word *martyrion*, which was a legal term of "**that which serves as testimony or proof, *testimony, proof*.**"[78] The testimony here that is to be shared by Christ's disciples has to with Jesus and the kingdom. Evidence, proof, testimony has the ability to overcome the false reasoning of those in the world, to win them over, as well as convict those who refuse to see the evidence for what it is. Elsewhere Jesus said very clearly,

Matthew 11:15	**Matthew 13:9**	**Matthew 13:43**
English Standard Version (ESV)	English Standard Version (ESV)	English Standard Version (ESV)
¹⁵ He who has ears to hear, let him hear.	⁹ He who has ears, let him hear."	⁴³ Then the righteous will shine like the sun in the kingdom of their Father. He who has ears, let him hear.

---

[77] William Arndt, Frederick W. Danker, and Walter Bauer, *A Greek-English Lexicon of the New Testament and Other Early Christian Literature* (Chicago: University of Chicago Press, 2000), 276.
[78] IBID, 619.

No One Knows That Day and Hour

Matthew 24:36 English Standard Version (ESV)

³⁶ "But concerning that day and hour no one knows, not even the angels of heaven, nor the Son, but the Father only.

While none of us can know the precise time of Jesus' return, we do know that we are to be busy in the work that he has given us. Regardless of the time left, how will you use it? Here is how we should use our time before Christ's return. We should **live as though it is tomorrow**, but **plan as though it is 50-years away**. What do we mean by this? We live as though Christ is returning tomorrow, by walking with God, having a righteous standing before him. We plan as though it is 50-years away by living a life that makes strategies for a long-term evangelism that fulfills our end of the great commission. (Matt 24:14; 28:19-20; Ac 1:8)

Our sinful nature would not do well if we knew the exact day and hour. We do badly enough when we simply think Christ's return is close. You have had religions that have set dates for Christ's return, or are constantly saying, 'the end is near!' The ones who set actual dates for Christ's return: quit their jobs, sell their homes, take all their money out of the bank, and take their kids out of school, either (1) to have a good time before the end, or (2) to spend the last couple years yelling from the rooftops that "the end is coming!"

Those who are constantly saying, 'the end is near,' are similar, in that they do not take job promotions because it would cut into their evangelism, they do not allow their children to have university educations or plan careers because to them the end is near. Nevertheless, these groups are at least concerned about their evangelism but fail to realize; we do not know when the end is coming.

We need to find a way in the time that remains, be it 5 years, 50 years, or 500 years, to encourage and foster "sincere brotherly love," and to display "obedience to the truth." What do we need to be obedient to? **(1)** We need to clean up the household of Christianity. **(2)** We need to then, carry out the great commission that Jesus assigned, to preach, to teach, and to make disciples! (Matt 24:14; 28:19-20; Ac 1:8) It is our assignment, in the time remaining, to assist God in helping those with a receptive heart, to accept the good news of the kingdom. Yes, we are offering those of the world, the hope of getting on the path of salvation, an opportunity at everlasting life. Just because we do not know the day or the hour, does not mean that we should be less urgent about this assignment. Remember Jesus' illustration,

Matthew 24:43 English Standard Version (ESV)

⁴³ But know this, that if the master of the house had known in what part of the night the thief was coming, he would have stayed awake and would not have let his house be broken into.

Moreover, remember Jesus' question,

Luke 18:8 English Standard Version (ESV)

⁸ I tell you, he will give justice to them speedily. Nevertheless, when the Son of Man comes, will he find faith on earth?"

CHAPTER 3 Correctly Understanding Bible Prophecy

Explaining Prophecy

Most understand the word "prophecy" to be another word for prediction. The Hebrew, *navi* and the Greek *prophētēs* (prophet), carry the meaning of one who is a proclaimer of God's message and need not necessarily be foretelling of the future. He may very well be proclaiming a moral teaching, an expression of a divine command or judgment, but they also mean a foretelling of something to come. Below, we will be considering the secondary meaning of prophecy, one who for *foretells* the future, not the primary meaning, one who *forth tells* the will and purpose of God, i.e. a proclaimer. Just as it is true of all these genres, there are principles that both writer and reader were aware of, and did not need to be explained. We, however, are far removed from their time and need to be introduced to these principles.

The Prophetic Judgment of Nineveh

Deuteronomy 18:20-22

[20]But the prophet who presumes to speak a word in my name that I have not commanded him to speak, or who speaks in the name of other gods, that same prophet shall die.' [21]And if you say in your heart, 'How may we know the word that the LORD has not spoken?'— [22]<u>when a prophet speaks in the name of the LORD, if the word does not come to pass or come true, that is a word that the LORD has not spoken; the prophet has spoken it presumptuously</u>. You need not be afraid of him.

Jonah 3:4

[4]Jonah began to go into the city, going a day's journey. And he called out, "Yet forty days, and Nineveh shall be overthrown!"

Jonah 3:5

[5] And the people of Nineveh believed God. They called for a fast and put on sackcloth, from the greatest of them to the least of them.

Jonah 3:10

[10]When God saw what they did, how they turned from their evil way, God relented of the disaster that he had said he would do to them, and he did not do it.

Based on Deuteronomy 18:20-222, does Jonah 3:4-5 and 10 not prove that Jonah was a false prophet. No, both Jonah and the Ninevites were aware of a principle that is often overlooked by the modern-day reader. Both Jeremiah and Ezekiel give the answer, or the principle that that readers of that time would have understood about judgment prophecy. Jeremiah explicitly explains the rule of judgment prophecies, when he writes, "If at any time I say that I am going to uproot, break down, or destroy any nation or kingdom, but then that nation turns from its evil, I will not do what I said I would." (17:7-8, GNT)

The opposite is true as well,

Jeremiah 18:9-10 Good News Translation (GNT)

⁹ On the other hand, if I say that I am going to plant or build up any nation or kingdom, ¹⁰ but then that nation disobeys me and does evil, I will not do what I said I would.

Yes, if one turns back from their evil ways, endeavoring to obey God's Word, he will not receive the condemnatory judgment that he deserves. That a repentant, evil person's previous wicked deeds will not be held against them, God states,

Ezekiel 33:13-15

¹³Though I say to the righteous that he shall surely live, yet if he trusts in his righteousness and does injustice, none of his righteous deeds shall be remembered, but in his injustice that he has done he shall die. ¹⁴Again, though I say to the wicked, 'You shall surely die,' yet if he turns from his sin and does what is just and right, ¹⁵if the wicked restores the pledge, gives back what he has taken by robbery, and walks in the statutes of life, not doing injustice, he shall surely live; he shall not die.

Regardless of all that one has done throughout their life, it is their standing in God's eyes at the time of the divine judgment, which God considers. Therefore, God goes on to say through Ezekiel,

Ezekiel 33:14-16

¹⁴ Again, though I say to the wicked, 'You shall surely die,' yet if he turns from his sin and does what is just and right, ¹⁵ if the wicked restores the pledge, gives back what he has taken by robbery, and walks in the statutes of life, not doing injustice, he shall surely live; he shall not die. ¹⁶ None of the sins that he has committed shall be remembered against him. He has done what is just and right; he shall surely live.

Supposed Unfulfilled Prophecy

In the days when Micah was prophesying, c. 777-717, the king, the heads of the Jerusalem government, the religious leaders, the priests, and some prophets, were deserving of nothing but death. All were guilty of causing the life of their fellow countrymen, all for the sake of greed. They were guilty of false worship, bribery, lies, and wicked behavior. These leaders used false prophets, who were not true spokesmen of God. Therefore, the real prophet, Micah, shouted,

Micah 3:12

12 Therefore because of you Zion shall be plowed as a field; Jerusalem shall become a heap of ruins, and the mountain of the house a wooded height.

The destruction occurred in the late seventh-century B.C.E., just as it was prophesied. As we can see below, Micah 3:12 was quoted over a century later in Jeremiah 26:18.

Jeremiah 26:16-19 Updated American Standard Version (UASV)

16 Then the officials and all the people said to the priests and the prophets, "This man is not worthy of death; for he hath spoken to us in the name of Jehovah our God." 17 Then rose up certain of the elders of the land, and spoke to all the assembly of the people, saying, 18 "Micah the Morashtite prophesied in the days of Hezekiah king of Judah; and he spoke to all the people of Judah, saying: 'Thus says Jehovah of hosts,

"'Zion shall be plowed as a field;
Jerusalem shall become a heap of ruins,
and the mountain of the house a wooded height.'

19 Did Hezekiah king of Judah and all Judah put him to death? Did he not fear Jehovah and entreat the favor of Jehovah, and Jehovah changed his mind about the misfortune, which he had pronounced against them? But we are committing a great evil against our own souls."

Is this another unfulfilled prophecy? Did not Jeremiah himself say, "Jehovah changed his mind about the misfortune, which he had pronounced against them"? Verse 19 of Jeremiah [chapter 26] "indicates that Micah's preaching may have been instrumental in the revival under King Hezekiah (see 2 Kgs 18:1–6; 2 Chr 29–31)." (Barker and Bailey 2001, 82) The New American Commentary authors go on to say,

> Lamentations describes the awful fulfillment of this prophecy (see Introduction, p. 30).[79] It is ironic that those who

---

[79] Cf. Lam 1:1, 4, 6, 18–19; 2:2, 6, 9–10, 20; 5:17–18, etc.

thought they were the builders of Zion (v. 10) actually turned out to be, in a sense, its destroyers. The Lord, because of their breach of covenant, used King Nebuchadnezzar's Neo-Babylonian army to raze Jerusalem and its temple. They were reduced to a "mound of ruins" (translating the Hb. word *'iyyîn*) similar to an archaeological tell and to Ai (see also comments on 1:6), foreshadowing the Roman destruction of a.d. 70. Jerusalem became a place suitable only for wild animals. And the temple mount that thronged with worshipers became as deserted as when Abraham almost offered Isaac there on Mount Moriah (Gen 22:2, 14). (Barker and Bailey 2001, 82)

Yes, there is no reason to view Micah's words as an unfulfilled prophecy. What we have here is a following of the above rule, with a qualifying clause, so to speak. As God said through Jeremiah, "If at any time I say that I am going to uproot, break down, or destroy any nation or kingdom, but then that nation turns from its evil, I will not do what I said I would." (17:7-8) However, "if I say that I am going to plant or build up any nation or kingdom, but then that nation disobeys me and does evil, I will not do what I said I would." In other words, the king, the governmental leaders, and the priests heeded Micah's warning, repented, and were forgiven for a time, with the judgment prophecy lifted. However, they fell back into their former ways, even more grievously than before. Therefore, Micah's prophecy was reinstated. It is as Jeremiah said in 26:19, "But we are committing a great evil against our own souls." Therefore, Jeremiah was saying, Micah prophesied, the people repented, God forgave them, and now Micah's words will be carried out, because of the current generation of God's people 'committing a great evil against their own souls.'

As we can see from the above, judgment prophecies are based on a continued wrong course by those receiving condemnation. However, both the condemned and the one proclaiming the prophecy knew that the judgment would be lifted if they reversed course, and repented. This was even expressed by Jonah himself. "But it displeased Jonah exceedingly, and he was angry. And he prayed to Jehovah and said, "O Jehovah, is not this what I said when I was yet in my country? That is why I made haste to flee to Tarshish; for I knew that you are a gracious God and merciful, slow to anger and abounding in steadfast love, and relenting from disaster." (4:1-2) However, it is also true, if one goes in the opposite direction after having repented, returning to the sinful ways, the judgment will be reinstated.

Prophetic Language

The prophet is much like the poet, in that he is given a license to express himself in nonliteral language. Generally, he is working with images that are far more effective than words themselves.

Matthew 24:29-31

The Coming of the Son of Man

²⁹ "Immediately after the tribulation of those days the sun will be darkened, and the moon will not give its light, and the stars will fall from heaven, and the powers of the heavens will be shaken. ³⁰ Then will appear in heaven the sign of the Son of Man, and then all the tribes of the earth will mourn, and they will see the Son of Man coming on the clouds of heaven with power and great glory. ³¹ And he will send out his angels with a loud trumpet call, and they will gather his elect from the four winds, from one end of heaven to the other.

The above cosmic terminology need not be taken literally. It is a part of their toolkit, which enables them to make it clear that God is acting in behalf of humans. (See Dan. 2:21; 4:17, 25, 34–35; 5:21) The sun is not going to be darkened, the moon will not stop giving its light, the stars are not going to fall from the heavens, nor will the heavens be shaken. What is being communicated here is that following the tribulation when God is going to judge humans, the righteous will receive life and the unrighteous will cut off from life. (34-45) While we do not take cosmic terminology literally, we do discover its meaning, and this is what we are to take literally.

Acts 2:14-21

Peter's Sermon at Pentecost

¹⁴ But Peter, standing with the eleven, lifted up his voice and addressed them: "Men of Judea and all who dwell in Jerusalem, let this be known to you, and give ear to my words. ¹⁵ For these people are not drunk, as you suppose, since it is only the third hour of the day. ¹⁶ But this is what was uttered through the prophet Joel:

¹⁷ "'And in the last days it shall be, God declares,
that I will pour out my Spirit on all flesh,
and your sons and your daughters shall prophesy,
  and your young men shall see visions,
  and your old men shall dream dreams;

¹⁸ even on my male servants and female servants
   in those days I will pour out my Spirit, and they shall prophesy.
¹⁹ And I will show wonders in the heavens above
   and signs on the earth below,
   blood, and fire, and vapor of smoke;
²⁰ the sun shall be turned to darkness
   and the moon to blood,
   before the day of the Lord comes, the great and magnificent day.
²¹ And it shall come to pass that everyone who calls upon the name of the Lord shall be saved.'

In all occurrences, prophecy proclaimed in Bible times had meaning to the people who heard it; it served for their guidance as well as each generation up unto the time of its fulfillment. Usually, it had some fulfillment in that time, in numerous instances being fulfilled during the days of that very generation. In looking at Peters quote from Joel, it must be asked; did they see those cosmic events on Pentecost? Yes, the cosmic terminology is expressing that God was acting in behalf of those first Christians. A new era was being entered and God did pour out His Spirit, and sons and daughters did prophesy, both in proclaiming a message, and in the foretelling of further events. However, let us delve even deeper into prophecy and how they are to be interpreted. Before moving on, let us briefly offer what we have learned this far:

- Judgment prophecies can be lifted, set aside if the parties affected repent and turnaround from their former course.
- On the other hand, if God has promised blessings but then that person or group disobeys him and does evil, he will not do what he had said he would do.
- Then again, if one has repented, turned around, and a judgment prophecy has been lifted, it can be reinstated if that person or group returns to their former evil ways.
- Prophets have a license to use prophetic language, cosmic terminology that evidences that God is working or acting within humanity.
- While we do not take cosmic terminology literally, we do discover its meaning, and this is what we are to take literally.

Interpreting Prophecy

If we are to understand and interpret prophecy correctly, we must first have a grasp of the figurative language, types, and symbols.

We will follow the same interpretation process here that we would elsewhere, grammatical-historical interpretation, which attempts to ascertain what the author meant by the words that he used, which should have been understood by his original readers. (Stein 1994, 38-9) It was the primary method of interpretation when higher criticism's Historical-Critical Method was in its infancy back in the 19th century (Milton Terry), and remains the only method of interpretation for true conservative scholarship in the later 20th century into the 21st century.

Grammatical Aspect

When we speak of interpreting the Bible grammatically, we are referring to the process of seeking to determine its meaning by ascertaining four things: (a) the meaning of words (lexicology), (b) the form of words (morphology), (c) the function of words (parts of speech), and (d) the relationships of words (syntax). In the meaning of words (lexicology), we are concerned with (a) etymology- how words are derived and developed, (b) usage how words are used by the same and other authors, (c) synonyms and antonyms -how similar and opposite words are used, and (d) context-how words are used in various contexts.

In discussing the form of words (morphology), we are looking at how words are structured and how that affects their meaning. For example, the word eat means something different from ate, though the same letters are used. The word part changes meaning when the letter "s" is added to it to make the word parts. The function of words (parts of speech) considers what the various forms do. These include attention to subjects, verbs, objects, nouns, and others, as will be discussed later. The relationships of words (syntax) are the way words are related or put together to form phrases, clauses, and sentences. (Zuck 1991, 100-101)

Historical Aspect

By "historical" we mean the setting in which the book of the prophet was written and the circumstances involved in the writing. ... taking into consideration the circumstances of the writings and the cultural environment. We must keep in mind that even though many of the prophetic utterances were meant for the generation, in which they were spoken, or shortly thereafter. Even if it is not the immediate generation, all prophetic utterances had some type of meaning to the prophet's generation, be it hope in some future person or event, or the knowledge of a judgment that is coming or could come as a result of their behavior. For example, maybe the Israelites are under persecution and oppression by the surrounding nations, and the prophecy is for a protector that is to rise up, and set matters straight. Even though they do not know, who the protector is, or the exact time of his appearance, they do know that God cannot lie, nor has he ever lied, and so, they can have hope and faith in his words. Moreover, they would have also known that if they fell back into false worship, God could withdraw his prophetic message of a savior.

The context in which a given Scripture passage is written influences how that passage is to be understood. Context includes several things:

- the verse(s) immediately before and after a passage
- the paragraph and book in which the verses occur
- the dispensation in which it was written
- the message of the entire Bible
- the historical-cultural environment of that time when it was written. (Zuck 1991, 77)

We will end this chapter here. However, our next chapter, chapter 10, will walk the reader through a portion of a prophetic book. We have chosen the book of Isaiah (66:1-14), which is a favorite of many, even viewed as the fifth Gospel, because it speaks of the coming Messiah so much.

CHAPTER 4 Correctly Understanding Signs of the End of the Age

Matthew 24:4 Updated American Standard Version (UASV)

⁴ And Jesus answered them, "See that no one leads you astray.

Jesus' disciples, like any other Jew of the day, would have seen the destruction of Jerusalem in 70 C.E. as impossible. However, the first-century Jewish historian, Josephus, tells us 1,100,000 Jews were killed in the destruction of Jerusalem, with another 97,000 taken captive. (War VI. 9.3)[80] Therefore, here in advance (33 C.E.); Jesus wanted his disciples to be on the watch, to not be misled, as though the destruction of Jerusalem (66-70 C.E.) also meant "the end of the age," i.e. his second coming, the kingdom, and the millennial reign.

Matthew 24:5 Update American Standard Version (UASV)

⁵ For many will come in my name, saying, 'I am the Christ,' and they will lead many astray.

Yes, this would be one of the ways that many coming in Jesus' name would have led the disciples astray, claiming to be the Christ (Hebrew *Messiah*), namely the "anointed one." Therefore, it would not be Christians alone, who would be filling this role as false Christs/messiahs/anointed ones.

> "From Josephus it appears that in the first century before the destruction of the Temple [in 70 C.E.] a number of Messiahs arose promising relief from the Roman yoke, and finding ready followers ... Thus about 44, Josephus reports, a certain impostor, Theudas, who claimed to be a prophet, appeared and urged the people to follow him with their belongings to the Jordan, which he would divide for them. According to Acts v. 36 (which seems to refer to a different date), he secured about 400 followers. Cuspius Fadus sent a troop of horsemen after him and his band, slew many of them, and took captive others, together with their leader, beheading the latter ... Another, an Egyptian, is said to have gathered together 30,000 adherents, whom he summoned to the Mount of Olives, opposite Jerusalem, promising that at his command the walls of Jerusalem would fall down, and that he and his followers would enter and possess themselves of the city. But Felix, the

---

[80] Flavius Josephus and William Whiston, *The Works of Josephus: Complete and Unabridged* (Peabody: Hendrickson, 1987).

procurator (c. 55-60), met the throng with his soldiery. The prophet escaped, but those with him were killed or taken, and the multitude dispersed. Another, whom Josephus styles an impostor, promised the people "deliverance and freedom from their miseries" if they would follow him to the wilderness. Both leader and followers were killed by the troops of Festus, the procurator (60-62; "Ant." xx. 8, § 10). Even when Jerusalem was already in process of destruction by the Romans, a prophet, according to Josephus suborned by the defenders to keep the people from deserting announced that God commanded them to come to the Temple, there to receive miraculous signs of their deliverance. Those who came met death in the flames.

Unlike these Messiahs, who expected their people's deliverance to be achieved through divine intervention, Menahem, the son of Judas the Galilean and grandson of Hezekiah, the leader of the Zealots, who had troubled Herod, was a warrior. When the war broke out he attacked Masada with his band, armed his followers with the weapons stored there, and proceeded to Jerusalem, where he captured the fortress Antonia, overpowering the troops of Agrippa II. Emboldened by his success, he behaved as a king, and claimed the leadership of all the troops. Thereby he aroused the enmity of Eleazar, another Zealot leader, and met death as a result of a conspiracy against him (ib. ii. 17, § 9). He is probably identical with the Menahem b. Hezekiah mentioned in Sanh. 98b, and called, with reference to Lam. i. 17, "the comforter ["menaḥem"] that should relieve" (comp. Hamburger, "R. B. T." Supplement, iii. 80). With the destruction of the Temple the appearance of Messiahs ceased for a time. Sixty years later a politico-Messianic movement of large proportions took place with Bar Kokba at its head. This leader of the revolt against Rome was hailed as Messiah-king by Akiba, who referred to him. *The Jewish Encyclopedia* lists 28 false Messiahs between the years 132 C.E. and 1744 C.E.[81]

Matthew 24:6 Update American Standard Version (UASV)

⁶ You will be hearing of wars and rumors of wars. See that you are not alarmed, for those things must take place, but the end is not yet.

There have been religious leaders that have been misled by the two Great Wars of the 20th century, World War I and II, associating each of them with the "end of the age." The First Jewish–Roman War (66–73

---

[81] Vol. X, pp. 252-255.

C.E.),[82] at times called The Great Revolt, could have misled the disciples into thinking that the end was imminent. Therefore, Jesus tells them that they should not be alarmed and that the end is not yet. This counsel of Jesus has had to be applied from First Jewish–Roman War to the two Great Wars of the 20th century, every time a war came along, which seems to be an end all for humanity. Nevertheless, this one sign alone is not enough to signal the end, because imperfect humans are prone to war.

Matthew 24:7 Update American Standard Version (UASV)

⁷ For nation will rise against nation, and kingdom against kingdom, and there will be famines and earthquakes in various places.

Here Jesus expounds on his previous comments about war because the conflicts of humankind have been so pervasive that there was a need for a reference book, *Dictionary of Wars* by George C. Kohn. Therefore, while we should take note of current events, wars, rumors of wars and even kingdom against kingdom is not enough alone to suppose that the end is here. Therefore, Jesus adds yet another two signs, famines, and earthquakes. These two have also been a part of humankind's history. Of course, the impact is going to be far greater with seven billion living people on earth, as opposed to a hundred million in 100 C.E. Nevertheless, these are just the beginning.

Matthew 24:8 Update American Standard Version (UASV)

⁸ But all these are but the beginning of the birth pains.

Wars, rumors of wars, kingdoms against kingdom, famines and earthquakes are just the beginning of the things to come. However, they are not the goal post that the end is imminent. Such tragedies being merely a "beginning of the birth pains," the end was "not yet." Men likely cannot appreciate this verse, because the woman only knows the pain of giving birth to a child. It is the most natural thing in her life and yet the most painful. Therefore, consider that what comes after this metaphorical concept is going to be far more painful for humankind. These pains will grow in severity until the birth of the end of the age, and the return of Jesus. Nevertheless, like any other birth that has finally reached the end, the joy of a newborn child makes one forget the past pains. This is true after the tribulation; the joys of the Kingdom will outweigh the previous pains.

---

[82] The Second Jewish–Roman War (132–135 C.E.) Simon Bar Kokba, who claimed to be the long awaited Messiah, led a revolt against Roman Emperor Hadrian (76-139), for setting up a shrine to Jupiter (supreme Roman god), on the temple site in Jerusalem, as well as outlawing circumcision and instruction of the Law in public.

Matthew 24:9 Update American Standard Version (UASV)

⁹ "Then they will deliver you up to tribulation, and will kill you, and you will be hated by all nations because of my name.

Verse 9 of the new section, 9-12, begins with "then" (Greek *tote*), which brings the reader into another section of signs, offering us more of the lines in the fingerprint, i.e., the full picture that we are at the time of to the end. "Then" can have the meaning coming *after*, *or at the same time*, or it could mean simply, *therefore*. It would seem that "then" is best understood as meaning 'at the same time,' because these signs, as well as those that we covered in 4-7, and those coming in verse 10 are of a composite sign. Meaning, we are looking for a time when they are all taking place and on a worldwide scale.

Who are "they" that deliver Christians up to tribulation? It would be those Christians of verse 5, who were led astray, abandoning the Christian faith. The last 50 years have truly brought about the abandonment of Christianity, as well as much tribulation for those that have remained faithful. This is primarily a reference to liberal Christianity (80 percent of Christianity), who has abandoned the biblical truth, for the lie so that they can maintain a good relationship with the world, and progressivism. Christianity has never been more hated than it is today. Sadly, conservative Christians have been deeply opposed and persecuted by liberal Christianity, atheists, not to mention Islam and other religions.

Verse 9 says "they will deliver you up" (ESV), or "they will hand you over" (HCSB), "to tribulation." If one is 'handed over,' he must first be seized and then delivered to those, who are seeking to do him harm, even death. Why are the Christians hated so? Former Christians (now agnostics and atheists), as well as liberal Christians hate the stand that conservative Christians take as they truly live by God's Word, in the world that is anything but. Radical Islam[83] is simply trying to impose themselves on everyone who stands in their way of dominating the world. Thus, being handed over is a result of one's true faith in Jesus Christ.

Islamic Excursion

"There are about 1.6 billion Muslims, or 23% of the world's population, making Islam the second-largest religion. ... Muslims make up a majority of the population in 49 countries around the world." It has been estimated that 5 to 15 percent of all Muslims are radical. However,

---

[83] World's Muslim population more widespread than you might ..., http://www.pewresearch.org/fact-tank/2013/06/07/worlds-muslim-population-more-wi (accessed December 23, 2015).

let us be generous and say that it is only 01 percent. One percent of 1.6 billion is still 16,000,000 million radical Muslims. However, one must realize that in survey after survey, the majority of Muslims support radical views.

Shariah Law is Islamic canonical law based on the teachings of the Quran and the traditions of the Prophet (Hadith and Sunna), prescribing both religious and secular duties and sometimes retributive penalties for lawbreaking. It has generally been supplemented by legislation adapted to the conditions of the day, though the manner in which it should be applied in modern states is a disputed between Islamic fundamentalists and modernists. Today Sweden is the rape capital of the world because of their Muslim population. Why? Under Shariah Law, it is not a sin or crime to force an infidel (i.e., non-Muslim) to have sex. This is what is missing from the debate. It is the culture, the worldview, the ideology, of a the Muslim people that conflict with God's Word, the US Constitution, The UK, Canada, Germany, Sweden, namely, human moral values of a civilized society.

Under Shariah Law women are viewed as property not humans. A wife can be beat for anything. She can be stoned to death for a number of things. A daughter could be killed for dating a non-Muslim, which is called an honor killing. A thief can have their hand or foot cut off. There are many horrific aspects to Shariah Law, but we will just look at honor killings as our example.

>An **honor killing** is the homicide of a member of a family by other members, due to the perpetrators' belief that the victim has brought shame or dishonor upon the family, or has violated the principles of a community or a religion, usually for reasons such as refusing to enter an arranged marriage, being in a relationship that is disapproved by their family, having sex outside marriage, becoming the victim of rape, dressing in ways which are deemed inappropriate, or engaging in non-heterosexual relations.

>Refusing an arranged marriage is often a cause of an honor killing. The family which has prearranged the marriage risks disgrace if the marriage does not proceed. A woman attempting to obtain a divorce or separation without the consent of the husband/extended family can also be a trigger for honor killings. In cultures where marriages are arranged and goods are often exchanged between families, a woman's desire to seek a divorce is often viewed as an insult to the men who negotiated the deal. By making their marital problems known outside the family, the women are seen as exposing the family to public

dishonor. In certain cultures, an *allegation* against a woman can be enough to tarnish her family's reputation, and to trigger an honor killing: the family's fear of being ostracized by the community is enormous. In many cultures, victims of rape face severe violence, including honor killings, from their families and relatives. In many parts of the world, women who have been raped are considered to have brought 'dishonour' or 'disgrace' to their families. This is especially the case if the victim becomes pregnant.

Central to the code of honor, in many societies, is a woman's virginity, which must be preserved until marriage. Suzanne Ruggi writes, "A woman's virginity is the property of the men around her, first her father, later a gift for her husband; a virtual dowry as she graduates to marriage."

Honor killings are often a result of strongly patriarchal views on women, and the position of women in society. In these traditional male-dominated societies women are dependent first on their father and then on their husband, whom they are expected to obey. Women are viewed as property and not as individuals with their own agency. As such, they must submit to male authority figures in the family – failure to do so can result in extreme violence as punishment. Violence is seen as a way of ensuring compliance and preventing rebellion. According to Shahid Khan, a professor at the Aga Khan University in Pakistan: "Women are considered the property of the males in their family irrespective of their class, ethnic, or religious group. The owner of the property has the right to decide its fate. The concept of ownership has turned women into a commodity which can be exchanged, bought and sold." In such cultures, women are not allowed to take control over their bodies and sexuality: these are the property of the males of the family, the father (and other male relatives) who must ensure virginity until marriage; and then the husband to whom his wife's sexuality is subordinated - a woman must not undermine the ownership rights of her guardian by engaging in premarital sex or adultery.[84]

We in the United States have known of Al Qaeda especially since September 11, 2001. Throughout 2014 and 2015, we have seen the rise of ISIS, whose slaughter of women, children, men, and older ones, anyone in their way has left us stunned. They have hung people on takes, put men

---

[84] Honor killing - Wikipedia, the free encyclopedia, https://en.wikipedia.org/wiki/Honor_killing (accessed December 23, 2015).

in cages and set them on fire, put cages filled with people in a pool and filled it slowly with water, and have raped and killed a countless number of little girls. What do Al Queda, ISIS in Iraq and Syria, Boko Haram in northeastern Nigeria, Al-Shabaab, a Somalia-based cell of the Islamist militant group, and many others want?

They want an Islamic State, which is a type of government, in which the primary basis for government is Islamic religious law, i.e., Shariah Law. They want a caliphate, which is an Islamic state led by a supreme religious as well as political leader known as a caliph and all the Prophets of Islam. The term caliphate is often applied to successions of Muslim empires that have existed in the Middle East and Southwest Asia.

Islam's eschatological (last days of humanity), belief is different from Christianity. Christians believe that an Armageddon (great was of God) is coming at the return of Christ but that Jesus determines when and how that return will take place. Islam, on the other hand, believes that one day Isa (Jesus) will return with their twelfth Imam.[85] They will rule the world from Jerusalem, where all are Muslims living under Shariah Law. Al Queda is trying to facilitate this through conversion, but also a slow process of turning countries into an Islamic majority state. They do so by growing the population until they reach the majority, who can then place Shariah Law on the same footing with whatever legal, governmental system that that country has. After that, the goal is to replace the governmental laws with Shariah Law. ISIS, on the other hand, believes they can simply conquer the lands through military might terrorism. They also believe that starting a World War III will facilitate the return of ISA and the twelfth Imam, i.e., their Armageddon.

The liberal-progressive world that we live in is a catalyst for Islamic growth. It is the political correctness run amuck that is aiding and abetting radical Islam and their silent supporters. Many of those liberals try to shift the blame over to the conservatives, by saying that the United States is Islamophobic and that we are simply a recruitment tool for radical Islam by our identifying them by the phrase *radical Islamic terrorists*. What they fail to realize is that this eschatological belief of Islam is religious, ideological, and embedded in their very being, which has nothing to do with what anyone says. The liberal-progressive movement will be politically correct all the way up unto the end. Radical Islam and their silent supporters have a murderous hatred for the West, the United States, and Israel especially, as well as Christians.[86]

---

[85] An Imam is a leader of an Islamic community.
[86] IS THE QURAN THE WORD OF GOD?: Is Islam the One True Faith?
http://www.christianpublishers.org/apps/webstore/products/show/7489030

End of Excursion

Matthew 24:10 Update American Standard Version (UASV)

¹⁰ And then many will fall away,[87] will betray[88] one another, and will hate one another.

While early Christianity suffered horrible deaths through being martyred for simply being a Christian, the hatred today is just as vile by those that slaughter Christians around the world. Nevertheless, persecution through social media, news media, and by way of lawsuits, and protests in the streets, has become the new form of persecution in the Western world. Many have fallen away from Jesus, becoming apostates toward their former brothers and sisters, loathing their very existence.

Matthew 24:11 Update American Standard Version (UASV)

¹¹ And many false prophets will arise and will lead many astray.

What is a prophet? The primary meaning is one who proclaims the Word of God, a spokesperson for God. Therefore, a false prophet would be a spokesperson giving the impression that he is a spokesman for God, but really he is far from it. These ones are very subtle and deceptive in their ability to present themselves as a person representing God. Some modern day examples would be, Jim Bakker, Kenneth Copeland, Benny Hinn, T.D. Jakes, Joyce Meyer, Juanita Bynum, Creflo Dollar, Eddie Long, Pat Robertson, and Joel Olsteen. Of course, these are just some of the televangelists, who are false prophets, with tens of millions of followers. Other false prophet religious leaders have tens of millions of followers as well. Then, there are charismatic Christian denominations that number over 500 million followers. These ones claim gifts of God (faith healing, speaking in tongues, etc.), which clearly are anything but. The true Christians are falling away in great numbers, being led astray by these false prophets, and those who have not fallen away, truly need to remain awake!

Matthew 24:12 Update American Standard Version (UASV)

¹² And because lawlessness will be increased, the love of many will grow cold.

The world we live in is overflowing with murders, rapes, armed robberies, and assaults, not to mention the wars between nations, as well as the war on terrorism. It has grown so pervasive that many have grown callused to seeing the newspapers, websites and television news filled with

---

[87] Lit *be caused to stumble*
[88] Or *hand over*

one heinous crime, one after another. In looking at just one city in the United States, in 2012, 532 people were murdered in Chicago, with a population of 2.7 million. However, in San Pedro Sula of the country Honduras, 1,143 people were murdered with only a population of 719,447. Statistics from the United Nations report 250,000 cases of rape or attempted rape annually. However, it must be kept in mind that because of the savagery of the times, in "many parts of the world, rape is very rarely reported, due to the extreme social stigma cast on women, who have been raped, or the fear of being disowned by their families, or subjected to violence, including honor killings."[89]

Verse 12 says that the love of "the love of many will **grow cold**," and indeed, it has. There are atrocious crimes against individuals, groups, nations, which would cripple the mind of anyone living decades ago. However, because of seeing it every day, all day long, the world has grown hardened to the lawlessness that exists around them. Christians carry the hope of salvation in their heart, which Jesus addresses next.

Matthew 24:13 Update American Standard Version (UASV)

[13] But the one who endures to the end will be saved.

What are we to endure? We are to **endure while we** maintain our walk with God through false Christs who will lead many astray, the wars, and the natural disasters. We are to **endure while we** maintain our walk with God through the loss of many of our spiritual brothers and sisters who fall away, the betrayal of former Christians, and the hatred of humankind who is alienated from God. We are to **endure while we** maintain our walk with God through false prophets that have arisen and lead many astray, the increase of the lawlessness in this world, and the love of humanity growing colder. Yes, each of us, who survives to the end of the Christian era, to the return of Christ, will be saved from Jesus' destruction of the wicked. However, we are not to simply sit around; we have work to accomplish that is the last sign of the end of the age. We are to proclaim the good news, to teach biblical truths, as we make disciples.

Matthew 24:14 Update American Standard Version (UASV)

[14] And this gospel of the kingdom will be proclaimed in all the inhabited earth[90] as a testimony to all the nations, and then the end will come.

This is the last of the signs that Jesus gave that should concern us as it is directly related to the end of the age, and the return of Christ, namely **'the gospel of the kingdom being proclaimed throughout the**

---

[89] http://en.wikipedia.org/wiki/Rape_statistics
[90] Or *in the whole world*

whole world.' Jesus makes it very clear what he meant by "the whole world," by then saying "all nations" (Gk., *ethnos*). What Jesus meant here was more directed toward all races, not so much the "nations" that we know the world to be divided into today. Therefore, Jesus speaking of the whole world was a reference to "**a body of persons united by kinship, culture, and common traditions, *nation, people*.**"[91] Today, while, for the most part, nations are made up of different races, the world is also becoming a melting pot.

In the phrase "**testimony** to all nations," we find the Greek word *martyrion*, which was a legal term of "**that which serves as testimony or proof, *testimony, proof*.**"[92] The testimony here that is to be shared by Christ's disciples has to with Jesus and the kingdom. Evidence, proof, testimony has the ability to overcome the false reasoning of those in the world, to win them over, as well as convict those who refuse to see the evidence for what it is. Elsewhere Jesus said very clearly,

Matthew 11:15 (UASV)	**Matthew 13:9** (UASV)	**Matthew 13:43** (UASV)
15 He who has ears to hear, let him hear.	9 He who has ears, let him hear."	43 Then the righteous will shine like the sun in the kingdom of their Father. He who has ears, let him hear.

John the Baptist Prepared the Way

As many are aware, John the Baptist was the fulfillment of a prophecy from Malachi 4:5–6, which reads, "'Behold, I will send you Elijah the prophet before the great and awesome day of the Lord comes. And he will turn the hearts of fathers to their children and the hearts of children to their fathers, lest I come and strike the land with a decree of utter destruction.'" Jesus well knew this, as is evidenced by his comments in verse 14 of chapter 11, "and if you are willing to accept it, he [John the Baptist] is Elijah who is to come." Nevertheless, many would refuse to accept that John was, in fact, the fulfillment prophecy about Elijah. Thus, Jesus says, "If you are **willing to accept it ... He who has ears to hear, let him hear.**"

Throughout Jesus' three and a half years ministry of teaching the people of Israel, bringing the truth to Israel, Jesus interpreted Scripture

---

[91] William Arndt, Frederick W. Danker, and Walter Bauer, *A Greek-English Lexicon of the New Testament and Other Early Christian Literature* (Chicago: University of Chicago Press, 2000), 276.
[92] IBID, 619.

and told them many things that would be difficult for them to accept, because they conflicted with the religious leaders of Judaism. He did these things because he wanted to sift out those, who were not truly interested in the truth. Those who rejected Jesus and his teachings were unteachable because they lacked a receptive heart and mind. They had hardened hearts, to the point that they were beyond repentance, beyond being able to see the truth, regardless of whether it was the very Son of God explaining it.

Was John the Baptist some reborn Elijah? The Jews asked John who he was, "What then? Are you Elijah?" (John 1:21) John answered them quite plainly, "I am not." However, the angel, likely Gabriel, said to Zechariah [John the Baptist's father], before John was born, "Do not be afraid, Zechariah, for "he will be filled with the Holy Spirit, even from his mother's womb. And he [John] will turn many of the children of Israel to the Lord their God, and he will go before him **in the spirit and power of Elijah**, to turn the hearts of the fathers to the children, and the disobedient to the wisdom of the just, to make ready for the Lord a people prepared.'" (Lu 1:17; Mal. 4:5-6) In other words, John the Baptist was the new Elijah, or an Elijah-like one, who in a sense did a work very similar to what Elijah had done.

The baptism that John carried out in the Jordan was for the Jews to offer a public display of repentance over their individual sins against the Mosaic Law, a law that was designed to lead them to the first coming of the Christ. Luke writes, "As it is written in the book of the words of Isaiah the prophet, 'The voice of one crying in the wilderness [John the Baptist]: 'Prepare the way of the Lord.' (Lu 3:3-6; Gal. 3:24) Yes, John's work prepared the Israelites for the first coming of Christ.

In the Hebrew Scriptures (Old Testament), there is a very common phrase, "the day of Jehovah." (ESV, "the day of the LORD," LEB "the day of Yahweh", or ASV "the day of Jehovah") This day of Jehovah is detailed in the Scriptures as a time of battle, a day of distress and anguish, a day of darkness, a day of wrath and fierce anger, a day of wrath is that day, a day of distress and anguish, a day of ruin and devastation, and a day to destroy its sinners. – Amos 5:18-20; Isaiah 13:9; Zephaniah 1:15; Ezekiel 7:19; Zephaniah 1:18

The work that John the Baptist did was to prepare the Israelites to accept the Christ, as *a day of Jehovah* was very near. The apostle Peter quoted the prophet Joel right after Pentecost, explaining that the miraculous events they had just seen unfold, were a fulfillment of the words of Joel, i.e., a fulfillment of the words God's inspired Joel to pen. Peter showed that the words of Joel were to come to pass before "the great and glorious day of the Lord comes." (Acts 2:16-21; Joel 2:28-32)

The prophecy of Joel was fulfilled in 70 C.E. when General Titus of the Roman army, destroyed Jerusalem, executing divine judgment on the nation of Israel for their centuries of rebellion, false worship, and finally, the rejection of the Son of God, in that they had him executed by way of the Roman government. – Daniel 9:24-27; John 19:15.

Peter's Sermon at Pentecost

Acts 2:16-21 Lexham English Bible (LEB)

16 But this is what was spoken through the prophet Joel:

17 'And it will be in the last days,' God says,
'I will pour out my Spirit on all flesh,
and your sons and your daughters will prophesy,
and your young men will see visions,
and your old men will dream dreams.
18 And even on my male slaves and on my female slaves
I will pour out my Spirit in those days, and they will prophesy.
19 And I will cause wonders in the heaven above
and signs on the earth below,
blood and fire and vapor of smoke.
20 The sun will be changed to darkness
and the moon to blood,
before the great and glorious day of the Lord comes.
21 And it will be *that* everyone who calls upon the name of the Lord will be saved.'

In all occurrences, prophecy proclaimed in Bible times had meaning to the people who heard it; it served for their guidance as well as each generation up unto the time of its fulfillment. Usually, it had some fulfillment in that time, in numerous instances being fulfilled during the days of that same generation. In looking at Peters quote from Joel, it must be asked, 'did they see those cosmic events on Pentecost?' Yes, the cosmic terminology is expressing that God was acting on behalf of those first Christians. A new era was being entered and God did pour out His Spirit, and sons and daughters did prophesy, both in proclaiming a message and in the foretelling of other events. However, let us delve even deeper into prophecy and how they are to be interpreted. Before moving on, let us briefly offer some insights:

- Judgment prophecies can be lifted, set aside if the parties affected repent and turnaround from their former course.
- On the other hand, if God has promised blessings but then that person or group disobeys him and does evil, he will not do what he had said he would do.

- Then again, if one has repented, turned around, and a judgment prophecy has been lifted, it can be reinstated if that person or group returns to their former evil ways.
- Prophets have a license to use prophetic language, cosmic terminology that evidences that God is working or acting within humanity.
- While we do not take cosmic terminology literally, we do discover its meaning, and this is what we are to take literally.

If we are to understand and interpret prophecy correctly, we must first have a grasp of the figurative language, types, and symbols. Walter C. Kaiser Jr. is distinguished professor emeritus of Old Testament and president emeritus of Gordon-Conwell Theological Seminary. He asks the following questions, which we will address at length,

> (1) the extent to which the NT authors also used ancient Jewish exegetical and interpretive methods in their use of the OT; (2) the NT authors' awareness or disregard of the larger OT context of the passages they quote; (3) the appropriate understanding of the function of typology; and (4) the question of whether contemporary interpreters may replicate the NT writers' techniques of appropriating and applying the OT Scriptures.[93]

2 Peter 3:11-14 English Standard Version (ESV)

[11] Since all these things are thus to be dissolved, what sort of people ought you to be in lives of holiness and godliness, [12] waiting for and hastening the coming of the day of God, because of which the heavens will be set on fire and dissolved, and the heavenly bodies will melt as they burn! [13] But according to his promise **we are waiting for new heavens and a new earth** in which righteousness dwells.

[14] Therefore, beloved, since you are waiting for these, be diligent to be found by him without spot or blemish, and at peace.

Is Peter's reference to a "new heavens and new earth" the same "new heavens and new earth" of which Isaiah spoke? It could be as we need to be cautious of being dogmatic. However, if Isaiah's was a prophecy that points to a remnant of restored Israelites, back from Babylonian captivity, who returned to pure worship, might this simply be Peter using Isaiah's prophecy to tack carry out an *Inspired Sensus Plenior Application*. It is hard to see Peter's use of Isaiah's words as a fulfillment of

---

[93] (2009-08-30). *Three Views on the New Testament Use of the Old Testament* (Counterpoints: Bible and Theology) (Kindle Locations 890-893). Zondervan. Kindle Edition.

what Isaiah himself had meant because Isaiah was referring to the return of the Israelites to Jerusalem some 600 years before Peter's words about the new heavens and a new earth.

What we do know is that if Peter assigns a different meaning to Isaiah's words, it is his meaning, and it is subjective He has the authority to offer subjective meaning, as he was an inspired Bible writer, who had been moved along by Holy Spirit. Peter was not reiterating Isaiah's words with the same intended meaning that Isaiah had; he was giving us an *Inspired Sensus Plenior Application*, a new meaning of Isaiah's words. This author believes that Peter's "new heavens" is the Kingdom of God, of which Jesus is the King, and he has co-rulers. The "new earth" is a restored earth, which Jesus will accomplish throughout his millennial reign. Peter did not mean that the earth was literally going to be destroyed, just the wicked. It is the same "new heavens" and "new earth," which the Apostle John actually beheld in a vision of a future time after first century C.E. It is the same "new heaven and new earth" that Christians are awaiting today. In order to get us back on topic, we will repeat two paragraphs.

As we learned in the above, John the Baptist was the fulfillment of a prophecy from Malachi 4:5–6, which reads, "'Behold, I will send you Elijah the prophet **before the great and awesome day of the LORD comes**. And he will turn the hearts of fathers to their children and the hearts of children to their fathers, lest I come and strike the land with a decree of utter destruction.'" Joel tells us,

Joel 2:31 English Standard Version (ESV)

³¹ The sun shall be turned to darkness, and the moon to blood, before **the great and awesome day of the LORD** comes.

Peter quotes Joel, telling us,

Acts 2:17, 20 English Standard Version (ESV)

¹⁷ "'And **in the last days** it shall be, God declares, that I will pour out my Spirit on all flesh

²⁰ the sun shall be turned to darkness
   and the moon to blood,
   before **the day of the Lord** comes, the great and magnificent day.

Peter writes in his second letter,

2 Peter 3:10 English Standard Version (ESV)

¹⁰ But **the day of the Lord** will come like a thief, and then the heavens will pass away with a roar, and the heavenly bodies will be

burned up and dissolved, and the earth and the works that are done on it will be exposed.

In the Hebrew Scriptures (Old Testament), there is a very common phrase, "the day of Jehovah." (ESV, "the day of the LORD," LEB "the day of Yahweh", or ASV "the day of Jehovah") This day of Jehovah is detailed in the Scriptures as a time of battle, a day of distress and anguish, a day of darkness, a day of wrath and fierce anger, a day of wrath is that day, a day of distress and anguish, a day of ruin and devastation, and a day to destroy its sinners. – Amos 5:18-20; Isaiah 13:9; Zephaniah 1:15; Ezekiel 7:19; Zephaniah 1:18

The work that John the Baptist did was to prepare the Israelites to accept the Christ, as *a day of Jehovah* was very near. The apostle Peter quoted the prophet Joel right after Pentecost, explaining that the miraculous events they had just seen unfold, were a fulfillment of the words of Joel, i.e., a fulfillment of the words God's inspired Joel to pen. Peter showed that the words of Joel were to come to pass before "the great and glorious day of the Lord comes." (Acts 2:16-21; Joel 2:28-32) The prophecy of Joel was fulfilled in 70 C.E. when General Titus of the Roman army, destroyed Jerusalem, executing divine judgment on the nation of Israel for their centuries of rebellion, false worship, and finally, the rejection of the Son of God, in that they had him executed by way of the Roman government.—Daniel 9:24-27; John 19:15.

Now, to tie all of this together, the day of the LORD (Jehovah) that took place in 70 C.E. when Jerusalem was destroyed was just one of many times of destructive judgment by God. For example, we had the first destruction of Jerusalem by the Babylonians. Malachi had prophesied that God would send the Jews Elijah-like prophet **before** the great and awesome **day of the LORD** comes. This came true with John the Baptist coming to prepare the way for Jesus, who prepared the way for the Christians, before the destruction of Jerusalem in 70 C.E., where one million Jews were killed and one hundred thousand taken captive. So at that time a "day of the LORD" was near at hand. Joel tells us that there would be an outpouring of Holy Spirit before this same "day of the LORD," which Peter quotes. (Ac 2:17) Again, that "day of the LORD" came in 70 C.E. when God used the Roman army to execute divine judgment on the nation of Israel for their centuries of rebellion, false worship, and finally, the rejection of the Son of God.

However, there is another "day of the Lord" to come. The apostle Paul associated this "day of the LORD" with the second coming of Jesus Christ. Paul writes,

2 Thessalonians 2:1-2 English Standard Version (ESV)

¹ Now concerning **the coming of our Lord** Jesus Christ and our being gathered together to him, we ask you, brothers, ² not to be quickly shaken in mind or alarmed, either by a spirit or a spoken word, or a letter seeming to be from us, to the effect that **the day of the Lord** has come.

The apostle Peter as we have mention associates this same "day of the LORD" with,

2 Peter 3:10 English Standard Version (ESV)

¹⁰ But **the day of the Lord** will come like a thief, and then the heavens will pass away with a roar, and the heavenly bodies will be burned up and dissolved, and the earth and the works that are done on it will be exposed. ¹³ But according to his promise we are waiting for **new heavens and a new earth** in which righteousness dwells.

When we look at all of this, we can see a future "day of the LORD." We know that Elijah prepared the way for "the day of the LORD" in the first century, with his evangelism, as did Jesus. Moreover, Jesus said that Christians would do an even greater work that he (John 14:12). We do so because we are to prepare the way for the greatest "day of the LORD," namely, the return of Jesus Christ. Let us take a deeper look at the first century one, looking for correlations.

Excursion of "One Meaning"

The idea that the reader is the one who determines the meaning is known as the "reader response." For those who hold to this position, all meaning is equal to another, and all are correct. We can have a set of verses, and 20 people may give us different interpretations, and many may seem the opposite of others. Those believing in the "reader "response" will say that all are correct. Under this position, the text allows each reader the right to derive his or her own meaning from the text. Again, this is where we hear "I think this means," "I believe this means," "this means to me," and "I feel this means to me." The problem with this is that the text loses its authority; God and his author lose their authority over the intended meaning of the text. When God inspired the writer, to express his will and purposes, there was the intention of **one meaning**, i.e., what the author under inspiration meant by the words he used. If anyone can come along and give it whatever meaning pleases them, then God's authority over the meaning is lost, and there is no real meaning at all.

The grammatical-historical method is a method, which attempts to ascertain what the author meant by the words that he used, which should have been understood by his first readers. It was the primary method of interpretation when higher criticism's Historical-Critical Method was in its infancy back in the 19th century (Milton Terry), and remains the only method of interpretation for true conservative scholarship in the later 20th century into the 21st century. The grammatical-historical method is objective, meaning that is free of any theological bias or prejudice caused by personal views.

Grammatical Aspect

When we speak of interpreting the Bible grammatically, we are referring to the process of seeking to determine its meaning by ascertaining four things: (a) the meaning of words (lexicology), (b) the form of words (morphology), (c) the function of words (parts of speech), and (d) the relationships of words (syntax). In the meaning of words (lexicology), we are concerned with,

(a) **Etymology**,[94] i.e., how words are derived and developed,

(b) **Usage**, namely, how words are used by the same author and other authors,

(c) **Synonyms and Antonyms**, that is how similar and opposite words are used, and

(d) **Context**, i.e., how words are used in various contexts, the words, phrases, sentences and paragraphs that surround them.

In discussing the form of words (morphology), we are looking at how words are structured and how that affects their meaning. For example, the word "eat" means something different from ate, though the same letters are used. The word "part" changes meaning when the letter "s" is added to it to make the word "parts." The function of words (parts of speech) considers what the various forms do. These include attention to subjects, verbs, objects, nouns, and others, as will be discussed later. The relationships of words (syntax) are the way words are related or put together to form phrases, clauses, and sentences. (Zuck 1991, 100-101)

---

[94] This would be used on very rare occasions in the extreme, See etymological Fallacy in D. A. Carson's *Exegetical Fallacies*.

Historical Aspect

By "historical," we mean the setting in which the Bible books were written and the circumstances involved in the writing ... taking into consideration the circumstances of the writings and the cultural environment.

The context in which a given Scripture passage is written influences how that passage is to be understood. Context includes several things:

- the verse(s) immediately before and after a passage
- the paragraph and book in which the verses occur
- the dispensation in which it was written
- the message of the entire Bible
- the historical-cultural environment of that time when it was written. (Zuck 1991, 77)

Some of the truly conservative scholars who have remained faithful to the grammatical-historical method of interpretation are Bernard Ramm, Harold Lindsell, Gleason L. Archer, Robert L. Thomas, Norman L. Geisler, Thomas Howe, Roy, B. Zuck, David F. Farnell, among other select ones. Such ones are referred to as "fundamentalist Protestants," as though fundamentalism is now a dirty word. Some modern day scholars believe that they can dip their feet in the pool of higher criticism, suggesting that they can use certain aspects of these forms of criticisms, without ending up doing any harm to the trustworthiness of the text, to inerrancy. This is very naïve, as some of them end up swimming in the deep end of higher criticism, while others walk along the edges of the deep end.

Here is just ten of the "tip-of-the-iceberg" of the things that these scholars would agree with:

- Matthew, not Jesus, Created the Sermon on the Mount.

- The commissioning of the Twelve in Matthew 10 is a group of instructions compiled and organized by Matthew, not spoken by Jesus on a single occasion.

- The parable accounts of Matthew 13 and Mark 4 are anthologies of parables that Jesus uttered on separate occasions.

- Jesus did not preach the Olivet Discourse in its entirety, as found in the of the gospel accounts.

- Jesus gave his teaching on divorce and remarriage without the exception clauses found in Matthew 5:32 and 19:9.

- In Matthew 19:16-17, Matthew changed the words of Jesus and the rich man to obtain a different emphasis or to avoid a theological problem involved in the wording of Mark's and Luke's accounts of the same event.

- The scribes and the Pharisees were in reality decent people whom Matthew painted in an entirely negative light because of his personal bias against them.

- The genealogies of Jesus in Matthew 1 and Luke 3 are figures of speech and not accurate records of Jesus' physical/and or legal lineage.

- The magi who, according to Matthew 2, visited the child Jesus after his birth are fictional, not real characters.

- Jesus uttered only three or four of the eight or nine beatitudes in Matthew 5:3-12[95]

The Original Meaning

The objective of the exegete in his use of the grammatical-historical method of interpretation is to discover what the author meant by the words that he used, as should have been understood by his originally intended audience. Each text has **one single meaning**. Milton S. Terry wrote, "A fundamental principle in grammatical-historical exposition is that the words and sentences can have but one significance in one and the same connection. The moment we neglect this principle we drift out upon a sea of uncertainty and conjecture." (Terry 1883, 205)

This author agrees with Robert L. Thomas and John H. Walton in the New Testament author's use of the Old Testament. I have no problem that the NT author either quote intending to convey the same meaning, i.e., there is but **one meaning** for the OT author, and the NT author is simply interpreting it as such. This author also use **I**nspired **S**ensus **P**lenior **A**pplication (ISPA), in that, the NT author will use the OT author's verse, but **not** in a grammatical-historical sense (objective), but using his own meaning, which is subjective, and rightly so because he is inspired. Moreover, we do not copy the subjective interpretation process because we are not inspired. All genuine conservatives should be of the **one meaning** camp.

This author ha revisited many author's chapters and papers that support one meaning and talk about NT author's use of OT authors. The main problem with Thomas' chapter, he does not give any real examples

---

[95] (Thomas and Farnell 1998)

in the "one meaning" chapter, he just quotes all of those violating the rule and then says that they are wrong, and in some cases why they are wrong. When he does get to an example, it seems to close out our options of taking Jesus words of Matthew 24:3-28, as anything other than a first-century meaning, referent, and application.

For example, Thomas speaks of Zuck's saying that Psalms 8, 16, and 22 are David talking about himself, and then the NT author's use those verses, applying them to Christ, but differently from what David intended. Well, this is simply ISPA, in that they are giving what they mean by their use of David's words, which is fine, as they are inspired, and can be subjective. However, Thomas says Zuck's conclusions about these Psalm's are accurate to the meaning, but they cannot have more than one referent, as that would result in more than one meaning. In other words, David had applied them to himself, and he did not intend them to be prophetic, applying to Jesus. The NT author is using those words as he sees fit, and not acting as though that is what David meant, so the NT author's meaning of the words are his own, an entirely different referent, but belonging to the NT author. However, Thomas' words are true; words spoken or written by King David cannot have more than one referent, unless David means to give them more than one referent.

Thomas gives another one, when he refers to Babylon in Revelation, and says some people interpret it as being Rome; others say it is literally Babylon while others claim it is Jerusalem, and even some saying all three and any other city that stands in the way of Christ and his disciples. Thomas goes on to say, it can only refer to one thing, either one of those cities, or a composite of any city in opposition. However, it cannot refer to each, i.e., Rome, Jerusalem and Babylon at the same time; otherwise, we would have more than one referent.

Now to our interpreting Jesus' prophecy of the desolation of Jerusalem in 66-70 C.E. and his second coming.

Did Jesus' prophecy (verses 3-28) about

- the signs of the end of the age,
- the abomination of desolation standing in the holy place,
- being cut short for the sake of the holy ones, false Christs, and false prophets,
- those on the housetops, in the field, in the winter, being pregnant, and the like,

Did these apply to what led up to 66 C.E. with General Gallus, his pulling away, and Titus coming back and destroying the temple Jerusalem in 70 C.E. by General Titus? Did these apply to the disciples he was speaking to and the events up unto the destruction of Jerusalem and the temple? If that is what Jesus was referring to; then, there cannot be a second referent, just before and up to the great tribulation, before the second coming of Christ, because we would then have two referents, i.e., two meanings. There are other options, without violating our single meaning, which will be discussed below.

The Coming of the Son of Man

Matthew 24:29-31 Update American Standard Version (UASV)

²⁹ "But immediately after the tribulation of those days the sun will be darkened, and the moon will not give its light, and the stars will fall from heaven, and the powers of the heavens will be shaken. ³⁰ And then will appear in heaven the sign of the Son of Man, and then all the tribes of the earth will mourn, and they will see the Son of Man coming on the clouds of heaven with power and great glory. ³¹ And he will send forth his angels with a great trumpet call, and they will gather his chosen ones[96] from the four winds, from one end of heaven to the other.

The prophet is much like the poet, in that he is given a license to express himself in nonliteral language. Generally, he is working with images that are far more effective than words themselves.

The above cosmic terminology need not be taken literally. It is a part of their toolkit, which enables them to make it clear that God is acting in behalf of humans. (See Dan. 2:21; 4:17, 25, 34–35; 5:21) The sun is not going to be darkened, the moon will not stop giving its light, the stars are not going to fall from the heavens, nor will the heavens be shaken. What is being communicated here is that following the tribulation when God is going to judge humans, the righteous will receive life, and the unrighteous will cut off from life. (34-45) While we do not take cosmic terminology literally, we do discover its meaning, and this is what we are to take literally. Moreover, we do not want to be dogmatic in our interpretation either, and will wait until the events have passed to see how much literalness there is from verses 29-31. Stuart K. Weber, in the *Holman New Testament Commentary*, offers some basic aspects that this author can get behind.[97]

> The Messiah's coming will be accompanied by supernatural manipulations of celestial bodies—or at least manipulations of their appearance, or their ability to give light. These signs in the sky will be such that all people of earth can see them and realize

---

[96] Or *the elect*

[97] He does make other comments, such as specifying that this cosmic show will last, i.e., "will extend over many hours."

that the Messiah is coming, If only one of these, signs were given, it might be explained away as an eclipse or a meteor shower. But all of them together can be caused only by the hand of God. (Weber 2000, 404)

"Jesus now returns to the question of the sign of his coming. He will return "immediately after" the tribulation of the interadvent period." (Blomberg 1992, 362)

(Option A) the disciples asked three questions, "Tell us, **(1)** when will these things be, and **(2)** what will be the sign of your coming, and **(3)** of the end of the age?" (Matthew 24:3) Jesus words of verses 24:3-28 apply to what happened from his ascension up unto 70 C.E., and the destruction of the temple and Jerusalem; this answering question **(1)**. He then began in verse 29 to talk about questions **(2)** and **(3)**, the second coming of Christ. This means that verses 3-28 would only have one referent, the first-century disciples.

(Option B) Jesus was applying verses 24:3-28 to what let up to 70 C.E., but he then made those words just as applicable to his second coming, starting verse 29. In other words, the disciples asked three questions, "Tell us, **(1)** when will these things be, and **(2)** what will be the sign of your coming, and **(3)** of the end of the age?" (Matthew 24:3) This author prefers option B.

The first question is legit about the destruction of the Temple complex, but the second and third is an assumption on their part of the disciples, because to them, if the temple and Jerusalem is being destroyed, the end has to be near and the second coming of Christ and his Kingdom must follow.

However, Jesus answered by giving them, in detail what would apply to them. When he uttered 3-28, he was talking about them, what was going to happen to them, which history bears out. Nevertheless, did he dragged those circumstances and events, which he had just spoken of (3-28), from the first century, to also applying just before his second coming. Is he the one that carried out an ISPA to his own words?

- Jesus words were for the end of the age of the Jewish age (Matt 24:3-28)
- Jesus gave them same words a Sensus Plenior Application, starting in verse 29 that were another end of the age, the end of wick humanity and the rule of age (era) of Satan.

If we remove the cosmic terminology, which is evidence of God acting on behalf of humankind, we have the following major points. 24:29-31 foretells us,

(1) the Son of Man comes immediately after the great tribulation,

(2) Jesus' second coming will be with great glory,

(3) as he will send forth his angels, and

(4) all the tribes of the earth will see him, in that they will perceive what is taking place, and

(5) Jesus will gather all of his chosen ones.

God will Gather the Remainder of His Chosen Ones Who Have a Heavenly Hope

Revelation 14:1-4 English Standard Version (ESV)

¹ Then I looked, and behold, on Mount Zion stood the Lamb, and with him 144,000 who had his name and his Father's name written on their foreheads. ² And I heard a voice from heaven like the roar of many waters and like the sound of loud thunder. The voice I heard was like the sound of harpists playing on their harps, ³ and they were singing a new song before the throne and before the four living creatures and before the elders. No one could learn that song except the 144,000 who had been redeemed from the earth. ⁴ It is these who have not defiled themselves with women, for they are virgins. It is these who follow the Lamb wherever he goes. These have been redeemed from mankind as firstfruits for God and the Lamb

> The whole of chapter 14 is proleptic. As a summary of the Millennium (20:4–6), the first five verses feature the Lamb in place of the beast, the Lamb's followers with His and the Father's seal in place of the beast's followers with the mark of the beast, and the divinely controlled Mount Zion in place of the pagan-controlled earth (Alford, Moffatt, Kiddle).[98]

Revelation 7:4 English Standard Version (ESV)

⁴ And I heard the number of the sealed, 144,000, sealed from every tribe of the sons of Israel

> Various efforts have sought to determine the significance of the number 144,000. An understanding of the number as symbolical divides it into three of its multiplicands, 12 × 12 × 1000. From the symbolism of the three it is concluded that the

---

[98] Robert L. Thomas, Revelation 8-22: An Exegetical Commentary (Chicago: Moody Publishers, 1995), 189.

number indicates fixedness and fullest completeness.[99] Twelve, a number of the tribes, is both squared and multiplied by a thousand. This is a twofold way of emphasizing completeness (Mounce). It thus affirms the full number of God's people to be brought through tribulation (Ladd). The symbolic approach points out the impossibility of taking the number literally. It is simply a vast number, less than a number indefinitely great (cf. 7:9), but greater than a large number designedly finite (e.g., 1,000, Rev. 20:2) (Lee). Other occurrences of the numerical components that are supposedly symbolic are also pointed out, 12 thousand in Rev. 21:16, 12 in Rev. 22:2, and 24, a multiple of 12, in Rev. 4:4. This is done to enhance the case for symbolism (Johnson). Though admittedly ingenious, the case for symbolism is exegetically weak. The principal reason for the view is a predisposition to make the 144,000 into a group representative of the church with which no possible numerical connection exists. No justification can be found for understanding the simple statement of fact in v. 4 as a figure of speech. It is a definite number in contrast with the indefinite number of 7:9. If it is taken symbolically, no number in the book can be taken literally. As God reserved 7,000 in the days of Ahab (1 Kings 19:18; Rom. 11:4), He will reserve 144,000 for Himself during the future Great Tribulation.[100] (Thomas, Revelation 1-7: An Exegetical Commentary 1992, 473-74)

These ones are made up of those under the new covenant, the Law of Christ, those called out of natural Israel, the new Israelites, also known as the Israel of God. They are a chosen number that are to reign with Jesus as kings, priests, and judges. Therefore, we ask, what is the other hope? What lies below was already mentioned in Chapter 3 but bears repeating again as a short repetition for emphasis as the thought are new to many minds.

---

[99] Alford, Greek Testament, 4:624; Charles, Revelation, 1:206; Lenski, Revelation, p. 154.

[100] Bullinger, Apocalypse, p. 282. Geyser is correct in observing that the predominant concern of the Apocalypse is "the restoration [on earth] of the twelve tribes of Israel, their restoration as a twelve-tribe kingdom, in a renewed and purified city of David, under the rule of the victorious 'Lion of the Tribe of Judah, the Root of David' (5:5; 22:16)" (Albert Geyser, "The Twelve Tribes in Revelation: Judean and Judeo Christian Apocalypticism," NTS 23, no. 3 [July 1982]: 389). He is wrong, however, in his theory that this belief characterized the Judean church only and was not shared by Gentile Christianity spearheaded by Paul (ibid., p. 390).

The New Earth: The Earthly Hope

In the O[ld] T[estament] the kingdom of God is usually described in terms of a redeemed earth; this is especially clear in the book of Isaiah, where the final state of the universe is already called new heavens and a new earth (65:17; 66:22) The nature of this renewal was perceived only very dimly by OT authors, but they did express the belief that a humans ultimate destiny is an earthly one.[101] This vision is clarified in the N[ew] T[estament]. Jesus speaks of the "renewal" of the world (Matt 19:28), Peter of the restoration of all things (Acts 3:21). Paul writes that the universe will be redeemed by God from its current state of bondage (Rom. 8:18-21). This is confirmed by Peter, who describes the new heavens and the new earth as the Christian's hope (2 Pet. 3:13). Finally, the book of Revelation includes a glorious vision of the end of the present universe and the creation of a new universe, full of righteousness and the presence of God. The vision is confirmed by God in the awesome declaration: "I am making everything new!" (Rev. 21:1-8).

The new heavens and the new earth will be the renewed creation that will fulfill the purpose for which God created the universe. It will be characterized by the complete rule of God and by the full realization of the final goal of redemption: "Now the dwelling of God is with men" (Rev. 21:3).

The fact that the universe will be created anew[102] shows that God's goals for humans is not an ethereal and disembodied existence, but a bodily existence on a perfected earth. The scene of the beatific vision is the new earth. The spiritual does not exclude the created order and will be fully realized only within a perfected creation. (Elwell 2001, 828-29)

God created the earth to be inhabited, to be filled with perfect humans, who are over the animals, and under the sovereignty of God. (Gen 1:28; 2:8, 15; Ps 104:5; 115:16; Eccl 1:4) Sin did not dissuade God from his plans (Isa. 45:18); hence, he has saved redeemable humankind by Jesus ransom sacrifice. It seems that the Bible offers two hopes to redeemed humans, (1) a heavenly hope [i.e., the chosen ones], or (2) an

---

[101] It is unwise to speak of the written Word of God as if it were of human origin, saying 'OT authors express the belief,' when what was written is the meaning and message of what God wanted to convey by means of the human author.

[102] reate anew does not mean a complete destruction followed by a re-creation, but instead a renewal of the present universe.

earthly hope. It also seems that those with the heavenly hope are limited in number, and are going to heaven to rule with Christ as kings, priests, and judges either **on** the earth or **over** the earth from heaven. It seems that those with the earthly hope are going to receive everlasting life here on a paradise earth as originally intended.

CHAPTER 5 Correctly Understanding the Rapture

Rapture Defined: "In premillennialism, Christ's removal of the church from the world. It is variously maintained that it will occur prior to, during, or following the great tribulation."[103] (M. J. Erickson 2001, 167) Is this doctrine biblically true? Many millions of Christian believes that they 'will be bodily taken up from the earth in the clouds to meet the Lord in the air.' The primary verse for this doctrinal position is 1 Thessalonians 4:17. The word "rapture" itself is not found in the Scriptures. Of course, this does not itself mean that the doctrine is unbiblical. The objective of this publication is to teach what the Scriptures really teach.

The doctrine that every Christian found in a righteous standing with God is going to heaven when they dies and that some will be caught away to heaven has always been the basic idea of the rapture doctrine. The *Holman Illustrated Bible Dictionary* writes, "God's taking the church out of the world instantaneously. The Latin term *rapio*, which means to "snatch away" or "carry off," is the source of the English word."[104] The *Tyndale Bible Dictionary* writes, "Christian term used to denote the ascension (or lifting up) of Christians at the time of Christ's second coming. This is the noun corresponding to the verb used in 1 Thessalonians 4:17, where those believers who are still alive at the coming of Christ are described as being "caught up" together with their resurrected fellow Christians to meet him "in the air." (It may be relevant to note that the verb of 1 Thes 4:17 is used in 2 Cor 12:2–3 to denote Paul's mysterious experience of being "caught up" into the third heaven, or paradise.)"[105]

---

[103] **Rapture, Midtribulational view of the** The idea that the church will go through half of the tribulation and then be raptured by Christ.
Rapture, Partial A reference to the idea that some persons will be raptured early and others later: The time depends on their readiness.
Rapture, Posttribulational view of the The doctrine that the church will go through the great tribulation and then will be caught up to meet Christ.
Rapture, Pretribulational view of the The idea that Christ will remove the church from the world prior to the great tribulation. (M. J. Erickson 2001, 167)
[104] Pete Schemm, "Rapture," ed. Chad Brand et al., *Holman Illustrated Bible Dictionary* (Nashville, TN: Holman Bible Publishers, 2003), 1366.
[105] Walter A. Elwell and Philip Wesley Comfort, *Tyndale Bible Dictionary*, Tyndale Reference Library (Wheaton, IL: Tyndale House Publishers, 2001), 1112.

Different Views of the Rapture

The Bible clearly says that prior the thousand-year reign of Jesus Christ, there will be a period, which is referred to as the "great tribulation. In speaking of the time before Jesus return, Jesus said, "For then there will be a great tribulation, such as has not occurred since the beginning of the world until now, nor ever will." (Matt 24:21, NASB) The apostle John wrote, "Blessed and holy is the one who has a part in the first resurrection; over these the second death has no power, but they will be priests of God and of Christ and will reign with Him for a thousand years." (Reve. 20:6, NASB) There are three main views to the rapture, and it has to do with when that rapture will occur. Some hold that the rapture will happen right before the great tribulation that Jesus spoke of (Pre-Tribulation view), while others argue that it will come during the tribulation (Pre-Wrath view), and others say the rapture will come after the great tribulation (Post-Tribulation view). Dr. Alan D. Hultberg (PhD, professor of New Testament at Talbot School of Theology) defends the Pre-Wrath view; Craig Blaising (PhD, Dallas Theological Seminary and president of Southwestern Baptist Theological Seminary) defends the Pre-Tribulation view; and Douglas Moo (PhD, University of St. Andrews and professor of New Testament at Wheaton College) sets forth the Post-Tribulation view.

The objective of this chapter is not to defend or debunk any of these views of the rapture. What we intend to do is used the Word of God, as the standard by which we will evaluate the truthfulness of the rapture doctrine itself (2 Tim. 1:13; 3:16-17) In other words, what does the Word of God say about the rapture?

When the apostle Paul said that Christians 'will be caught up together to meet the Lord,' what was context?

1 Thessalonians 4:13-18 Revised Standard Version (RSV)

[13] But we would not have you ignorant, brethren, concerning those who are asleep ["those who sleep in death," NIV; "those who have died," GNT; "the believers who have died" NLT], that you may not grieve as others do who have no hope. [14] For since we believe that Jesus died and rose again, even so, through Jesus, God will bring with him those who have fallen asleep. [15] For this we declare to you by the word of the Lord, that we who are alive, who are left until the coming of the Lord, shall not precede those who have fallen asleep. [16] For the Lord himself will descend from heaven with a cry of command, with the archangel's call, and with the sound of the trumpet of God. And the dead in Christ will rise first; [17] then we who are alive, who are left, shall be caught up together with them in the clouds to meet the Lord in the air;

and so we shall always be with the Lord.¹⁸ Therefore comfort one another with these words.

Clearly, some Christian in the Thessalonica congregation had died. Paul encouraged his brothers and sisters to comfort one another with the resurrection hope, as they need not grieve at the same level as the unbelievers that have no such hope. Paul reminds them that they know that "Jesus died and rose again, even so, through Jesus, God will bring with him those who have fallen asleep." (vs 14, RSV) In other words, "when Jesus returns, God will bring back with him the [Thessalonian] believers who have died."

Who are those that will 'be caught up together with them in the clouds to meet the Lord in the air"? (1 Thess. 4:17)

Looking to verse 15, these ones 'caught up to be with the Lord' are those "who are left until the coming of the Lord." In other words, these are the ones, who are alive at the time of the second coming of Jesus Christ. However, they must die before they are resurrected to heaven. Paul wrote, "Do you not know that all of us who have been baptized into Christ Jesus were baptized into his death? For if we have been united with him in a death like his, we shall certainly be united with him in a resurrection like his." (Rom. 6:3, 5, RSV) Paul said that some might ask, "'how are the dead raised? With what kind of body do they come?'" (1 Cor. 15:35, RSV) He then answers his own question, "It is sown a physical body, it is raised a spiritual body. If there is a physical body, there is also a spiritual body." (1 Cor. 15:44, RSV) In other words, those who are taken to heaven at Jesus' second coming, who are still alive, must die first. However, Paul goes on to tell the Corinthians this will be very brief. "I tell you a mystery. We shall not all sleep, but we shall all be changed, **in a moment, in the twinkling of an eye**, at the last trumpet. For the trumpet will sound, and the dead will be raised imperishable, and we shall be changed." (1 Cor. 15:51-52, RSV) Again, these are these are born again Christians who are alive at the end of the last days, when Christ returns in Kingdom power.

The apostle Paul wrote, "In **the last days** difficult times will come." On this Knute Larson wrote, "The 'last days' is not some future event to which we look. It is now, Jesus Christ initiated this epoch, and it will continue uninterrupted until his return.¹⁰⁶ (2 Tim. 3"1, NASB) In other words, the last days began with the outpouring of Holy Spirit at Pentecost 33 C.E. and will continue up unto his second coming. The apostle Peter wrote, "Know this first of all, that in **the last days** mockers will come with their mocking, following after their own lusts." (2 Pet. 3:3, NASB)

---

¹⁰⁶ Knute Larson, *I & II Thessalonians, I & II Timothy, Titus, Philemon*, vol. 9, Holman New Testament Commentary (Nashville, TN: Broadman & Holman Publishers, 2000), 300.

On this David Walls and Max Anders wrote, "**In the last days** refers to all the days between the first advent of the Messiah and the second advent [coming]. Characteristic of that time frame, however long it will be, is the fact that people will make fun of the doctrine of the Second Coming. **Scoffing** means 'to make fun of someone.' It describes the characteristic attitude of the day toward the Second Coming. False teachers argued that the promise of the Second Coming had been delayed so long that we may safely conclude that it would never happen. As far as they could see, the world was going on just as it always had—people lived and died, but nothing really changed. They concluded that God's promises were unreliable and that the universe was a stable, unchanging system where events like the Second Coming just don't happen."[107] On the last days, Thomas D. Lea writes, "In a sense Christians have been living in the **last days** since the outpouring of the Spirit at Pentecost (see Acts 2:17)."[108]

Will Jesus appear in the cloud and take all remaining Christians to heaven with him as the world watches? What did Jesus say as far as the world of humanity ever seeing him again with their physical eyes? Jesus told his faithful disciples at the end of his life and ministry, "Yet a little while, and the world will see me no more, but you will see me; because I live, you will live also." (John 14:19, RSV) In 33 C.E., Jesus returned to heaven as a spirit person, where no human can see. Jesus did appear to his disciples once more in human form, after his resurrection. However, in due time, Jesus will resurrect them to life with him in heaven as spirit persons.

What did Paul mean when he said, "the Lord himself will descend from heaven"?

Is it possible for Jesus to "descend from heaven" without human eyes seeing him? In the days of Abraham, in ancient Sodom and Gomorrah, the Father said, "**I will go down to see** whether they have done altogether according to the outcry which has come to me." (Gen. 18:21, RSV) When the Father made that assessment, there were no human eyes, which saw him. However, they did see three of his angelic representatives, who had materialized in human form. (John 1:18) Therefore, it is not that Jesus is coming back in human flesh, but rather that he is turning his attention to his faithful followers, the righteous and the unrighteous, some of which will be resurrected to serve as kings, priest

---

[107] David Walls and Max Anders, *I & II Peter, I, II & III John, Jude*, vol. 11, Holman New Testament Commentary (Nashville, TN: Broadman & Holman Publishers, 1999), 141.
[108] Thomas D. Lea, *Hebrews, James*, vol. 10, Holman New Testament Commentary (Nashville, TN: Broadman & Holman Publishers, 1999), 341.

and judges in heaven with him for a thousand years. – John 5:28-29; Acts 24:1; Revelation 5:9-10; 20:6.[109]

How, then, are we to understand Jesus own words that says, "They will see the Son of man coming in a cloud with power and great glory"?

Luke 21:27 Revised Standard Version (RSV)

[27] And then they will see the Son of man coming in a cloud with power and great glory.

Luke 21:27 and other verses like it (Rev. 1:7; Matt. 24:30; Mark 13:26; Lu 21:27), are not at odds with John 14:19, which says, "Yet a little while, and the world will see me no more." Let us consider when the Father Lord said to Moses, "Lo, **I am coming to you in a thick cloud**, that the people may hear when I speak with you, and may also believe you forever." (Ex. 19:9, RSV) On this, Douglas K. Stuart wrote, "Moses learned of God's intention to make personal appearances to Moses in/by means of (or in the form of) a cloud, out of which the people could hear him speaking to Moses. Thus, he would make plain to the people of Israel the fact of his communication to Moses, thus reducing the likelihood that the people would doubt Moses when he claimed to be delivering to them words from God. God wanted this confidence in Moses as his reliable prophet to be continuous and permanent ("so that the people will hear me speaking with you and will always put their trust in you").[110] Yes, the Father was invisibly present. However, the people of Israel saw visible evidence of God's presence. Yet, no human eyes have ever seen God. Therefore, Jesus words mean that his presence will be known; humans will know that he has invisibly accomplished the Father's will and purposes. In other words, they will mentally discern his presence.

Acts 1:9-11 Revised Standard Version (RSV)

[9] And when he had said this, as they were looking on, he was lifted up, and a cloud took him out of their sight. [10] And while they were gazing into heaven as he went, behold, two men stood by them in white robes,[11] and said, "Men of Galilee, why do you stand looking into heaven? This Jesus, **who was taken up from you into heaven, will come in the same way as you saw him go into heaven**."

Notice that Jesus will come "**in the same way**," not in the same physical human body that he had used to pay humanities debt. Well, what is the "same way"? Verse 9 tells us "a cloud took him out of their sight." Jesus ascended in from earth in front of his disciples, not the whole

---

[109] http://www.christianpublishers.org/resurrection-bible-s-view

[110] Douglas K. Stuart, *Exodus*, vol. 2, The New American Commentary (Nashville: Broadman & Holman Publishers, 2006), 425.

world of mankind. The same will be true of his return. The whole of mankind will not physically see him, only those taken to heaven will because they will then be as he is, a spirit person. However, all of mankind will know Jesus has returned, just not physically.

Revelation 1:7 Revised Standard Version (RSV)

⁷ Behold, he is coming with the clouds, and **every eye will see him**, everyone who pierced him; and all tribes of the earth will wail on account of him. Even so. Amen.

The clouds represent invisibility. Again, the Father told Moses: "**I am coming to you in a thick cloud,** that the people may hear when I speak with you, and may also believe you forever." Did Moses see the Father? No. However, the people were well aware of his presence, listening as he spoke with Moses. (Ex. 19:9; see also Lev. 16:2; Num. 11:25) If Jesus literally appeared in a physical body in the sky, not every human could see him. For example, say he appeared over New York City, even people in Ohio would not see him, let alone in China, the United Kingdom, Australia, the African countries and the like. The seeing is discerning from the events taking place here on earth. This is why Jesus and his apostles gave so many descriptions and signs, so people could recognize the sign of the times. Yes, many will mock and reject his return but Armageddon will quickly follow, where these wicked ones will be destroyed, so, even they will be well aware of his presence. Moreover, they will have been warned by the evangelism of Christians beforehand. Who are those "who pierced him"? This cannot refer to the Roman soldiers, who have long been dead for over 2,000 years. It must be referring to those of mankind that have "pierced him" by abusing and oppressing his disciples in the close of "the last days." – Matthew 25:40, 45.

Will Christians be taken to heaven in their physical bodies?

1 Corinthians 15:50 Revised Standard Version (RSV)

⁵⁰ I tell you this, brethren: flesh and blood cannot inherit the kingdom of God, nor does the perishable inherit the imperishable.

Some might ask, were not Enoch and Elijah taken to heaven in their physical bodies?

Of **Enoch**, the Holman Illustrated Bible Dictionary says, "The son of Jared who was taken up to God without dying (Gen. 5:18)."[111] *The Baker Encyclopedia of the Bible* says of **Elijah**, "Elisha requested a double portion (the firstborn's share, cf. Dt 21:17) of his master's spirit, for he desired to be Elijah's full successor. Elisha knew his request was granted

---

[111] Chad Brand, Charles Draper, et al., eds., "Enoch," *Holman Illustrated Bible Dictionary* (Nashville, TN: Holman Bible Publishers, 2003), 489.

because he saw Elijah pass into the heavens in a whirlwind bearing a chariot and horses of fire. The young prophets who had accompanied Elisha searched in vain for Elijah in the mountains and valleys around the Jordan, but God had taken his faithful prophet home. Elijah thus joined Enoch as the only other man in the Bible who did not experience death."[112] **Is this true?**

ENOCH

Hebrews 11:5 English Standard Version (ESV)

⁵ By faith, Enoch was taken away so that he did not experience death, and he was not to be found because God took him away. For prior to his transformation he was approved, having pleased God.

Some translators have chosen to go beyond the Scripture, being more in the realms of an interpretative translation. The Message Bible reads, "By an act of faith, Enoch skipped death completely." Worse still the James Moffatt translation states, "It was by faith that Enoch was taken to heaven so that he never died." All the original says is that "Enoch was taken away;" (why), "so that he did not experience death." We need to work within what was written and no subject the text to our preconceived doctrinal ideas. Let us look at what Jesus adds to this ...

John 3:13 Holman Christian Standard Bible (HCSB)

¹³ No one has ascended into heaven except the One who descended from heaven, the Son of Man.

This is stated by the Son of God, who existed in heaven at the very time "Enoch was taken away so that he did not experience death." We know two primary points from Jesus' exchange with Nicodemus: (1) Jesus had been in heaven before coming to the earth, and (2) no one was to ever ascend to heaven but those who were 'born again.' It is only by faith in Jesus' ransom sacrifice that ones can be born again.

Since only Jesus himself had been in heaven before coming to the earth, he speaks with authority. Tenney offers a great line here: "Revelation, not discovery, is the basis for faith" (Tenney, EBC, p. 48). Some Jews of Nicodemus's day taught that great saints would attain heaven by their godliness and righteous living. But no one ever sees heaven apart from the new birth.[113]

---

[112] Walter A. Elwell and Barry J. Beitzel, *Baker Encyclopedia of the Bible* (Grand Rapids, MI: Baker Book House, 1988), 691–692.
[113] Kenneth O. Gangel, vol. 4, John, Holman New Testament Commentary; Holman Reference (Nashville, TN: Broadman & Holman Publishers, 2000), 53.

Here again, digging deeper we look at another New Testament writer, the Apostle Paul, who wrote ...

Hebrews 11:13, 39-40 Revised Standard Version (RSV)

¹³ These all died in faith, not having received what was promised, but having seen it and greeted it from afar, and having acknowledged that they were strangers and exiles on the earth. ³⁹ And all these, though well attested by their faith, did not receive what was promised, ⁴⁰ since God had foreseen something better for us, that apart from us they should not be made perfect.[114]

All prior true followers of God before Jesus' ransom sacrifice would "died in faith." Thomas D. Lea writes, "The promises for which believers eagerly waited appeared only in Christ. Old Testament saints did not experience the eternal inheritance. Their faith earned for them a remarkable reputation and favor with God. They lived and died in the hope of a fulfillment which none of them saw on earth. The reaping of the benefits did not occur until Christ opened the box of spiritual treasures."[115]

Why would these ones not receive a heavenly inheritance at death, prior to Jesus' ransom sacrifice? All of humankind has inherited sin from Adam, including Enoch. (Psalm 51:5; Romans 5:12) As man would come to find out in the era of the New Testament, the only means of salvation is by means of Jesus' ransom sacrifice. (Acts 4:12; 1 John 2:1, 2) Enoch lived three thousand years before Jesus' days on the earth, and that ransom had not been paid at that time. Therefore, Enoch was simply asleep in death, awaiting a future resurrection. John 5:28-29

How then are we understand the phrase, "he did not experience death"? Enoch was an outstanding example of faith. "Enoch walked with God, and he was not there, because God took him." (Gen 5:18, 21-24; Heb. 11:5; 12:1) He was a prophet of God, prophesying of God's coming "with thousands of His holy ones to execute judgment on all, and to convict them of all their ungodly deeds that they have done in an

---

[114] These verses comprise the final paragraph of the chapter. It serves a twofold function: (1) to summarize the chapter in succinct fashion, and (2) to serve as a transition to 12:1–13. The author concludes his lengthy list of examples by stating two truths in v. 39: (1) all the heroes mentioned "were commended" by God for their faith, (2) "yet none of them received what had been promised." God's commendation of their faith gives warrant for the author to use these men and women as examples for his readers to emulate. Yet contrary to expectation, none of these heroes received in their lifetimes the fulfillment of the promise (singular) God had made to them. – David L. Allen, Hebrews, *The New American Commentary* (Nashville, TN: B & H Publishing Group, 2010), 566.
[115] Thomas D. Lea, *Hebrews, James*, vol. 10, Holman New Testament Commentary (Nashville, TN: Broadman & Holman Publishers, 1999), 206.

ungodly way, and of all the harsh things ungodly sinners have said against Him." Jude 14-15.

Enoch only lived 365 years in an era where everyone lived over 900 years because God "God took him." Why would God take the only man walking with Him at the time? There is no doubt that this evil world was about to persecute Enoch for his prophecies, to the point of executing him. Instead of letting Satan and the wicked men of that day torture and kill this one faithful follower, God chose to take him in such a way, so as to not experience death. While we do not know how God did this, it is possible that he could have given Enoch a vision, and while in that vision, God took him so that he would not experience the pains of death. God had chosen to do a similar thing with Moses as well, disposing of his body. (Deut. 34:5-6; Jude 9) Like some other Bible details, we cannot be dogmatic. However, we can be certain of the following: (1) God took Enoch, (2) so he would not experience death, (3) but he did enter the sleep of death in such a way as to not experience that entry, (4) and had the hope of a future resurrection, (5) based on Jesus' ransom sacrifice.

ELIJAH

2 Kings 2:11-12 Lexham English Bible (LEB)

¹¹ Then they *were* walking, talking as they went. Suddenly a fiery chariot with horses of fire *appeared* and separated between the two of them. Elijah went up in the storm *to* the heavens **12** while Elisha *was* watching and crying out, "My father, my father; the chariot of Israel and its horsemen!" But he could not see him any longer, and he grasped his clothes and tore them in two pieces.

What were "the heavens" to which "Elijah went up in the storm"? The Hebrew *shamayim* (always in the plural), is rendered "heavens," and references several different meanings. It can refer to the universe, the atmosphere, the place where birds fly, and the spiritual heavens. The biblical evidence does not indicate that Elijah was taken into the physical heavens outside of earth's atmosphere or the spiritual heavens. The heavens to where Elijah was taken were the sky where the birds fly. Elijah was taken up out of sight and delivered to another place, where he continued to live and serve God for a time. Some years later, in fact, Elijah penned a letter to Jehoram, the king of Judah, communicating God's judgment, which was achieved soon afterward. – 2 Chronicles 21:1, 12-15

Jesus Christ himself, who clearly stated, also confirms this "No one has ascended into heaven except he who descended from heaven, the Son of Man." (John 3:13) The opportunity for life in heaven was not available to imperfect humans when they died, until the death, resurrection, and ascension of Jesus Christ. (Jn. 14:2-3; Heb. 9:24; 10:19-20) This is why we are told at 2 Kings 2:10, "then David slept with his fathers [died] and was buried in the city of David." In other words, David had the hope of a future resurrection, once the ransom was paid. (Gen 3:15) The hope of a heavenly resurrection is not discussed in the Old Testament, nor any time prior to Christ, as he is the first to bring it up. (Matt. 19:21, 23-28; Lu 12:32; Jn. 14:2-3) The resurrection hope was not fully understood until after Pentecost 33 C.E.—Acts 1:6-8; 2:1-4, 29-36; Rom 8:16, 17.

Even Job expected that at his death, he would be asleep in death in the grave, until a future resurrection. (Job 14:13-15) Therefore, again, "No one has ascended into heaven but he who descended from heaven, the Son of man." – John 3:13, RSV.

Should Christians that are alive at Christs return that they will just disappear and be taken to heaven without ever having to die?

Romans 6:3-5 Revised Standard Version (RSV)

³ Do you not know that all of us who have been baptized into Christ Jesus were baptized into his death? ⁴ We were buried therefore with him by baptism into death, so that as Christ was raised from the dead by the glory of the Father, we too might walk in newness of life.

⁵ For if we have been united with him in a death like his, we shall certainly be united with him in a resurrection like his.

What Jesus experienced, a death and resurrection, is what all Christian will have to experience, following the pattern that Jesus hat set.

1 Corinthians 15:35-36, 44 Revised Standard Version (RSV)

³⁵ But someone will ask, "How are the dead raised? With what kind of body do they come?" ³⁶ You foolish man! What you sow does not come to life unless it dies. ⁴⁴ It is sown a physical body, it is raised a spiritual body. If there is a physical body, there is also a spiritual body.

Here, we can see that death comes before the person receives the spiritual body.

Will Christians, who are to serve with Christ as priests, kings, and judges (Rev 5:9-10; 20:6), be taken to heaven prior to the great tribulation, during, or after?

Matthew 24:21-22 Revised Standard Version (RSV)

²¹ For then there will be great tribulation, such as has not been from the beginning of the world until now, no, and never will be. ²² And if

those days had not been shortened, no human being would be saved; but for the sake of the elect [chosen ones][116] those days will be shortened.

We notice that the texts above do not say that all of the elect will be taken before the great tribulation. Rather, it says that the great tribulation will be cut short for their sake This suggests that some of the elect will still be present on earth during the great tribulation, some even surviving the great tribulation, meaning the are there afterward as well.

Revelation 7:4, 9-10, 14 Revised Standard Version (RSV)

⁴ And I heard the number of the sealed, **a hundred and forty-four thousand**[117] sealed, out of every tribe of the sons of Israel, ⁹ After this I looked, and behold, a great multitude which no man could number, from every nation, from all tribes and peoples and tongues, standing before the throne and before the Lamb, clothed in white robes, with palm branches in their hands, ¹⁰ and crying out with a loud voice, "Salvation belongs to our God who sits upon the throne, and to the Lamb!" ¹⁴ I said to him, "Sir, you know." And he said to me, "These are they **who have come out of the great tribulation**; they have washed their robes and made them white in the blood of the Lamb.

The elect (chosen ones), who had the great tribulation cut short for their sake, are part of the hundred and forty-four thousand, of Revelation 7:4. The great multitude is other Christians, who are not a part of the elect, who **are not** going to heaven to serve as kings, priests, and judges with Jesus Christ. The good news is that this great multitude of Christians will survive the great tribulation as well. God created the earth to be inhabited, to be filled with perfect humans, who are over the animals, and under the sovereignty of God. (Gen 1:28; 2:8, 15; Ps 104:5; 115:16; Eccl 1:4) Sin did not dissuade God from his plans (Isa. 45:18); hence, he has saved redeemable humankind by Jesus ransom sacrifice. It seems that the Bible offers two hopes to redeemed humans, (1)

---

[116] "But even in judgment, the Lord will display mercy, particularly for the sake of the elect (plural of eklektos, 'select, chosen ones'). These are those who have placed faith in him and followed him as his disciples. The use of the term elect also highlights the Lords sovereign choice as to who these people will be. – Stuart K. Weber, *Matthew*, vol. 1, Holman New Testament Commentary (Nashville, TN: Broadman & Holman Publishers, 2000), 401.

[117] **The case for symbolism is exegetically weak.** The principal reason for the view is a predisposition to make the 144,000 into a group representative of the church with which no possible numerical connection exists. No justification can be found for understanding the simple statement of fact in v. 4 as a figure of speech. **It is a definite number [at 7:4] in contrast with the indefinite number of 7:9.** If it is taken symbolically, no number in the book can be taken literally. As God reserved 7,000 in the days of Ahab (1 Kings 19:18; Rom. 11:4), He will reserve 144,000 for Himself during the future Great Tribulation. (Bold mine) – Robert L. Thomas, *Revelation 1-7: An Exegetical Commentary* (Chicago: Moody Publishers, 1992), 474.

a heavenly hope, or (2) an earthly hope.[118] It also seems that those with the heavenly hope are limited in number, and are going to heaven to rule with Christ as kings, priests, and judges either on the earth or over the earth from heaven. It seems that those with the earthly hope are going to receive everlasting life here on a paradise earth as originally intended.

What protection is there for true Christian during this coming great tribulation?

Matthew 7:21-23 Revised Standard Version (RSV)

[21] "Not everyone who says to me, 'Lord, Lord,' shall enter the kingdom of heaven, but **he who does the will of my Father** who is in heaven. [22] On that day many will say to me, 'Lord, Lord, did we not prophesy in your name, and cast out demons in your name, and do many mighty works in your name?' [23] And then will I declare to them, 'I never knew you; depart from me, you evildoers.'

1 John 2:15-17 Revised Standard Version (RSV)

[15] Do not love the world or the things in the world. If anyone loves the world, love for the Father is not in him. [16] For all that is in the world, the lust of the flesh and the lust of the eyes and the pride of life, is not of the Father but is of the world. [17] And the world passes away, and the lust of it; but **he who does the will of God** abides forever.

---

[118] In the O[ld] T[estament] the kingdom of God is usually described in terms of a redeemed earth; this is especially clear in the book of Isaiah, where the final state of the universe is already called new heavens and a new earth (65:17; 66:22) The nature of this renewal was perceived only very dimly by OT authors, but they did express the belief that a humans ultimate destiny is an earthly one. [It is unwise to speak of the written Word of God as if it were of human origin, saying 'OT authors express the belief,' when what was written is the meaning and message of what God wanted to convey by means of the human author. – Edward D. Andrews] This vision is clarified in the N[ew] T[estament]. Jesus speaks of the "renewal" of the world (Matt 19:28), Peter of the restoration of all things (Acts 3:21). Paul writes that the universe will be redeemed by God from its current state of bondage (Rom. 8:18-21). This is confirmed by Peter, who describes the new heavens and the new earth as the Christian's hope (2 Pet. 3:13). Finally, the book of Revelation includes a glorious vision of the end of the present universe and the creation of a new universe, full of righteousness and the presence of God. The vision is confirmed by God in the awesome declaration: "I am making everything new!" (Rev. 21:1-8).

The new heavens and the new earth will be the renewed creation that will fulfill the purpose for which God created the universe. It will be characterized by the complete rule of God and by the full realization of the final goal of redemption: "Now the dwelling of God is with men" (Rev. 21:3).

The fact that the universe will be created anew [Create anew does not mean a complete destruction followed by a re-creation, but instead a renewal of the present universe. – Edward D. Andrews] shows that God's goals for humans is not an ethereal and disembodied existence, but a bodily existence on a perfected earth. The scene of the beatific vision is the new earth. The spiritual does not exclude the created order and will be fully realized only within a perfected creation. (Elwell 2001, 828-29)

Based on who can enter into the kingdom, 'those doing the will of the Father,' what should we know? What the will of the Father is? Did the many on the path to destruction believe they were doing the will of the Father? What did Jesus say he would say to those who thought they were doing the right thing or thought they were teaching the right thing but were not? ANSWER: 'I never knew you; depart from me, you evildoers.' Certainly, all Christian would want to make sure that they are doing the will of the Father. One way to do this is to heed the words of the apostle Paul.

2 Corinthians 13:5 Updated American Standard Version (UASV)

⁵ Keep testing yourselves to see if you are in the faith. Keep examining yourselves! Or do you not realize this about yourselves, that Jesus Christ is in you, unless indeed you fail to meet the test?

The New Earth: The Earthly Hope

In the O[ld] T[estament] the kingdom of God is usually described in terms of a redeemed earth; this is especially clear in the book of Isaiah, where the final state of the universe is already called new heavens and a new earth (65:17; 66:22) The nature of this renewal was perceived only very dimly by OT authors, but they did express the belief that a humans ultimate destiny is an earthly one.[119] This vision is clarified in the N[ew] T[estament]. Jesus speaks of the "renewal" of the world (Matt 19:28), Peter of the restoration of all things (Acts 3:21). Paul writes that the universe will be redeemed by God from its current state of bondage (Rom. 8:18-21). This is confirmed by Peter, who describes the new heavens and the new earth as the Christian's hope (2 Pet. 3:13). Finally, the book of Revelation includes a glorious vision of the end of the present universe and the creation of a new universe, full of righteousness and the presence of God. The vision is confirmed by God in the awesome declaration: "I am making everything new!" (Rev. 21:1-8).

The new heavens and the new earth will be the renewed creation that will fulfill the purpose for which God created the universe. It will be characterized by the complete rule of God and by the full realization of the final goal of redemption: "Now the dwelling of God is with men" (Rev. 21:3).

---

[119] It is unwise to speak of the written Word of God as if it were of human origin, saying 'OT authors express the belief,' when what was written is the meaning and message of what God wanted to convey by means of the human author.

The fact that the universe will be created anew[120] shows that God's goals for humans is not an ethereal and disembodied existence, but a bodily existence on a perfected earth. The scene of the beatific vision is the new earth. The spiritual does not exclude the created order and will be fully realized only within a perfected creation. (Elwell 2001, 828-29)

Why are these elect or chosen ones being taken to heaven to be with Christ?

Revelation 5:9-10 Updated American Standard Version (UASV)

⁹ And they sang a new song, saying,

"Worthy are you to take the scroll
and to open its seals,
for you were slain, and purchased for God with your blood men
from every tribe and language and people and nation,
¹⁰ and you have made them a kingdom and priests to our God,
and they shall reign over the earth."

Revelation 20:6 Updated American Standard Version (UASV)

⁶ Blessed and holy is the one who has a part in the first resurrection; over these the second death has no power, but they will be priests of God and of Christ and will reign with him for a thousand years.

Will these elect or chosen ones return to the earth as humans some time later?

1 Thessalonians 4:17 Revised Standard Version (RSV)

¹⁷ then we who are alive, who are left, shall be caught up together with them in the clouds to meet the Lord in the air; and so **we shall always be with the Lord**.

We notice that those who are caught away to be with the Lord Jesus Christ, will always be with him.

What if we are asked, 'do you believe in the rapture?' We can comment that there are at least four different views or interpretations of the doctrine of the rapture. Then, kindly ask them, what do you mean by the rapture? Allow for a response ... After hearing what they have to say, we might ask them a question like, "Is it not important that we inspect our beliefs against what the Bible says? Then, use the material above to respond.

---

[120] Create anew does not mean a complete destruction followed by a re-creation, but instead a renewal of the present universe.

We might add that many Christian denominations feel that the rapture is what God will use so that his true followers do not have to experience the horrors of the great tribulation. However, Scripture makes it clear that the great multitude of Christians, who actually have a hope of living forever here on the earth, as well as some of the elect (chosen ones who will rule with Christ as kings, priest, and judges over the earth), will live through the great tribulation. This means we will have protection from God. (Zeph. 2:3; Pro. 2:21-22) However, some will die during the great tribulation. If it is one of the great multitude, who have an earthly hope, they will be resurrected after Armageddon, living throughout the thousand year reign of Christ here on earth. If it is one of the elect, he or she will be resurrected to heaven to be with the Lord (1 Thess. 4:17), in a moment, in the twinkling of an eye (1 Cor. 15:51-52), going from a physical body to a spiritual body. (Rom. 6:3-5; 1 Cor. 15:35-36, 44) Having a great multitude of Christian survive Armageddon (Rev 7:9-10, 14;), with millions of others being resurrected back here to earth (John 8:28-29; Acts 24:15), taking care of the things originally commanded of Adam (Gen. 1:28; 2:8, 15), God's originally intended purpose (Isa. 45:18), is biblical. (2 Tim. 3:16; 2 Pet. 1:21) While we await these future things, we want to carry out the will and a purpose of the Father (Matt 7:21-23; 1 John 2:15-17), as well as Paul's counsel to the Corinthians.

1 Corinthians 15:58 Revised Standard Version (RSV)

[58] Therefore, my beloved brethren, be steadfast, immovable, always abounding in the work of the Lord, knowing that in the Lord your labor is not in vain.

CHAPTER 6 Correctly Understand the Great Tribulation

The Abomination of Desolation

Matthew 24:15 Update American Standard Version (UASV)

¹⁵ "Therefore when you see the abomination of desolation, which was spoken of through Daniel the prophet, standing in the holy place (let the reader understand),

Matthew 24:13 reads, "But **the one who endures to the end** will be saved." Matthew 24:14 said, "this gospel of the kingdom will be proclaimed throughout the whole world as a testimony to all nations, **and then the end will come**." Matthew 24:15 begins with the Greek word *hotan* "whenever" followed by *oun* "therefore, which reads in English, "Therefore when," which connects what preceded, "**the end**," and leads into what follows. Let us take a moment to investigate verse 15.

In verse 3-14, Jesus outlined the signs of "the end of the age." Here in Mathew 24:15, Jesus begins with "**Therefore when** you see the abomination of desolation, which was spoken of through Daniel the prophet, standing in the holy place (let the reader understand)." If we look at the corresponding accounts in Mark and Luke, they offer us additional insights. Mark 13:14 says, "standing where it ought not to be." Luke 21:20 adds Jesus' words, "But when you see Jerusalem surrounded by armies, then know[121] that its desolation has come near." The complete picture is an "abomination" "standing in the holy place," i.e., "where it ought not be," namely, "Jerusalem surrounded by armies,"

This is a reference to the Roman army, which assaulted Jerusalem and its temple starting in 66 C.E., under General Cestus Gallus. The temple was the "holy place" and the abomination was the Roman army "standing where it ought not to be." As for the "desolation," this came in 70 C.E. when General Titus of the Roman army completely desolated Jerusalem and its temple. Specifically, what was this "abomination"? Moreover, in what sense was it "standing in the holy place"?

Jesus had urged the readers to *understand*. What was it that they were to *understand*? They were to *understand* that "which was spoken of through Daniel the prophet," i.e. Daniel 9:27. Part "b" of verse 27 reads "And upon the wing of abominations shall come the one causing desolation, even until a complete destruction, one that is decreed, is

---

[121] Or *then recognize*

poured out on the one causing desolation." – Daniel 9:26-27; see also Daniel 11:31; 12:11.

> The *abomination of desolation* is an expression that recurs in Daniel with some variation in wording (Daniel 8:13; 9:27; 11:31; 12:11), where most scholars agree that there is a reference to the desecration perpetrated by Antiochus Epiphanes when he built an altar to Zeus in the temple and offered swine and other unclean animals on it as sacrifices (cf. 1 Macc. 1:41–61).[122]

We can have it but one of two ways, as Jesus' words were a clear reference to the Roman armies of 66–70 C.E. It may very well be that Daniel's prophecy points to Antiochus Epiphanes "who in 167 [B.C.E., 200-years before Jesus uttered his prophecy] plundered the temple, ordered the sacrificial system to cease, and polluted the altar of the Lord by turning it into a pagan altar, where unclean sacrifices were offered to pagan deities."[123] This would be no different from Matthew referring to Hosea 11:1 (When Israel was a child ... and out of Egypt I called my son). In that case, Matthew did not use Hosea's intended meaning, but carried out an *Inspired Sensus Plenior Application*, by having a whole other meaning, an entirely different meaning for those words, making them applicable to Jesus being called back out of Egypt. It could be that Jesus used Daniel's prophecy about Antiochus Epiphanes, and gave is an *Inspired Sensus Plenior Application*, by having a whole other meaning, a completely different meaning for those words, making them applicable to the Roman armies desolating Jerusalem between 66 and 70 C.E. Then, again, it could be that was what Daniel was pointing to all along, and Jesus used Daniel's words in a grammatical-historical application. Either way, it still comes out the same.

> During the days of the Maccabees this expression was used to describe the sacrilege of Antiochus IV Epiphanes, the Seleucid king who decreed that an altar to Olympian Zeus and perhaps a statue of himself were to be erected in the temple on 15 Chislev, 167 b.c.: "They erected a desolating sacrilege on the altar of burnt offering. They also built altars in the surrounding towns of Judah." Antiochus further decreed that the Sabbath and other festal observances were to be profaned, that circumcision was to be abolished, and that swine and other unclean animals were to be sacrificed in the temple (cf. 1 Macc. 1:41–50). This was one of the lowest points of Jewish history and was considered by

---

[122] Leon Morris, *The Gospel According to Matthew*, The Pillar New Testament Commentary (Grand Rapids, MI; Leicester, England: W.B. Eerdmans; Inter-Varsity Press, 1992), 603.
[123] Larry Chouinard, *Matthew*, The College Press NIV Commentary (Joplin, MO: College Press, 1997), Mt 24:15.

many the primary focus of Daniel's prophecy. Jesus now quotes Daniel directly to clarify that the fulfillment of the "abomination that causes desolation" is yet future.[124]

When Jesus uttered those words of verse 15, the abomination of desolation was yet to appear. Jesus was clearly pointing to the Roman army of 66 C.E., with its distinctive standards, which were idols to the Romans and the empire, but an abomination to the Jews.

Image 1 STANDARD OF THE 10TH ROMAN LEGION This Legion attacked and destroyed Jerusalem in the Jewish War (A.D. 70).

Judæa was under the charge of a Roman official, a subordinate of the governor of the Roman province of Syria, who held a relation to that functionary similar to that which the Governor of Bombay holds to the Governor-General at Calcutta. Roman soldiers paraded the streets of Jerusalem; **Roman standards** waved over the fastnesses of the country; Roman tax-gatherers sat at the gate of every town. To the Sanhedrin, the supreme Jewish organ of government, only a shadow of power was still conceded, its presidents, the high priests, being mere puppets of Rome, set up and put down with the utmost caprice. So low had the proud nation fallen whose ideal it had ever been to rule the world, and whose patriotism was a religious and national passion as intense and unquenchable as ever burned in any country.[125]

---

[124] Clinton E. Arnold, *Zondervan Illustrated Bible Backgrounds Commentary: Matthew, Mark, Luke*, vol. 1 (Grand Rapids, MI: Zondervan, 2002), 148.
[125] James Stalker, *The Life of Jesus Christ* (Chicago: Henry A. Sumner and Company, 1882), 30–31.

Matthew 24:16 (UASV)	Mark 3:14b (UASV)	Luke 21:21 (UASV)
[16] then let those who are in Judea flee to the mountains.	[14] "... then let those who are in Judea flee to the mountains.	[21] Then let those who are in Judea flee to the mountains, and let those who are in the midst of the city depart, and let not those who are out in the country enter it;

Looking at verse 20 of Luke 21, we know that it fits the fact that General Cestius Gallus had "the holy city" Jerusalem (Matt. 4:5)[126] surrounded, which had become the center of the Jewish revolt against Rome. Thirty-three years had passed since Jesus uttered his prophecy, but now the "abomination of desolation" of Rome was near. Gallus and his armies were responding to the Jewish revolt, at the time of the celebration of the festival of booths (tabernacles), October 19-25. On about November 3-4, the Roman army entered the city of Jerusalem, where they attacked the temple wall for five days, weakening it on the sixth day. However, for some unforsaken reason, he pulls away. On this attack of Cestius Gallus, Josephus' *Wars of the Jews 2.539*, says that "had he but continued the siege a little longer, had certainly taken the city; but it was, I suppose, owing to the aversion God had already at the city and the sanctuary, that he was hindered from putting an end to the war that very day." A footnote in Flavius Josephus and William Whiston reads,

> There may another very important, and very providential, reason be here assigned for this strange and foolish retreat of Cestius; which, if Josephus had been now a Christian, he might probably have taken notice of also; and that is, the affording the Jewish Christians in the city an opportunity of calling to mind the prediction and caution given them by Christ about thirty-three years and a half before, that "when they should see the abomination of desolation" [the idolatrous Roman armies, with the images of their idols in their ensigns, ready to lay Jerusalem desolate,] "stand where it ought not;" or, "in the holy place;" or, "when they should see Jerusalem encompassed with armies," they should then "flee to the mountains."
>
> By complying with which those Jewish Christians fled to the mountains of Perea, and escaped this destruction. See Lit. Accompl. of Proph. pp. 69–70. Nor was there, perhaps, any

---

[126] **Matthew 4:5** English Standard Version (ESV)
[5] Then the devil took him to the holy city and set him on the pinnacle of the temple

one instance of a more unpolitic, but more providential conduct than this retreat of Cestius, visible during this whole siege of Jerusalem; which yet was providentially such a "great tribulation, as had not been from the beginning of the world to that time; no, nor ever should be."—Ibid., pp. 70–71.[127]

Matthew 24:17-18 (UASV)	Mark 13:15-16 (UASV)
[17] Let the man who is on the housetop not go down to take what is in his house, [18] and let the man who is in the field not turn back to take his cloak.	[15] let the man who is on the housetop not go down, nor enter his house, to take anything out; [16] and let the man who is in the field not turn back to take his cloak.

When General Gallus suddenly, for no seemingly good reason, withdrew his armies, they suffered substantial fatalities at the hands of the Jews, who were pursuing them. This would wake the Jewish and Gentile Christians to Jesus' words, and that a great tribulation would soon be upon them. (Matt. 24:21) This gave them the opportunity to flee, and for no Christian, to return until the tribulation had passed. Eusebius of Caesarea (260/265 – 339/340 C.E.), a Christian, who was a Roman historian, writes,

> But the people of the church in Jerusalem had been commanded by a revelation, vouchsafed [promised] to approved men there before the war, to leave the city and to dwell in a certain town of Perea called Pella.[128] And when those that believed in Christ had come thither from Jerusalem, then, as if the royal city of the Jews and the whole land of Judea were entirely destitute of holy men, the judgment of God at length overtook those who had committed such outrages against Christ and his apostles, and totally destroyed that generation of impious men. (Eusebius, Ecclesiastical History 3.5.3)

Josephus, first-century Jewish historian (33–100 C.E.), tells us that the Jews waited for God's help, not realizing this was the day of the Lord, a judgment day upon them,

---

[127] Flavius Josephus and William Whiston, *The Works of Josephus: Complete and Unabridged* (Peabody: Hendrickson, 1987).

[128] Pella was a town situated beyond the Jordan, in the north of Perea, within the dominions of Herod Agrippa II. The surrounding population was chiefly Gentile. See Pliny V. 18, and Josephus, B. J. III. 3. 3, and I. 4. 8. Epiphanius (De pond. et mens. 15) also records this flight of the Christians to Pella.

> A false prophet[129] was the occasion of these people's destruction, who had made a public proclamation in the city that very day, that God commanded them to get up upon the temple, and that there they should receive miraculous signs of their deliverance. Now, there was then a great number of false prophets suborned by the tyrants to impose upon the people, who denounced this to them, that they should wait for deliverance from God: and this was in order to keep them from deserting, and that they might be buoyed up above fear and care by such hopes. Now, a man that is in adversity does easily comply with such promises; for when a such a seducer makes him believe that he shall be delivered from those miseries which oppress him, then it is that the patient is full of hopes of such deliverance. (Josephus, Wars of the Jews 6.285–87)

Dio Chrysostom expresses wonder at the level of Jewish fight that they possessed to the very end of the revolt,

> The Jews resisted [Titus] with more ardor than ever, as if it were a kind of windfall [an unexpected piece of luck] to fall fighting against a foe far outnumbering them; they were not overcome until a part of the Temple had caught fire. Then some impaled themselves voluntarily on the swords of the Romans, others slew each other, others did away with themselves or leaped into the flames. They all believed, especially the last, that it was not a disaster but victory, salvation, and happiness to perish together with the Temple. (Dio Chrysostom, Orations 66.6–2–3.)

Zondervan's Illustrated Bible Background Commentary on Matthew 24:17 tell us, "Likewise, there will not be time to gather provisions in the home. The flat rooftops on many homes in Israel were places to find a cool breeze in the evening and were considered part of the living quarters." (Arnold 2002, 150) In Jewish homes of those who could afford a multiform house, there was a staircase outside that led to the roof. The poor would have had a ladder in the courtyard, which led to the roof. Therefore, anyone on the housetop of their home, which was very common, could leave without having to enter their home. Moreover, many homes were built side-by-side, and it was possible to walk from one rooftop to the next. These backgrounds fit what Jesus meant by the words that he used. Whether Jesus meant his words in a hyperbolic sense of, 'when you see these things, act immediate, do not delay,' or literally, 'do not even look back, get out,' it is clear that Christians considered

---

[129] Reland here justly takes notice that these Jews who had despised the true Prophet, were deservedly abused and deluded by these false ones.

Jesus' warning serious, knowing that mere materials were not worth the loss of their lives.

Zondervan's Illustrated Bible Background Commentary on Matthew comments on verse 18 that "The outer coat was an essential garment for traveling, often used as a blanket when sleeping outdoors, and only those in the greatest hurry would think of leaving it behind." (Arnold 2002, 150) ZIBBC comments on Mark 13:18, saying, "Winter is the time of heavy rains in Palestine, flooding roads and wadis. Gadarene refugees during the first revolt sought shelter in Jericho but could not cross the swollen Jordan and were slain by the Romans.304 Winter travel is also hazardous if people are to traverse mountain passes." (Arnold 2002, 283)

Matthew 24:19 Update American Standard Version (UASV)

[19] But woe to those who are pregnant and to those who are nursing babies in those days![130]

Certainly, the modern day woman has taken on some very rigorous activities. Recently, this author saw news of a woman in her eighth months of pregnancy, running a marathon. However, in the days of the first century C.E., an extended flight over mountainous terrain on foot would be very difficult and quite dangerous. This would be especially true for any woman close to her due date. When the Romans finally desolated Jerusalem in 70 C.E., pregnant women, and those with young, were shown no mercy by the Roman troops. As the months of laying siege to the city drug on feminine prevailed, which for a pregnant woman, the baby would be robbing the woman of nourishment. For example, the baby would take the mother's calcium for bone development, meaning the woman could lose all of her teeth. Moreover, some mother gave birth, and had to watch her child starve to death, and in some cases, the people would take the child, cook it and eat it.

Matthew 24:20 Update American Standard Version (UASV)

[20] But pray that your flight will not be in the winter, or on a Sabbath.

This verse is self-explanatory, as we can only imagine the Christians trying to escape over mountainous terrain during the winter. Imagine, if they ignored the warning, procrastinated until the Roman troops arrived, and had to make their escape in the winter; when, they could have left

---

[130] In this connection it should be borne in mind that this tender concern for women with babies was revealed by Christ in days when women were often looked down upon. The words uttered came from the lips of the same Son of man who showed special kindness to widows (Mark 12:42, 43; Luke 7:11–17; 18:1–8; 20:47; 21:2, 3); to women who were, or had been, living in sin (Luke 7:36–50; John 4:1–30); and, at the time of his own crowning agony, to his own mother (John 19:26, 27). (Hendriksen and Kistemaker 1953–2001, p. 859)

earlier. *Zondervan's Illustrated Bible Background Commentary* on Matthew comments on verse 18, saying, "Flight in winter, when roads are washed out and rivers are swollen, presents, even more difficulty for those fleeing the horrors of the coming desolation. In prayer the disciples must cling to God's presence and ever-ready help, even though they may have to disrupt even the most devoutly held religious traditions, such as the Jewish Sabbath." (Arnold 2002, 150)

Matthew 24:21 Update American Standard Version (UASV)

²¹ For then there will be great tribulation, such as has not been from the beginning of the world until now, no, and never will be.

As we looking at Matthew 24:15-22 with Luke 21:20-24, the great tribulation of Jesus' prophecy is applicable to what took place in Jerusalem. The fulfillment of these words came in 70 C.E., when General Titus and his Roman armies laid siege to the city, desolating it, killing 1,100,000 Jews, whereas 97,000 who survived were taken into captivity. (Whiston 1987, Wars of the Jews 6.420) Some might are argue that the 6,000,000 million Jews killed by Hitler during World War II was certainly a greater tribulation than 70 C.E. However, the difference is God used the Roman army as a tool to judge ("a day of the Lord") the Jews for their 1,500 years of false worship, child sacrifice, murder, and the execution of the Son of God. After 70 C.E. Jerusalem was never again the holy city that it once was, nor were the Jews God's chosen people. Therefore, the suffering that the Jews faced during World War II was not as a judgment of God, but rather an unexpected or unforeseen event of human imperfection, as the result of Adamic sin, no different from any other atrocity on humanity.

Matthew 24:22 Update American Standard Version (UASV)

²² And if those days had not been cut short, no flesh would have been saved: but for the chosen ones[131] sake those days shall be shortened.

Again, these words are applicable to a preliminary fulfillment in 66-70 C.E. If we recall the city was under siege by General Cestius Gallus, who had the city, were undermining the Temple wall, with many of the Jews ready to surrender, but for some unknown reason pulled away, suffering great casualties at the hands of the pursuing Jews. Had Gallus not pulled away, leaving several years before Titus would come back and finish the job, the chosen ones,[132] i.e., predominantly Jewish and some Gentile Christians would have not been saved from the desolation. Yes, they heeded Jesus words, "But when you see Jerusalem surrounded by

---

[131] Or *the elect*

[132] Chapter 6 will cover explicitly who these "chosen ones" are.

armies, then know[133] that its desolation has come near. Then let those who are in Judea flee to the mountains, and let those who are in the midst of the city depart, and let not those who are out in the country enter it." (Luke 21:20-21) Thus, the Christians fled the city that was doomed to suffer destruction of 70 C.E.

Matthew 24:23-26 Update American Standard Version (UASV)

23 Then if any man says to you, 'Look, here is the Christ!' or 'There he is!' do not believe it. **24** For false Christs and false prophets will arise and will show great signs and wonders, so as to mislead, if possible, even the chosen ones.[134] **25** Behold, I have told you in advance. **26** So if they say to you, 'Behold, he is in the wilderness,' do not go out, or, 'Behold, he is in the inner rooms,' do not believe it.

We have discussed this aspect extensively earlier. Jesus' prophecy about the end of the Jewish age and the end of wicked humanity, reads, "See that no one leads you astray. For many will come in my name, saying, 'I am the Christ,' and they will **lead many astray**." (Matt 24:4-5) Here in our current verses, Jesus tells us who specifically is being "led astray," "For false Christs [Gr., *pseudochristoi*] and false prophets will arise and will show great signs and wonders, so as to mislead, if possible, even **the chosen ones**." Any who falsely claim to be Christ (anointed one or Messiah), or claim to be a special representative of Christ, are included in the "antichrist" [Gr., *antichristos*], which is mentioned five times by the apostle John. (1 John 2:18, 22; 4:3; 2 John 1:7) For more information on the Antichrist, see, IDENTIFYING THE ANTICHRIST: The Man of Lawlessness and the Mark of the Beast Revealed.[135]

There were false Christs and false prophets that came on the scene before 70 C.E., and the destruction of the Jewish age. Jewish historian Flavius Josephus confirms this as he writes that before the Romans ever attacked, false Messiahs prompted rebellion. To mention just a couple, there is Menahem ben Judah, who claimed to be the Jewish Messiah and is mentioned by Josephus. Then, there is Theudas, who claimed to be the Messiah a Jewish rebel of the 1st century C.E., who between 44 and 46 CE, led his followers in a short-lived revolt. However, as is self-evident, they showed themselves to be false, charlatans, as they did not deliver the Jewish people from the Roman armies. After the destruction of Jerusalem,

---

[133] Or *then recognize*
[134] Or *the elect*
[135] http://www.christianpublishers.org/apps/webstore/products/show/5355019

up unto this day, the Jews[136] have put faith in Jesus Christ, the Son of God, but have rather continued their search for a Messiah in the flesh.

Conversely, both Jewish and non-Jewish Christians have evidenced their faith in Jesus Christ, as they have continued to look at the end of Satan's rule over the earth, the end of wicked humankind, the return of Jesus Christ and his millennial reign. There have been many notable people in the 18th to the 21st century, who have been claimed to be the reincarnation or incarnation of Jesus or the Second Coming of Christ. Either they have made these claims or their followers have made the claim. To mention just a couple, Jim Jones (1931–1978), founder of Peoples Temple, this started as a branch of a mainstream Protestant group before becoming a cult. Then, we have Marshall Applewhite (1931–1997), an American, who posted a famous message declaring, "I, Jesus, Son of God," whose Heaven's Gate cult committed mass suicide on March 26, 1997. Wayne Bent (1941–), AKA Michael Travesser of the Lord Our Righteousness Church. He claimed, "I am the embodiment of God. I am divinity and humanity combined."

If any reader does not believe that they can fall victim to charismatic persons, they are deceiving themselves. Millions of Christians have fallen victim to such ones, and they have not even had the satanic power of 'showing great signs and wonders,' which will be the result before humanities "great tribulation." Then, we have Christians that pick up these end times books, going around speaking of how much truth are within them, when the author(s) has gone beyond what the Word of God says. Finally, there are Pentecostals and Charismatic Christians that number over 500 million, a quarter of the world's two billion Christians. This author sees the religious leaders of these groups as the false Christs, antichrists, false prophets that will be the catalyst to the major false Christs, antichrists, false prophets before the great tribulation. **Excessive** emotionalism within Christianity brings about a blind desire for the return of Christ, opening many up to a situation in which religious leaders offer biblical passages that incorrectly match a return of Christ, e.g. signs of the times, a charismatic person, world events, bad prooftexting, and the like.

The information herein is based on the disciples coming to Jesus privately, saying, "Tell us, **(1)** when will these things be, and **(2)** what will be the sign of your coming, and **(3)** of the end of the age?" (Matthew 24:3)

These questions refer to the end of an age, which was referred to in Matthew 24:1-2,

---

[136] This is not to say that no individual Jewish persons have not converted to Christianity, as hundreds of thousands have in the last two millennium.

¹ Jesus came out from the temple and was going away when¹³⁷ his disciples came up to point out the temple buildings to him. ² And he said to them, "Do you not see all these things? [the temple buildings] Truly I say to you, not one stone here will be left upon another, which will not be torn down."

Jesus is referring to the end of the Jewish age, which was to come in 66-70 C.E., with the desolation and destruction of Jerusalem and its temple. The disciples' questions were based on a presumption the end of the temple equal the end of the age, encompassing Christ's return, the judgment of the wicked and the setting up of his kingdom. The rest of Matthew 24 and 25 is Jesus answering their question. In his words, he does address what will lead up to the end of the Jewish age, as well as the end of wicked humankind age, and his second coming, his kingdom, and his thousand year reign. We have to understand the end of the Jewish age as well because all prophecy has an application to those who hear it, which will help us understand how it applies to the end of sinful, wicked humanity and Christ's return.

Matthew 24:27-28 Update American Standard Version (UASV)

²⁷ For just as the lightning comes from the east and flashes even to the west, so will be the coming of the Son of Man. ²⁸ Wherever the corpse is, there the vultures will gather.

The phrase "for just as," helps us to appreciate in what sense we should expect the arrival of the Son of Man. Again, without coming across as dogmatic, we will adopt a wait and see attitude, but this author does not hold the position that Jesus is coming back here to the earth, but that rather he and his kingdom of co-rulers will be ruling over the earth from heaven. However, just as you can see lightening coming from the east, and vultures from a great distance circling over a corpse, there will be no doubt in the minds of Christians who have stayed awake, remained on the watch, of "the coming of the Son of Man," in that he is ruling under the new millennial reign.

---

¹³⁷ Lit *and*

CHAPTER 7 Correctly Understanding Armageddon

Revelation 16:13-16 Updated American Standard Version (UASV)

13 And I saw coming out of the mouth of the dragon and out of the mouth of the beast and out of the mouth of the false prophet, three unclean spirits like frogs; **14** for they are spirits of demons, performing signs, which go out to the kings of the whole inhabited earth, to gather them together for the war of the great day of God, the Almighty. **15** ("Behold, I am coming like a thief. Blessed is the one who stays awake and keeps his clothes, so that he will not walk about naked and men will not see his shame.") **16** And they gathered them together to the place which in Hebrew is called Har-Magedon.[138]

ARMAGEDDON Hebrew word in Revelation 16:16 meaning "Mount Megiddo." It is generally thought that the term refers to the town of Megiddo, strategically located between the western coastal area and the broad plain of Jezreel in northern Palestine. The area of Megiddo was important commercially and militarily and was the scene of many important battles in Israel's history. There the Lord routed Sisera before the armies of Deborah and Barak (Jgs 4–5); Gideon was victorious over the Midianites and Amalekites (Jgs 6–7); King Saul and his army were defeated by the Philistines (1 Sm 31); and King Josiah was slain in battle by the Egyptian army of Pharaoh Neco (2 Kgs 23:29). Because of that long history the name seems to have become symbolic of a battlefield. Such is the depiction in the book of Revelation.

Revelation 15 and 16 describe seven angels who pour out seven bowls of the wrath of God upon the earth. The sixth angel pours out his bowl upon the great river Euphrates, and its waters are dried up (Rv 16:12–16), preparing the way for the coming of the "kings of the East." Also three demonic spirits go forth to cause the kings of the whole world to gather for a battle on the great day of God the Almighty (16:13–14). Their gathering takes place at Armageddon (16:16).[139]

It would seem that there was not a literal place called "Mountain of Megiddo," either inside or outside the Promised Land, before or during the days of the apostle John. Hence, Har–Magedon clearly draws its meaning from the events linked with the ancient city of Megiddo.

---

[138] Two early MSS read *Armagedon*

[139] Walter A. Elwell and Philip Wesley Comfort, *Tyndale Bible Dictionary*, Tyndale Reference Library (Wheaton, IL: Tyndale House Publishers, 2001), 111.

MEGIDDO, MEGIDDON City standing at the southwest edge of the plain of Esdraelon on the main route between Mesopotamia and Egypt. It overlooks the historic route where a pass through the Mt Carmel range led from the plain of Sharon into the plain of Jezreel. This strategic position made Megiddo one of the most important commercial and military centers of Palestine in the second millennium and the early first millennium B.C. From earliest times, the environs have been the scene of major battles. Great military men, such as Thutmose III of 15th-century bc Egypt, Napoleon in 1799, and General Allenby during World War I, have fought for mastery there.

Aerial View of Megiddo

At the time of the conquest, Joshua defeated the king of Megiddo but did not take the city (Jos 12:21). In the subsequent allotments to the tribes of Israel, Megiddo was assigned to Manasseh, but they could not conquer it from the Canaanites (Jos 17:11–12; Jgs 1:27). During the days of the judges, Deborah and Barak defeated the forces of Hazor under the command of Sisera near Megiddo (Jgs 4:15; 5:19) but did not take the city either. Perhaps David conquered it as part of his program for establishing the kingdom. At any rate, by the time of Solomon, Megiddo served as the headquarters of one of his 12 administrative regions (1 Kgs 4:12). Solomon rebuilt it to serve as one of his chariot and garrison cities (9:15–19).

> **Revelation 13:1** (UASV)
>
> **1** And the dragon stood on the sand of the sea. Then I saw a beast coming up out of the sea, having ten horns and seven heads, and on his horns were ten diadems, and on his heads were blasphemous names.
>
> What or who do these seven heads represent? The seven heads are seven world empires throughout Bible history that have had some kind of impact on God's people, five of which were before John's day: Egypt Assyria, Babylon, Medo-Persia, and Greece. The sixth of those world empires was in existence during John's day, Rome, with the seventh world empire yet to come. Look at John's reference again in the same book.
>
> **Revelation 17:9-10** (UASV)
>
> **9** Here is the mind which has wisdom. The seven heads are seven mountains on which the woman sits, **10** and they are seven kings; five have fallen **[Egypt, Assyrian, Babylon, Medo-Persia, and Greece]**, one is **[Rome]**, the other has not yet come **[?]**; and when he comes, he must remain a little while.
>
> We can conclude that the first wild beast from the sea (vss. 1-10) and the second wild beast from the earth (vss. 11-18) of Revelation 13 represent two governmental powers.
>
> Continued ...

King Ahaziah of Judah died there (841 BC) after being wounded by Jehu while on a visit to the northern kingdom (2 Kgs 9:27). King Josiah of Judah met and intercepted Pharaoh Neco of Egypt (609 bc) at Megiddo in a vain effort to prevent him from going north to aid the Assyrians; he was mortally wounded in the battle (23:29–30). The plain of Megiddo (KJV "valley of Megiddon") is referred to in Zechariah's prophecies of restoration for Israel and Jerusalem (Zec 12:11). Revelation predicts a great future war that will take place at Armageddon (Har Megiddon, the "mount of Megiddo," Rv 16:16).[140]

Interpretation of Revelation 16:13-16

Revelation 16:13-14 Updated American Standard Version (UASV)

13 And I saw coming out of the mouth of the dragon and out of the mouth of the beast and out of the mouth of the false prophet, three unclean spirits like frogs; **14** for they are spirits of demons, performing signs, which go out to the kings of the whole inhabited earth, to gather them together for the war of the great day of God, the Almighty.

When Moses was being used by the Father to free the Israelites from Egyptian slavery, he brought a disgusting plague of frogs on Pharaoh's Egypt, so that "the land stank." (Exodus 8:5-15) Satan with his "three unclean spirits," will bring misleading propaganda intended to maneuver all human rulers, "kings," into opposition to God. This is the beginning of "the war of the great day of God, the Almighty."

---

[140] Walter A. Elwell and Philip Wesley Comfort, *Tyndale Bible Dictionary*, Tyndale Reference Library (Wheaton, IL: Tyndale House Publishers, 2001), 876–877.

> The first wild beast "the dragon **[Satan, Rev. 12:3, 9]** gave it his power and his throne and great authority." The second wild beast "exercises all the authority of the first beast on his behalf and compels the earth and those who live on it to worship the first beast." Therefore, these beasts or governmental powers are against Christ, consequently, they are antichrists.
>
> We must not overreact to this, believing that everyone within the government is somehow a tool, being possessed and used by Satan or his demons. We must realize that God uses the human governments for his own purposes as well.
>
> http://www.christianpublishers.org/mark-of-the-beast-666

The **dragon** is the devil; the **beast** is Antichrist ["anti" "Christ" governmental powers against Christ, see Box]; the **false prophet** is the one previously called the beast "out of the earth" (13:11). With all the persuasive speech they can muster, assisted by ingenious **evil spirits** (literally, "unclean spirits"), they summon all their forces together. John sees these **spirits of demons** in the guise of **frogs**. Frogs are a reminder of another of the Egyptian plagues (Exod. 8:1–13). In fact, the only time the Bible mentions frogs is in reference to the plagues on Egypt—and here in a plague at the end of the world.

Not only are these evil spirits persuasive in speech; they are persuasive in deeds. With one final triumph of wicked deception, they perform **miraculous signs**, perhaps even going beyond the miracles that first brought the beast to power (13:13). This time their goal is to counter the threat of the eastern armies. They must meet force with super force. The **kings of the whole world** are enlisted.

Perhaps the world's armies will suppose they are simply on the march to restore their beloved beast to power. What John tells us is that they are actually being gathered **for the battle on the great day of God Almighty**. The more common biblical reference to God's judgment on the nations is the day of the Lord. In the Old Testament, it appears only in eight prophetic books (Isa., Ezek., Joel, Amos, Obad., Zeph., Zech., Mal.). In the New Testament it occurs six times.[141]

• Acts 2:20—The sun will be turned to darkness and the moon to blood before the coming of the great and glorious day of the Lord.

• 1 Corinthians 1:8—He will keep you strong to the end, so that you will be blameless on the day of our Lord Jesus Christ.

• 1 Corinthians 5:5—Hand this man over to Satan, so that the sinful nature may be destroyed and his spirit saved on the day of the Lord.

---

[141] Kendell H. Easley, *Revelation*, vol. 12, Holman New Testament Commentary (Nashville, TN: Broadman & Holman Publishers, 1998), 289.

- 2 Corinthians 1:14—As you have understood us in part, you will come to understand fully that you can boast of us just as we will boast of you in the day of the Lord Jesus.

- 1 Thessalonians 5:2—For you know very well that the day of the Lord will come like a thief in the night.

- 2 Thessalonians 2:2—[You are] not to become easily unsettled or alarmed by some prophecy, report or letter supposed to have come from us, saying that the day of the Lord has already come.

- 2 Peter 3:10—But the day of the Lord will come like a thief. The heavens will disappear with a roar; the elements will be destroyed by fire, and the earth and everything in it will be laid bare.[142]

In the Hebrew Scriptures (Old Testament), there is a very common phrase, "the day of Jehovah." (ESV, "the day of the LORD," LEB "the day of Yahweh", or ASV "the day of Jehovah") This day of Jehovah is detailed in the Scriptures as a time of battle, a day of distress and anguish, a day of darkness, a day of wrath and fierce anger, a day of wrath is that day, a day of distress and anguish, a day of ruin and devastation, and a day to destroy its sinners. – Amos 5:18-20; Isaiah 13:9; Zephaniah 1:15; Ezekiel 7:19; Zephaniah 1:18

The work that John the Baptist did was to prepare the Israelites to accept the Christ, as *a day of Jehovah* was very near. The apostle Peter quoted the prophet Joel right after Pentecost, explaining that the miraculous events they had just seen unfold, were a fulfillment of the words of Joel, i.e., a fulfillment of the words God's inspired Joel to pen. Peter showed that the words of Joel were to come to pass before "the great and glorious day of the Lord comes." (Acts 2:16-21; Joel 2:28-32) The prophecy of Joel was fulfilled in 70 C.E. when General Titus of the Roman army, destroyed Jerusalem, executing divine judgment on the nation of Israel for their centuries of rebellion, false worship, and finally, the rejection of the Son of God, in that they had him executed by way of the Roman government.—Daniel 9:24-27; John 19:15.

Now, to tie all of this together, the day of the LORD (Jehovah) that took place in 70 C.E. when Jerusalem was destroyed was just one of many times of destructive judgment by God. For example, we had the first destruction of Jerusalem by the Babylonians. Malachi had prophesied that God would send the Jews Elijah-like prophet **before** the great and awesome **day of the LORD** comes. This came true with John the Baptist coming to prepare the way for Jesus, who prepared the way for the Christians, before the destruction of Jerusalem in 70 C.E., where one

---

[142] Kendell H. Easley, *Revelation*, vol. 12, Holman New Testament Commentary (Nashville, TN: Broadman & Holman Publishers, 1998), 295–296.

million Jews were killed and one hundred thousand taken captive. So at that time a "day of the LORD" was near at hand. Joel tells us that there would be an outpouring of Holy Spirit before this same "day of the LORD," which Peter quotes. (Ac 2:17) Again, that "day of the LORD" came in 70 C.E. when God used the Roman army to execute divine judgment on the nation of Israel for their centuries of rebellion, false worship, and finally, the rejection of the Son of God.

However, there is another "day of the Lord" to come. The apostle Paul associated this "day of the LORD" with the second coming of Jesus Christ. Paul writes,

2 Thessalonians 2:1-2 Updated American Standard Version (UASV)

¹ Now we request you, brothers, with regard to the coming[143] of our Lord Jesus Christ and our gathering together to him, **2** that you not be quickly shaken from your composure or be disturbed either by a spirit or a word or a letter as if from us, to the effect that the day of the Lord has come.

The apostle Peter associates this same "day of the LORD" with,

2 Peter 3:10, 13 Updated American Standard Version (UASV)

¹⁰ But **the day of the Lord** will come like a thief, in which the heavens will pass away with a loud noise, the elements will burn and be dissolved, and the earth and its works will be exposed.[144] **13** But according to his promise we are looking for **new heavens and a new earth**, in which righteousness dwells.

When we look at all of this, we can see a future "day of the LORD." We know that Elijah prepared the way for "the day of the LORD" in the first century, with his evangelism, as did Jesus. Moreover, Jesus said that Christians would do an even greater work that he (John 14:12). We do so because we are to prepare the way for the greatest "day of the LORD," namely, the return of Jesus Christ. Jesus disciples asked him, "Lord, will you at this time restore the kingdom to Israel?" Jesus' said to them, "It is not for you to know times or seasons that the Father has fixed by his own authority." (Ac 1:7) The apostle Paul wrote the Thessalonians, who had been inclined to worry excessively about the second coming of Christ. He said, "Now concerning the times and the seasons, brothers, you have no need to have anything written to you. For you yourselves are fully aware

---

[143] Or *presence* (Gr *parousia*), which denotes both an "arrival" and a consequent "presence with."

[144] Gr *heurethesetai* ("will be discovered") is attested to by ℵ B KP 424c 1175 1739txt 1852 syrph, hmg arm Origen. Gr *katakaesetai* ("will be burned up") is attested to by A 048 049 056 0142 33 614 Byz Lect syrh copbo eth *al*.

that the day of the Lord will come like a thief in the night." – 1 Thessalonians 5:1-2.

Like a thief (v. 15)

During his days on earth, Jesus had warned that "the Son of Man will come at an hour when you do not expect him" (Matt. 24:44). Both Peter and Paul had compared the "day of the Lord" to the surprise arrival of a thief (2 Pet. 3:10; 1 Thess. 5:2, 4). Jesus had warned the almost-dead church of Sardis that he was about to come like a thief in judgment on them (Rev. 3:3).

The image of Christ returning as an unexpected thief is sometimes accompanied by the picture of his return being as unexpected as labor pains on an expectant mother (Matt. 24:8; Mark 13:17-18). The classic text is 1 Thessalonians 5:3: "While people are saying, 'Peace and safety,' destruction will come on them suddenly, as labor pains on a pregnant woman, and they will not escape."

When some people have learned of my interpretation that the New Testament—and Revelation in particular—teaches that Christians are destined to endure end-time tribulations, they have responded with the following. "Oh, then, so you don't really believe in the imminent return of Christ." To which I must always reply, "Of course I do. The day of the Lord is imminent." I always go back in my thinking to the eighth and ninth months in my wife's pregnancy. There were certainly signs that a baby was coming. Labor was imminent. Yet the highest degree of medical technology was totally helpless to predict the onset of labor.

It is like that with the return of Christ. Certainly many signs show that the Lord is about to return. His coming is, indeed, imminent. Nothing keeps him from returning at any moment. What this means is that the final sequence—grain harvest (Rapture) to grape vintage (wrath)—may begin at any moment. His coming—the day of the Lord—covers these two and all points between.

While Revelation seems reasonably clear about the sequence of events before the grain harvest, none of the information is sufficiently precise to enable us to say "this marks the specific time of the seven trumpet judgments." This calls for humility on our part. It is perhaps parallel to a woman knowing that she is, in fact, pregnant but not knowing quite how far along in the process she is. The times have been "pregnant" since John's visions. Nothing hinders birth pains from beginning (the Great Tribulation) and the arrival of the male child who will rule the nations (the Lord Jesus).[145]

Revelation 16:16 Updated American Standard Version (UASV)

¹⁶ And they [the expressions inspired by demons] gathered them [the earthly kings, or rulers] together to the place which in Hebrew is called Har-Magedon.[146]

Armageddon has been connected also with the ancient city of Megiddo, the site of many significant battles in Bible times. It is for this reason that Armageddon is commonly associated with a World War III by Hollywood, where a nuclear holocaust takes place. It is because of the battles fought in ancient Megiddo, many Bible scholars see Armageddon taking place in the "Middle East site of the final battle between the forces of good and evil (Rev. 16:16)."[147] **However**, rather than being literal, it is simply being used to represent the situation in which the world finds itself, in opposition against the Creator, who will destroy the wicked, with a great multitude of Christians surviving. – Jeremiah 25:31-33; Daniel 2:44.

---

[145] Kendell H. Easley, *Revelation*, vol. 12, Holman New Testament Commentary (Nashville, TN: Broadman & Holman Publishers, 1998), 296–297.

[146] Two early MSS read *Armagedon*

[147] Kenneth Hubbard, "Armageddon," ed. Chad Brand et al., *Holman Illustrated Bible Dictionary* (Nashville, TN: Holman Bible Publishers, 2003), 114.

CHAPTER 8 Correctly Understanding the Resurrection Hope

All of us have lost a loved one to this force to be reckoned with, and it is only a matter of time before we have to face the greatest enemy humankind has ever known, death! However, we have been given a hope that is as great at the penalty that we are under. We have the hope of life eternal, and if we die, it is the hope of a resurrection. This hope means that we will be reunited with the loved ones that we have lost. Some in the past have had a foretaste of this great hope:

Mark 5:35, 41-42 English Standard Version (ESV)

35 While he was still speaking, there came from the ruler's house some who said, "Your daughter is dead. Why trouble the Teacher any further?" **41** Taking her by the hand he said to her, "Talitha cumi," which means, "Little girl, I say to you, arise." **42** And immediately the girl got up and began walking (for she was twelve years of age), and they were immediately overcome with amazement.

Acts 9:36-41 English Standard Version (ESV)

36 Now there was in Joppa a disciple named Tabitha, which, translated, means Dorcas.[148] She was full of good works and acts of charity. **37** In those days she became ill and died, and when they had washed her, they laid her in an upper room. **38** Since Lydda was near Joppa, the disciples, hearing that Peter was there, sent two men to him, urging him, "Please come to us without delay." **39** So Peter rose and went with them. And when he arrived, they took him to the upper room. All the widows stood beside him weeping and showing tunics[149] and other garments that Dorcas made while she was with them. **40** But Peter put them all outside, and knelt down and prayed; and turning to the body he said, "Tabitha, arise." And she opened her eyes, and when she saw Peter she sat up. **41** And he gave her his hand and raised her up. Then calling the saints and widows, he presented her alive.

We have already heard of the charges that Satan has risen against God in chapter six of this book. The resurrection hope allows God to let Satan play out his challenges, to resolve the issues that would have otherwise plagued us for an eternity. It is like when you suffer through a painful medical treatment, to enjoy thereafter with all the complications of the issues you had. It is only by means of the greatest resurrection, namely Jesus Christ that we can have this hope.

---

[148] The Aramaic name Tabitha and the Greek name Dorcas both mean gazelle
[149] Greek chiton, a long garment worn under the cloak next to the skin

Matthew 20:28 English Standard Version (ESV)

²⁸ even as the Son of Man came not to be served but to serve, and to give his life as a ransom for many.

Resurrection is a Foundational Doctrine

Hebrews 6:1-2 English Standard Version (ESV)

⁶ Therefore let us leave the elementary doctrine of Christ and go on to maturity, not laying again a foundation of repentance from dead works and of faith toward God, ² and of instruction about washings,[150] the laying on of hands, the resurrection of the dead and eternal judgment.

The resurrection is a foundational doctrine to our Christian faith. However, it does not compute with the world of humankind that is alienated from God. They see this as the only life there is, and so they are in pursuit of fleshly pleasures, to make the most of it. (1 Cor. 15:32) We on the other hand do not need to chase after the things that Satan's world has to offer.

Acts 17:32 English Standard Version (ESV)

³² Now when they heard of the resurrection of the dead, some mocked. But others said, "We will hear you again about this."

We need to look to at least two **hopes** that humans have the opportunity of having. Some are of new Israel and is seen as being given a kingdom, a chosen race, a royal priesthood, and ruling with Christ for a thousand years. There will be a need to investigate this, and this section will be a little more complex than any other part of this book. It is very important to all of us, so bear with me. I am going to quote some of the leading evangelical scholars at length.

Revelation 5:9-10 English Standard Version (ESV)

⁹ And they **sang a new song**, saying,

"Worthy are you to take the scroll
 and to open its seals,
for you were slain, and by your blood you ransomed people for God
 from every tribe and language and people and nation,
¹⁰ and **you have made them a kingdom and priests** to our God,
 and **they shall reign on**[151] **the earth.**"

---

[150] Or baptisms (that is, cleansing rites)
[151] According to this verses Jesus will rule "on" the earth. For another consideration, see the next subheading: Over the earth or On the Earth?

A further result of the Lamb's sacrifice is the establishment[152] of the redeemed as a kingdom and priests: kai epoiēsas autous tǭ theǭ hēmōn basileian kai hiereis ("and You made them a kingdom and priests to our God"). The threefold occurrence of this theme in Revelation (cf. also Rev. 1:6; 20:6) indicates that talk about such a spiritual heritage was common parlance among Christians of John's day (Swete). As God's possession,[153] the redeemed will not merely be God's people over whom He reigns, but will also share God's rule in the coming millennial kingdom (cf. 1 Cor. 4:8; 6:3) (Charles; Ladd). This kingdom is the goal toward which the program of God is moving as emphasized by basileusousin ("they shall reign") later in v. 10 (cf. Rev. 20:4). The idea of priesthood found in hiereis ("priests") means full and immediate access into God's presence for the purpose of praise and worship (Ladd). It also includes the thought of priestly service to God (Mounce). Though believers are currently viewed as a royal priesthood (1 Pet. 2:5, 9; cf. Ex. 19:6), this is only preliminary to the fullness of the way they will function alongside Christ in the millennial kingdom.[154]

Kai basileusousin epi tēs gēs ("and they shall reign on the earth") explains more fully the earlier basileian ("kingdom"). The fact that believers will serve as reigning powers means that they will be the equivalent of kings (Charles; Beckwith). Spelled out more particularly in 20:4 regarding the millennial kingdom and in 22:5 regarding the eternal state, they will join with Christ in His continual reign following His second advent to the earth. This all stems from the epoch determining redemptive work of the Lamb.[155]

On the earth or Over the Earth

ἐπί epí [2093] is in the genitive and can range from: on, upon; over; at, by; before, in the presence of; when, under, at the time of;[156] Below you are going to find a list the genitive epi within Revelation that has

---

[152] The aorist ἐποίησας connotes finished result. As commonly the case in the heavenly songs of this book, it is proleptic, anticipating the culmination of the process being carried out at the time the song is sung (Swete, Apocalypse, p. 81; Beckwith, Apocalypse, pp. 512–13).[152]

[153] Τῷ θεῷ (5:10) has a possessive sense: "belonging to God" as His peculiar people (Beckwith, Apocalypse, p. 513).[153]

[154] Newell, Revelation, p. 13.

[155] Robert L. Thomas, Revelation 1-7: An Exegetical Commentary (Chicago: Moody Publishers, 1992), 402.

[156] William D. Mounce, Mounce's Complete Expository Dictionary of Old & New Testament Words (Grand Rapids, MI: Zondervan, 2006), 1150.

a similar construction. Please pay particular attention to **5:10, 9:11,** and **11:6**, but there will be others that are similar.

If we are to establish that some translations are choosing a rendering because it suits their doctrine, we must compare how they render the same thing elsewhere. You do not need to be a Greek scholar below, so you can ignore the grammar talk, and just notice the similarities and differences.

I do believe that the English is a problem in trying to say, "they shall reign on the earth." First, because this is not a location issue: i.e., where. The genitive *epi* is dealing not with where, but with authority over, which is expressed by having it over _____ not on _____

Please also take special note that the context of all of these epi genitives that follow the active indicative verb and then are followed by the genitive definite article and noun are dealing with authority.

> The verb "to reign" is properly used of kings and queens, and here implies complete power over the world and its inhabitants. So another way of expressing this is "and they shall rule over the world and its inhabitants" or "they shall have power over ...."[157]

Rev 5:10: basileusousin epi tēs gēs ("They are reigning [opon, on, over] the earth")[158]

ESV: they shall reign **on** the earth

NASB: they will reign **upon** the earth

ASV: they reign **upon** earth

DBY: they shall reign **over** the earth

ἐπί epí is in the genitive and comes after the future active indicative verb followed by the definite article and followed by a definite genitive article and noun

Rev 9:11: echousin ep autōn basilea (They are having [upon, on, over] them king)

ESV: They have as king **over** them

NASB: They have as king **over** them

ASV: They have **over** them as king

---

[157] Bratcher, Robert G.; Hatton, Howard: A Handbook on the Revelation to John. New York: United Bible Societies, 1993 (UBS Handbook Series; Helps for Translators), S. 105

[158] English Standard Version (ESV), New American Standard Bible (NASB), American Standard Version (ASV), and the Darby Bible (DBY)

DBT: They have a king **over** them

ἐπί **epí** is in the genitive and comes after the present active indicative verb followed by a definite genitive article and noun

Rev 11:6: exousian echousin epi tōn hudatōn (they are having authority [upon, on, over] the water)

ESV: they have power **over** the waters

NASB: they have power **over** the waters

ASV: they have power **over** the waters

DBY: they have power **over** the waters

ἐπί **epí** is in the genitive and comes after the future active indicative verb followed by a definite genitive article and noun

Rev 2:26: dōsō autō exousian epi tōn ethnōn (I shall give to him authority [upon, on, over] the nations)

ESV: I will give authority **over** the nations

NASB: I WILL GIVE AUTHORITY **OVER** THE NATIONS

ASV: I give authority **over** the nations

DBY: will I give authority **over** the nations,

ἐπί **epí** is in the genitive and comes after the future active indicative verb followed by a definite genitive article and noun

Rev 6:8: edothē autois exousia epi to tetarton tēs gēs (was given to them authority [upon, on, over] the fourth of the earth)

ESV: they were given authority **over** a fourth of the earth

NASB: Authority was given to them **over** a fourth of the earth

ASV: here was given unto them authority **over** the fourth part of the earth

DBY: authority was given to him **over** the fourth of the earth

ἐπί **epí** is in the genitive and comes after the future active indicative verb followed by a definite genitive article and noun

Rev 13:7: edothē autō exousia epi pasan phulēn kai laon kai glōssan kai ethnos (was given to it authority [upon, on, over] every tribe and people and tongue and nation)

ESV: authority was given it **over** every tribe and people and language and nation

NASB: authority **over** every tribe and people and tongue and nation was given to him

ASV: there was given to him authority **over** every tribe and people and tongue and nation

DBY: was given to it authority **over** every tribe, and people, and tongue, and nation

ἐπί **epí** is in the genitive and comes after the future active indicative verb followed by a genitive noun. While there is no definite article, it still seems definite in that we know which one: everyone.

Rev 14:18: ho echōn exousian epi tou puros the one having authority [upon, on, over] the fire

ESV: who has authority **over** the fire

NASB: the one who has power **over** fire

ASV: he that hath power **over** fire

DBY: having power **over** fire

Rev 16:9: tou echontos tēn exousian epi pas plēgas (the one having the authority (upon, on, over) the plagues)

ESV: who had power **over** these plagues

NASB: who has the power **over** these plagues

ASV: who hath the power **over** these plagues

DBY: who had authority **over** these plagues

Rev 17:18: hē polis megalē hē echousa basileian epi tōn basileōn tēs gēs (the woman whom you saw is the city the great the one having kingdom (upon, on, over) the kingdoms of the earth)

ESV: the great city that has dominion **over** the kings of the earth

NASB: the great city, which reigns **over** the kings of the earth.

ASV: the great city, which reigneth **over** the kings of the earth.

DBY: the great city, which has kingship **over** the kings of the earth

Revelation 5:9-10 has a high level of theological content. It either says that Jesus and his co-rulers are going to rule from heaven, over the earth or on the earth. It is theological bias to have several cases of similar context and the same grammatical construction, rendering the verses the same every time, yet to then render one verse contrary to the others, simply because it aligns with one's theology. Whether that is the case here or not, the readers will have to determine for themselves. I will offer this, either way, Jesus is ruling the earth, and we are blessed to have had a resurrection. Take your time, as things are going to get a little deeper below for about four more pages. You can grasp it, just slow down meditate on what is being said, and get out your dictionary if you have to, and write the definitions in the book beside the word, and read again.

Heavenly Hope

Revelation 14:1-4 English Standard Version (ESV)

¹ Then I looked, and behold, on Mount Zion stood the Lamb, and with him **144,000** who had his name and his Father's name written on their foreheads. ² And I heard a voice from heaven like the roar of many waters and like the sound of loud thunder. The voice I heard was like the sound of harpists playing on their harps, ³ and **they were singing a <u>new song</u>** before the throne and before the four living creatures and before the elders. **No one could learn that song except the 144,000 who had been redeemed from the earth.** ⁴ It is these who have not defiled themselves with women, for they are virgins. It is these who follow the Lamb wherever he goes. These have been redeemed from mankind as firstfruits for God and the Lamb

> The whole of chapter 14 is proleptic. As a summary of the Millennium (20:4–6), the first five verses feature the Lamb in place of the beast, the Lamb's followers with His and the Father's seal in place of the beast's followers with the mark of the beast, and the divinely controlled Mount Zion in place of the pagan-controlled earth (Alford, Moffatt, Kiddle).[159]

Revelation 7:4 English Standard Version (ESV)

⁴ And I heard the number of the sealed, 144,000, sealed from every tribe of the sons of Israel

> Various efforts have sought to determine the significance of the number 144,000. An understanding of the number as symbolical divides it into three of its multiplicands, 12 × 12 × 1000. From the symbolism of the three it is concluded that the number indicates fixedness and fullest completeness.[160] Twelve, a number of the tribes, is both squared and multiplied by a thousand. This is a twofold way of emphasizing completeness (Mounce). It thus affirms the full number of God's people to be brought through tribulation (Ladd). The symbolic approach

---

[159] Robert L. Thomas, Revelation 8-22: An Exegetical Commentary (Chicago: Moody Publishers, 1995), 189.
[160] Alford, Greek Testament, 4:624; Charles, Revelation, 1:206; Lenski, Revelation, p. 154.

points out the impossibility of taking the number literally. It is simply a vast number, less than a number indefinitely great (cf. 7:9), but greater than a large number designedly finite (e.g., 1,000, Rev. 20:2) (Lee). Other occurrences of the numerical components that are supposedly symbolic are also pointed out, 12 thousand in Rev. 21:16, 12 in Rev. 22:2, and 24, a multiple of 12, in Rev. 4:4. This is done to enhance the case for symbolism (Johnson). Though admittedly ingenious, the case for symbolism is exegetically weak. The principal reason for the view is a predisposition to make the 144,000 into a group representative of the church with which no possible numerical connection exists. No justification can be found for understanding the simple statement of fact in v. 4 as a figure of speech. It is a definite number in contrast with the indefinite number of 7:9. If it is taken symbolically, no number in the book can be taken literally. As God reserved 7,000 in the days of Ahab (1 Kings 19:18; Rom. 11:4), He will reserve 144,000 for Himself during the future Great Tribulation.[161] (Thomas, Revelation 1-7: An Exegetical Commentary 1992, 473-74)

These ones are made up of those under the new covenant, the Law of Christ, those **called out of natural Israel**, the new Israelites, also known as the Israel of God. They are a chosen number that are to reign with Jesus as kings, priests, and judges. Therefore, we ask, what is the other hope?

The New [Renewed] Earth: The Earthly Hope

In the O[ld] T[estament] the kingdom of God is usually described in terms of a redeemed earth; this is especially clear in the book of Isaiah, where the final state of the universe is already called new heavens and a new earth (65:17; 66:22) The nature of this renewal was perceived only very dimly by OT authors, but they did express the belief that a humans ultimate destiny is an earthly one.[162] This vision is clarified in the N[ew]

---

[161] Bullinger, Apocalypse, p. 282. Geyser is correct in observing that the predominant concern of the Apocalypse is "the restoration [on earth] of the twelve tribes of Israel, their restoration as a twelve-tribe kingdom, in a renewed and purified city of David, under the rule of the victorious 'Lion of the Tribe of Judah, the Root of David' (5:5; 22:16)" (Albert Geyser, "The Twelve Tribes in Revelation: Judean and Judeo Christian Apocalypticism," NTS 23, no. 3 [July 1982]: 389). He is wrong, however, in his theory that this belief characterized the Judean church only and was not shared by Gentile Christianity spearheaded by Paul (ibid., p. 390).

[162] It is unwise to speak of the written Word of God as if it were of human origin, saying 'OT authors express the belief,' when what was written is the meaning and message of what God wanted to convey by means of the human author.

T[estament]. Jesus speaks of the "renewal" of the world (Matt 19:28), Peter of the restoration of all things (Acts 3:21). Paul writes that the universe will be redeemed by God from its current state of bondage (Rom. 8:18-21). This is confirmed by Peter, who describes the new heavens and the new earth as the Christian's hope (2 Pet. 3:13). Finally, the book of Revelation includes a glorious vision of the end of the present universe and the creation of a new universe, full of righteousness and the presence of God. The vision is confirmed by God in the awesome declaration: "I am making everything new!" (Rev. 21:1-8)

The new heavens and the new earth will be the renewed creation that will fulfill the purpose for which God created the universe. It will be characterized by the complete rule of God and by the full realization of the final goal of redemption: "Now the dwelling of God is with men" (Rev. 21:3).

The fact that the universe will be created anew[163] shows that God's goals for humans is not an ethereal and disembodied existence, but a bodily existence on a perfected earth. The scene of the beatific vision is the new earth. The spiritual does not exclude the created order and will be fully realized only within a perfected creation. (Elwell 2001, 828-29)

What have we learned so far in this publication? God created the earth to be inhabited, to be filled with perfect humans, who are over the animals, and under the sovereignty of God. (Gen 1:28; 2:8, 15; Ps 104:5; 115:16; Eccl 1:4) Sin did not dissuade God from his plans (Isa. 45:18); hence, he has saved redeemable humankind by Jesus ransom sacrifice. It seems that the Bible offers two hopes to redeemed humans, **(1) a heavenly hope**, or **(2) an earthly hope**. It also seems that those with the heavenly hope are limited in number, and are going to heaven to rule with Christ as kings, priests, and judges either **on** the earth or **over** the earth from heaven. It seems that those with the earthly hope are going to receive everlasting life here on a paradise earth as originally intended.

---

[163] Create anew does not mean a complete destruction followed by a re-creation, but instead a renewal of the present universe.

CHAPTER 9 Correctly Understanding the Millennium

The millennium is the kingdom of Christ Jesus and his elect or chosen ones (i.e., co-rulers), where they will rule over the earth for a period of a thousand years. The thousand-year period begins the second coming of Christ, after Armageddon.

Revelation 21:4 Updated American Standard Version (UASV)

⁴ and he will wipe away every tear from their eyes, and death shall be no more, neither shall there be mourning, nor crying, nor pain anymore, for the former things have passed away."

Here, we see that God links the millennium at a time when "he will wipe away every tear from their eyes, and death shall be no more, neither shall there be mourning, nor crying, nor pain anymore." Thus, it seems important that we have a correct understanding of the millennium. If we open our Bible to chapter 20, there we will discover most of what the Bible has to say about the millennium.

Satan Bound for 1,000 Years

Revelation 20:1-3 Updated American Standard Version (UASV)

20 Then I saw an angel coming down from heaven, holding the key of the abyss and a great chain in his hand. ² And he seized the dragon, the original serpent, who is the Devil and Satan, and bound him for a thousand years; ³ and threw him into the abyss, and shut it and sealed it over him, so that he might not deceive the nations any longer, until the thousand years were ended; after these things he must be released for a short time.

Who is this angel? Robert L. Thomas offers the best insight into this question. "Various suggested identifications of the "angel" (ἄγγελον [angelon]) charged with the responsibility of binding Satan have been Christ, the Holy Spirit, the twelve apostles, one of the popes, and Constantine the Great.[164] None of these has convincing support, however. The better course is to understand him to be a special angel commissioned for this particular task (Walvoord)."[165] It could not have been worded any better, "a special angel commissioned for this particular task." There

---

[164] William Lee, "The Revelation of St. John," in *The Holy Bible*, ed. F. C. Cook (London: John Murray, 1881), 4:791–92.
[165] Robert L. Thomas, *Revelation 8-22: An Exegetical Commentary* (Chicago: Moody Publishers, 1995), 405–406.

are two special angels mentioned in the Bible, who would have the tremendous power needed to be able to dispose of Satan.

We have **Gabriel**, the only angel other than **Michael** named in the Bible. Twice Gabriel appeared to the prophet Daniel. (Dan. 8:1, 15-26) Gabriel was given the task of bringing the good news to Zechariah and Elizabeth that they would have a son, John the Baptist. (Lu 1:11-20) Gabriel also declared a special message to Mary, who was pregnant with Jesus. (Lu 1:26-38) Gabriel is a high-ranking angel who 'stands in the presence of God,' 'the angel sent from God' to deliver special messages here on earth. Gabriel is a "personal name meaning "strong man of God.'"[166] Thus, Gabriel is the only *other* true candidate being sent by God to abyss Satan.

Jude 9 Updated American Standard Version (UASV)

⁹ But **Michael the archangel**, when he disputed with the devil and argued about the body of Moses, did not dare to bring a judgment against him in abusive terms, but said, "The Lord[167] rebuke you!"

Yes, the best interpretation of who this special angel might be is **Michael**. Michael is a "personal name meaning, "Who is like God?'"[168] Michael is an "archangel who served as the guardian of the nation of Israel (Dan. 10:13, 21; 12:1). Together with Gabriel, Michael fought for Israel against the prince (angelic patron) of Persia. ... In Rev. 12:7, Michael commands the forces of God against the forces of the dragon in a war in heaven. Jude 9 refers to a dispute between the devil and Michael over Moses' body."[169] The *Holman Illustrated Dictionary* also notes that archangel means "chief or first angel. The English term "archangel" is a derivative of the Greek word *archangelos*, which occurs only twice in the NT. Only one archangel is named in the Bible, though it is possible that there are others."[170] This author would disagree that there is any possibility that there is more than one archangel. The prefix "arch," meaning "chief" or "principal," indicates that there is only one archangel, the chief angel. Yes, Gabriel is very powerful, but no Scripture ever refers to him as an archangel. If there were multiple archangels, how could they

---

[166] Chad Brand, Charles Draper, et al., eds., "Gabriel," *Holman Illustrated Bible Dictionary* (Nashville, TN: Holman Bible Publishers, 2003), 610.

[167] I.e., the Father; Zechariah 3:2 (UASV) Then Jehovah said to Satan, "rebuke you, Satan! Indeed, Jehovah, who has chosen Jerusalem rebuke you! Is this not a brand plucked from the fire?"

[168] Chad Brand, Charles Draper, et al., eds., "Gabriel," *Holman Illustrated Bible Dictionary* (Nashville, TN: Holman Bible Publishers, 2003), 1119.

[169] Chad Brand, Charles Draper, et al., eds., "Michael," *Holman Illustrated Bible Dictionary* (Nashville, TN: Holman Bible Publishers, 2003), 1119.

[170] John Laing, "Archangel," ed. Chad Brand et al., *Holman Illustrated Bible Dictionary* (Nashville, TN: Holman Bible Publishers, 2003), 105.

even be described as an arch (chief or principal) angel? In the Scriptures, "archangel" is never found in the plural.

Clearly, Michael is the only archangel and as the highest-ranking angel, like the highest-ranking general in the army, Michael stands directly under the authority of God, as he commands the other angels, including Gabriel, according to the Father's will and purposes. This archangel, who is like God, who disputed with Satan over Moses body, who stood guard over the sons of Israel, who fought for Israel against demons, who cast Satan out of heaven, who defeated the kings of the earth and their armies at Armageddon would be the one given the privilege of abyssing Satan, the archenemy of God. – Jude 9; Daniel 10:13, 21; 12:1; Revelation 12:7-9; 18:1, 2; 19:11-21.

Michael "seized the dragon, the original serpent, who is the Devil and Satan, and bound him for a thousand years; and threw him into the abyss, and shut it and sealed it over him." The abyss could be likened to a super-maximum-security (Supermax) prison, which represents the most secure levels of custody in the prison systems, which is solitary confinement, which is used to isolate and keep the worst of the worst from having any contact with other inmates. According to *A Greek-English Lexicon of the New Testament*, the Greek abyssos means, "an immensely deep space, depth, abyss."[171] On this, Kendell H. Easley writes, "The binding of the devil is triply secure: the angel **threw him into the Abyss, and locked and sealed it**. The purpose is not to punish him, but to **keep him from deceiving the nations any more**. First Peter 5:8 supports the idea that the devil is reasonably free during this age: "Your enemy the devil prowls around like a roaring lion looking for someone to devour." Premillennialists believe that this binding must mean complete removal of satanic influence from the affairs of humans during the time Christ rules the nations after his return, even though there is no reference to Christ's ruling *nations* anywhere in this passage. This is the most natural reading."[172]

Even though Revelation 20:1-3 states that only Satan will be seized and thrown into the abyss prison, we can reasonably conclude that his demonic angels will also be bound and abyssed. Neither Satan nor his demon hordes will be allowed to interfere with the work of Christ and his kingdom during the millennium. Why are Satan and his demonic angels released for a short time? At the end of Christ's thousand-year reign, humankind will have been restored to perfection, living on a paradise

---

[171] William Arndt, Frederick W. Danker, and Walter Bauer, *A Greek-English Lexicon of the New Testament and Other Early Christian Literature* (Chicago: University of Chicago Press, 2000), 2.
[172] Kendell H. Easley, *Revelation*, vol. 12, Holman New Testament Commentary (Nashville, TN: Broadman & Holman Publishers, 1998), 370.

earth, which was the original purpose of the Father. (Gen. 1:28; 2:8, 15Isa. 45:18; Ps 104:5; 115:16; Eccl. 1:4) God did not tempt Adam with the tree of knowledge, but rather it was used as a symbol to help Adam and Eve to respect the sovereignty of God, his right to rule, and to willingly remain under that umbrella of rule. As we know, Adam rebelled. Again, God chose a very faithful servant, Abraham that he intended to use for his will and purpose, who would be the father of a great nation. Here again, God did not tempt Abraham with the sacrificing of his son, it was merely a means of letting Abraham see what God already knew, an evident demonstration of great faith.

Nevertheless, God allows trials to come; he does not try or tempt his servants with evil intent. What he allows is for our good, our advancement; never would he do anything that would bring us harm. God allowed Satan to tempt Job over the argument from Satan that man is only loyal to God based on what they get from him, i.e., greed, not out of love. Would Adam, Abraham, and Job see God as the rightful sovereign of the universe? after all that imperfect humanity has been through, and now that humanity has been restored to perfection, Satan and the demons are released for a little while, where humans will evidence that they recognize and willingly accept God as the rightful sovereign if the universe. (Rev. 20:3) Each one will be proved as to their integrity to God, many of which had been born during the thousand year reign and have no experience under a Satan ruled age that humanity had just come. (Job 1:12) Satan had induced Adam and Eve to sin, even though they were perfect. We can only assume that he will use similar tactics as before his being abyssed. Clearly, no doubt he will again appeal to selfishness, trying to convince those perfect humans that they would be better off without the rulership of God. Satan will seek to have humans rebel again. We will discuss this more below under verses 7-8.

Millennial Rulers with Christ

Revelation 20:4 Updated American Standard Version (UASV)

⁴ Then I saw thrones, and they sat on them, and judgment was given to them. And I saw the souls of those who had been beheaded[173] because of their testimony of Jesus and because of the word of God, and those who had not worshiped the beast or his image, and had not received the mark on their forehead and on their hand; and they came to life and reigned with Christ for a thousand years.

Daniel 7:13-14, 18 Updated American Standard Version (UASV)

---

[173] Lit *executed with the ax*

¹³ "I kept looking in the night visions,

>   and behold, with the clouds of heaven
> there came one like a son of man,
> and he came to the Ancient of Days
>   and was presented before him.
> ¹⁴ And to him was given dominion
>   and glory and a kingdom,
> that all peoples, nations, and languages
>   should serve him;
> his dominion is an everlasting dominion,
>   which shall not pass away,
> and his kingdom one
>   that shall not be destroyed.

> ¹⁸ But the holy ones of the Most High shall receive the kingdom and possess the kingdom forever, even for ever and ever.'[174]

Who are these "holy ones" sitting on thrones and ruling in the heavens with Jesus? The "holy ones," who are to be co-rulers with Christ in his kingdom, are the elect or the chosen ones, for the sake of the elect those days of the great tribulation will be cut short. (Matt. 24:21-22) They include the 12 apostles, to whom Jesus gave the promise: "in the renewal,[175] when the Son of man sits down on his glorious throne, you who have followed me will sit on twelve thrones, judging the twelve tribes of Israel." They are the "fellow heirs with Christ." (Rom. 8:17) They are pictured by the symbolic number of the twenty-four elders, clothed in white garments, with golden crowns on their heads. (Rev. 4:4) They are to be a kingdom and priests to our God, and they shall reign over the earth (Rev. 5:9-10), will reign with him for a thousand years. (Rev. 20:6) They are the ones, who will be caught up together with them in the clouds to meet the Lord in the air, and so we will always be with the Lord. (1 Thess. 4:17) Hence, Christ Jesus and these elect or chosen ones will rule the world of humankind throughout the millennium.

Who is the "son of man" referred to in Daniel 7:13-14? John F Walvoord writes, "Conservative scholars are agreed that the Son of Man is a picture of the Lord Jesus Christ rather than an angelic agency.55 The description of Him as being worthy of ruling all nations is obviously in keeping with many passages in the Bible referring to the millennial rule of Jesus Christ, for example, Psalm 2:6-9 and Isaiah 11. Like the scene in Revelation 4–5, Christ is portrayed as a separate person from God the Father. The expression that He is attended by "clouds of heaven" implies

---

[174] Lit *and unto the age of the ages*

[175] Gr., *palingenesiai* (recreation), "an era involving the renewal of the world (with special reference to the time of the Messiah)—'new age, Messianic age.'" – GELNTSD

His deity (1 Thess. 4:17). A parallel appears in Revelation 1:7, "Behold, he is coming with the clouds," in fulfillment of Acts 1 wherein His ascension Christ was received by a cloud and the angels tell the disciples that Christ "will come in the same way as you saw him go into heaven" (Acts 1:9–11). ... Jesus' frequent use of this title for Himself in the New Testament is the divine commentary on the phrase (cf. Matt. 8:20; 9:6; 10:23; 11:19; 12:8, 32, 40; 13:37, 41; 16:13, 27, 28; 17:9, 12, 22, etc.). "Son of Man" was, in fact, Jesus' favorite description of Himself during His earthly ministry ... In verse 13, the Son of Man is presented as being near the Ancient of Days, and in verse 14 He is given dominion over all peoples and nations. This could not be an angel, nor could it be the body of saints, as it corresponds clearly to other Scriptures that predict that Christ will rule over all nations (Ps. 72:11; Rev. 19:15–16). Only Christ will come with clouds of heaven, and be the King of kings and Lord of lords over all nations throughout eternity."[176]

Clearly, among these elect or chosen ones, who are to serve as kings, priests, and judges with Christ, were some who suffered as martyrs, like Stephen before the Sanhedrin, James (son of Zebedee), James (Jesus' half-brother), the apostle Paul, Peter, Polycarp, Justin, Ignatius of Antioch, John Hus, and William Tyndale, to mention just a few. While very few of the elect or chosen ones were executed by beheading, it should be seen as an expression may be true of a couple early apostles and simply stands for all those elect, holy ones who endure martyrdom in one way or another. The ax (Greek, *pelekus*) was apparently the customary instrument of execution in Rome: However, by the time of John writing the book of Revelation (c. 96-98 C.E.) the sword was more commonly used. *Pepelekismenon* means "to kill by beheading, normally an act of capital punishment–'to cut the head off, to behead.'"[177] (Matt. 10:22, 28) Certainly, there is little doubt that Satan would like to behead every one of the chosen ones who will serve with Christ, but not all will suffer martyrdom, as many will simply die of old age like the apostle John.

John goes on to say of these elect, chosen ones, "**they came to life and reigned with Christ for a thousand years**." Does this mean that these holy ones will not be resurrected until Michael; the archangel has abyssed Satan and the demons? No. These ones began to be resurrected at the beginning of what is commonly called the "last days." (2 Tim. 3:1) "The 'last days' is not some future event to which we look. It is now, Jesus Christ initiated this epoch [at his ascension], and it will continue

---

[176] John F Walvoord, *Daniel (The John Walvoord Prophecy Commentaries)* (Chicago, IL: Moody Publishers, 2012), Kindle Locations 3668-3683.

[177] Johannes P. Louw and Eugene Albert Nida, *Greek-English Lexicon of the New Testament: Based on Semantic Domains* (New York: United Bible Societies, 1996), 236–237.

uninterrupted until his return."[178] Thus, the elect or holy ones have been and will be resurrected the moment die. In fact, these ones have been playing a role in Jesus work all along since he ascended back to heaven. They will play a role in Armageddon.

Is this a literal thousand years? Yes, Robert L. Thomas writes, "there are many good reasons for taking one thousand to be literal (Walvoord). It is the plain statement of the text six times. [Rev. 20:3, 4, 5, 6, 7] It is doubtful that any symbolic number if there be such, is ever repeated that many times. Other symbolism in Revelation is not opposed to a literal understanding of the thousand years.[179] The mention of the thousand years is not limited to the binding of Satan. John received the information by direct revelation apart from symbols also (cf. 20:4, 5, 6) (Walvoord). Alleged problems in identifying this kingdom with the one promised in the OT—such as its limited length, rather than being eternal, and its lack of the ideal conditions cited in the OT[180]—are only apparent. The kingdom will have a limited phase and will enter its eternal phase after the conclusion of the thousand years. And it will have the ideal conditions described in the OT, but John has no occasion to mention them here."[181] Paul said that "he [God] has fixed **a day** on which he will judge the world. (Ac 17:31) Peter tells us "that with the Lord one day is like a thousand years, and a thousand years like one day." Peter's reference to a thousand years is literal. This Day of Judgment is therefore a literal thousand years. **Papias** (70–163 C.E.), along with **Ignatius** (c. 35–c.108 C.E.) and **Polycarp** (69–155 C.E.), was considered among the pupils of the apostle John, perhaps even his scribe. Papias later became bishop of Hierapolis in Asia Minor. Papias believed in a literal Thousand Year Reign of Christ.

The Beast, the Image, and the Mark

How are we to "understand those who had not worshiped the beast or his image, and had not received the mark on their forehead and on their hand"?

---

[178] Knute Larson, *I & II Thessalonians, I & II Timothy, Titus, Philemon*, vol. 9, Holman New Testament Commentary (Nashville, TN: Broadman & Holman Publishers, 2000), 300.

[179] Contra Swete, *Apocalypse*, p. 266.

[180] Swete, *Apocalypse*, p. 264; Martin Kiddle, *The Revelation of St. John*, HNTC (New York: Harper, 1940), pp. 393–94; Johnson, "Revelation," 12:478; cf. Robert M. Johnson, "The Eschatological Sabbath in John's Apocalypse: A Reconsideration," *AUSS* 25, no. 1 (Spring 1987): 44–46; Barbara Wooten Snyder, "How Millennial Is the Millennium? A Study in the Background of the 1000 Years in Revelation 20," *Evangelical Journal* 9, no. 2 (Fall 1991): 70–72.

[181] Robert L. Thomas, *Revelation 8-22: An Exegetical Commentary* (Chicago: Moody Publishers, 1995), 409.

In our efforts to understand what is meant by the mark of the beast, the name, the number six hundred and sixty-six (666), we need to look for clues within the Scripture that will help us find the correct answer.

The Importance of Bible Names

If anyone has read much of Scripture, they will discover that Bible names play a significant importance, especially those handed out by God himself. On this Dr. Cornwall and Smith write, "Every Bible name has a meaning. So much so, that sometimes when God changed the nature of a person He also changed his or her name. For example, when Abram believed God's promise of a son, God changed his name to Abraham ["father of a multitude"] and changed his wife's name from Sarai to Sarah ["Princess"]. Years later, after the angel of the Lord had wrestled with him all night; Jacob's name was changed to Israel ["Contender with God"]. In the New Testament, Saul of Tarsus, whose name meant, "demanded," came to be known as Paul, which means "little." And this is what the greatest apostle became in his own eyes as he looked increasingly upon the greatness of Christ. It's amazing how often a Bible character lives up to the meaning of his or her name. Sometimes, as in the case of Paul, they deliberately took a name that meant what they wanted to be." (Cornwall and Smith 1998, Page viii)

We find this to be the case from Genesis to Revelation; therefore, the mark of the beast, the name, the number six hundred and sixty-six (666) given by God has to be in relation to the nature of the beast. If we are to understand the nature of the beast, we must identify the beat itself, so we can discover what we can about its undertakings.

The Beast Uncovered

We can actually discover much about the symbolic beast of Revelation by looking to the prophetic book of Daniel. In chapter 7 of Daniel, there are four beasts: a lion, a bear, a leopard, and "a fourth beast, terrifying and dreadful and exceedingly strong. It had great iron teeth; it devoured and broke in pieces and stamped what was left with its feet. It was different from all the beasts that were before it, and it had ten horns." (Daniel 7:2-7) If we look at verse 17 of chapter 7, Daniel tells us "These four great beasts are four kings who shall arise out of the earth." In verse 23 of the same chapter, Daniel says, "Thus he said: 'As for the fourth beast, there shall be a fourth kingdom on earth, which shall be different from all the kingdoms, and it shall devour the whole earth, and trample it down, and break it to pieces.'" In other words, these symbolic beasts represent kingdoms that were to rule over the earth.

Regarding the beast of Revelation 13:1-2, the *Holman New Testament Commentary: Revelation* states, "The monster appears even more royal than the dragon, wearing **ten crowns** (diadems) as compared to the dragon's seven (12:3). **The blasphemous name** on each head suggests a claim to divine status (vv. 5–6). The body parts of this brute are a composite of three of the four creature of Daniel 7:1–6, but in reverse order: body of **a leopard**, feet of **a bear**, and mouth of **a lion**. In Daniel's vision, these represented historical empires that opposed Judah, such as Babylon and Persia. Here they are all combined into one monster–raw political-military power. The Christians of John's day immediately grasped that the form of the monster current in their day was imperial Rome. Where did Rome's power come from? **The dragon gave the beast his power and his throne and great authority**. Although God has ordained that government be used for good (Rom. 13:1–7), clearly the devil has mastered the art of twisting what God means for good and turning it to evil."– (Easley 1998, p. 227)

Revelation 13:2 Updated American Standard Version (UASV)

² And the beast which I saw was like a leopard, and his feet were like those of a bear, and his mouth like the mouth of a lion. And the dragon gave him his power and his throne and great authority.

As we saw in the above, these symbolic beasts represent kingdoms that were to rule over the earth. However, what do these features denote? Regarding the features of the beast of Revelation 13:1-2, the *Baker New Testament Commentary: Revelation* states, "The first portrayal is that of the leopard, noted for stalking its prey, its amazing speed in capturing prey, and its swiftness in dealing the deathblow. The second picture is that of a bear, who with its powerful paws is able to tear its victims apart. And third, the lion's mouth symbolizes cruelty as it kills and devours wild animals. The three pictures of these beasts are a depiction of force, speed, and savagery." (Kistemaker 2001, p. 379)

Revelation 13:1 Updated American Standard Version (UASV)

¹ And the dragon stood on the sand of the sea. Then I saw a beast coming up out of the sea, having ten horns and seven heads, and on his horns were ten diadems, and on his heads were blasphemous names.

What or who do these seven heads represent? The seven heads are seven world empires throughout Bible history that have had some kind of impact on God's people, five of which were before John's day: Egypt Assyria, Babylon, Medo-Persia, and Greece. The sixth of those world empires was in existence during John's day, Rome, with the seventh world empire yet to come. Look at John's reference again in the same book.

Revelation 17:9-10 Updated American Standard Version (UASV)

⁹ Here is the mind which has wisdom. The seven heads are seven mountains on which the woman sits, **10** and they are seven kings; five have fallen **[Egypt, Assyrian, Babylon, Medo-Persia, and Greece]**, one is **[Rome]**, the other has not yet come **[?]**;and when he comes, he must remain a little while.

We can conclude that the first wild beast from the sea (vss. 1-10) and the second wild beast from the earth (vss. 11-18) of Revelation 13 represent two governmental powers. The first wild beast "the dragon **[Satan, Rev. 12:3, 9]** gave it his power and his throne and great authority." The second wild beast "exercises all the authority of the first beast on his behalf and compels the earth and those who live on it to worship the first beast." Therefore, these beasts or governmental powers are against Christ, consequently, they are antichrists.

We must not overreact to this, believing that everyone within the government is somehow a tool, being possessed and used by Satan or his demons. We must realize that God uses the human governments for his own purposes as well. We have seen in the United States of late, what other countries have long known, without the law enforcement, a part of the government, there would be anarchy. Moreover, without the military might of the United States government, the world would be overrun by evil, such as Islam. If there were not legislatures, we would have no laws, which give structure to our human society. Some leaders and governments throughout human history have been used by Satan to try and stop pure worship, but others have protected the rights of its citizens, which include the freedom of worship. (Romans 13:3, 4; Ezra 7:11-27; Acts 13:7) Nevertheless, because of satanic influence and human imperfection, no human society has ever, nor will they ever bring true peace and security.[182]

The Number of a Man

Revelation 13:18 Updated American Standard Version (UASV)

¹⁸ Here is wisdom. Let the one who has understanding calculate the number of the beast, for it is the number of a man, and his number is six hundred and sixty-six.[183]

---

[182] Because of Satan's influence over human governments, while Christians are to be in subjection to superior authorities (Rom 13:1), this is only as long as they do not ask anything that is in opposition to God's will and purpose. For example, if the government said "no more evangelizing about the Bible," we would obey God rather than man.–Acts 5:29.

[183] One early MS reads 616

Our next clue is in the fact that the meaning of six hundred and sixty-six (666) lays in the fact that it "is the number of a man." "A man" is generic for humanity, i.e., a human number, and should not be taken as a reference to a specific man. (Luke 4:5-6; 1 John 5:19; Revelation 13:2, 18) What does the fact that it is a human number bring to the table? What do we know about humanity over the 6,000 plus years? Paul tells us, "all have sinned **[missing the mark of perfection]** and fall short of the glory of God." (Rom. 3:23) He also stated, "Sin came into the world through one man, and death through sin, and so death spread to all men because all sinned **[all are missing the mark of perfection, i.e., human imperfection]**." The world power governments mentioned above, the ones reflective in these symbolic beasts are made up of imperfect humans, name, sin, human imperfection. Jeremiah the prophet tells us why, "I know, O Jehovah, that the way of man is not in himself, that it is not in man who walks to direct his steps."–Jeremiah 10:23

Biblical Numbers

Just as Bible names play a significant importance, this is also true of numbers. For example, the number seven is often associated with what is complete or perfect. On the number seven, the *Holman Illustrated Bible Dictionary* says, "God's work of creation was both complete and perfect, and it was completed in seven days. All of mankind's existence was related to God's creative activity. The seven-day week reflected God's first creative activity. The Sabbath was that day of rest following the workweek, reflective of God's rest (Gen. 1:1–2:4). Israelites were to remember the land also and give it a sabbath, permitting it to lie fallow in the seventh year (Lev. 25:2–7). Seven was also important in cultic matters beyond the Sabbath: major festivals such as Passover and Tabernacles lasted seven days as did wedding festivals (Judg. 14:12, 17). In Pharaoh's dream the seven good years followed by seven years of famine (Gen. 41:1–36) represented a complete cycle of plenty and famine. Jacob worked a complete cycle of years for Rachel; then, when he was given Leah instead, he worked an additional cycle of seven (Gen. 29:15–30). A major Hebrew word for making an oath or swearing, *shaba*, was closely related to the word 'seven,' *sheba*. The original meaning of 'swear an oath' may have been 'to declare seven times' or 'to bind oneself by seven things.' A similar use of the number seven can be seen in the NT. The seven churches (Rev. 2–3) perhaps symbolized all the churches by their number. Jesus taught that forgiveness is not to be limited, even to a full number or complete number of instances. We are to forgive, not merely seven times (already a generous number of forgivenesses) but 70 times seven (limitless forgiveness, beyond keeping count) (Matt. 18:21–22). As the last example shows, multiples of seven frequently had symbolic meaning. The year of Jubilee came after the completion of every 49 years. In the year of Jubilee, all Jewish bond slaves were released and land which had been sold reverted to its former owner (Lev. 25:8–55). Another multiple of seven used in the Bible is 70. Seventy elders are mentioned (Exod. 24:1, 9). Jesus sent out the 70 (Luke 10:1–17). Seventy years is specified as the length of the exile (Jer. 25:12, 29:10; Dan. 9:2). The messianic kingdom was to be inaugurated after a period of 70 weeks of years had passed (Dan. 9:24)." (Brand, Draper and Archie 2003, p. 1201)

Simply put, six is one short of seven. If seven represents perfection and completion, it only seems reasonable that six falls short of that. On this, *The College Press NIV Commentary: Revelation* says, "*Six* is one less than seven; it does not 'measure up' to seven or attain to the fullness of seven. Six, then, symbolizes 'incompleteness,' "imperfection," and sometimes evil." (Davis 2000, p. 21) This really ties in well with the fact that, the number of the beast is a human number, being that we are under human imperfection. In short, what do we know? We know that "man" (Gk., *anthrōpos*), often signifies the whole of humankind, i.e., humanity. We also know that the number six in the Bible, one less than seven (perfect) can denote imperfection. We also know that when something is mentioned three times, it is a way of intensifying what is being said. Therefore, six hundred and sixty-six (666) could be signifying gross human imperfection.

Revelation 20:5 Updated American Standard Version (UASV)

⁵ (The rest of the dead did not come to life until the thousand years were completed.) This is the first resurrection.

What is meant by the expression "come to life"? It was actually used back in Revelation 20:4, where John said, "They came to life." The "they" here is a reference to the elect, the chosen ones, who are to rule with Christ over the earth, as kings, priest and judges. Their coming to life is far faster than the expression used for the great multitude referred to in verse five, who survive Armageddon. Paul could speak of born-again Christians as being 'dead in their trespasses and sins' (Eph. 2:1), because of their inheriting Adamic sin. He also wrote, "All have sinned and fall short of the glory of God, being justified as a gift by His grace through the redemption which is in Christ Jesus. (Rom. 3:23-24, NASB) Paul told the Corinthians, "For as in Adam all die, so also in Christ all **will be made alive**." (1 Cor. 15:22, NASB) The "elect," chosen ones of Matthew 24:21-22, i.e., "the holy ones of the Most High shall receive the kingdom" spoken of in Daniel 7:18, who have been 'made a kingdom and priests,' 'to rule over the earth (Rev 5:9-10),' to 'reign with Christ for a thousand years' (Rev. 20:6), these ones were given perfect spiritual bodies. Thus, their return to perfection was immediate. However, the great multitude of other born-again Christians, who survive Armageddon, even though they are still dead in their tress passes, they will not "**not come to life until the thousand years were completed**." At that time, they will be perfect humans just as Adam and Eve were prior to the rebellion in the Garden of Eden; however, with far more knowledge and experience. This section of verse 20:5 is in a parenthetical. This verse is John's brief parenthetical explanation to take pause and talk about another group of Christians other than the elect, the chosen holy ones, who had been being discussed since 20:4, and are returned to, with the closing thought of 20:5, "This is the first resurrection."

How is this, the first resurrection? As was just mention, John is mow returning to the subject of the elect, the chosen holy ones, who are the first group of Christians that received a resurrection based on the ransom sacrifice of Jesus Christ. The resurrections in the Old Testament and those performed by Jesus and the apostle in the New Testament were not of this sort. They had purposes like evidencing the power and authority of the one performing the resurrection. All of those persons died again. "These have been purchased from among men as first fruits to God and to the Lamb." (Rev. 14:14, NASB) Moreover, these first resurrected ones are of great importance as well, as they will be co-rulers with Christ, in his heavenly kingdom, judging all others that are a part of the second resurrection in the beginning of the millennium. In addition, those resurrected to a heavenly life will receive immortality, while the great multitude of Christians, who survive Armageddon, will not receive immortality, but rather eternal life. Immortality (Gr, *athanasia*; deathlessness) means indestructible, "the state of not being subject to death (that which will never die)."[184] This means that Adam was not created inherently immortal, possessing deathlessness, but rather the opportunity at endless life. This is quite amazing, considering the fact that even God's angels do not possess immortality, even though they possess spirit bodies, not carnal ones. – 1 Corinthians 15:53; 1 Timothy 6:16

Revelation 20:6 Updated American Standard Version (UASV)

⁶ Blessed and holy is the one who has a part in the first resurrection; over these the second death has no power, but they will be priests of God and of Christ and will reign with him for a thousand years.

What is the second death? "The lake of fire" into which death, Hades, the symbolic "wild beast" and "the false prophet," Satan, his demons, and those who live in wickedness on earth are thrown into "the second death." (Rev 20:10, 14, 15; 21:8; Matt. 25:41) Judgment day is a specific "day" (hardly ever a literal 24 hour day), when certain groups,

---

[184] Johannes P. Louw and Eugene Albert Nida, *Greek-English Lexicon of the New Testament: Based on Semantic Domains* (New York: United Bible Societies, 1996), 267.

nations, or humankind are held accountable by God. Jesus said, "The one who rejects me and does not receive my words has a judge; the word that I have spoken will judge him **on the last day**." (John 12:48, ESV) If we look at Revelation 11:17-18, we see that God begins his judging the moment that he begins ruling in a special way, i.e., after Armageddon, Jesus' kingdom of co-rulers over the earth for a millennium, the judgment day. During that thousand years reign, the elect, chosen ones, holy ones will served as judges, priests, and rulers with Christ. In other words, the great multitude who survive Armageddon, the righteous and unrighteous who are resurrected, will be judged throughout the millennium. A thousand-year period can be viewed as a "day," for it is stated in the Bible. (2 Peter 3:8; Psalm 90:4) There is no resurrection from the second death. As we just mentioned, the elect, chosen ones, holy ones who are serving in heaven with Christ as part of his kingdom, are spirit persons, and have received immortality, deathlessness, so those who are part of the first resurrection, the second death has no power. The wicked are destroyed at Armageddon, to never be resurrected again, so, the neither second death nor judgment day is applicable to them. Jesus promised the elect, "The one who conquers will not be hurt by the second death." The second death has no authority over these ones because they cannot die and have been declared righteous. They will they "will be priests of God and of Christ and will reign with him for a thousand years," judging those on earth.

Revelation 20:7 Updated American Standard Version (UASV)

⁷ When the thousand years are completed, Satan will be released from his prison,

When the thousand years are completed, the earth will be like the Garden of Eden, a paradise earth, with all humans again living as perfect humans. This does not mean that cities and technological advancements will have been discarded. Humanity will no longer need the ransom sacrifice of Jesus Christ to cover their sins, as adamic sin will be no more. Paul wrote, "For as in Adam all die, so also in Christ shall all be made alive. But each in his own order: Christ the firstfruits, then at his coming those who belong to Christ. **Then comes the end**, when he delivers the kingdom to God the Father after destroying every rule and every authority and power. For he must reign until he has put all his enemies under his feet. The last enemy to be destroyed is death." – 1 Corinthians 15:22-26; Romans 15:12, ESV

Adam had the tree in the Garden of Eden, which was designed to help him evidence his willingness to see the sovereignty of God as the right way to live life and the best way to live life, i.e., the rightfulness of God's sovereignty. Abraham was asked to sacrifice his son, not knowing

God was not going to actually have him go through with it, but it enabled him to evidence a faith God already knew was there. Even Jesus Christ himself was tempted in the wilderness by Satan.

Matthew 4:1 How do we reconcile that Jesus is being led "to be" tempted by the Spirit?

Matthew 4:1 Updated American Standard Version (UASV)

¹ Then Jesus was led up by the Spirit into the wilderness to be tempted (Gr, *peirazo*)[185] by the devil.

The Father does **not tempt** us, but he does allow us to go through temptations. As we know from Adam and Abraham, the Father can **test** us, but never tempt us with sin.

The text specifically states that the Spirit led Jesus into the wilderness "to be tempted." How do we reconcile that Jesus is being led by the Spirit "to be" tempted? First, (*Peirazo*) can be rendered either as "tempted" (ESV, NIV, LEB) or "tested" (CEV, MSG), but seeing that Satan is carrying this out, it is best to be rendered "tempted." This is not a literal versus a dynamic equivalent issue, because almost all dynamic equivalents have "tempted."

Second, the Father would have foreknown that Satan was going to tempt Jesus, and that he would wait until his weakest moment to do so. What Satan would see as an opportunity to tempt Jesus, the Father may very well see as an opportunity to test Jesus, as he did with Abraham, establishing his faithfulness, which the Father was well aware was perfectly fine. Therefore, God allowed Jesus "to be" tempted, which he used as a test to confirm what he would already know to be true, an evident demonstration of Jesus faith. Jesus' actions would establish or demonstrate God's confidence in him. Jesus clearly revealed that his faith was a living faith. The apostle Paul wrote of Jesus, "Since he himself was tested in that which he has suffered, He is able to come to the aid of those who are tested." (Heb. 2:18) Paul went on to write, "Although he [Jesus] was a son, he learned obedience from the things which he suffered. And having been made perfect, he became to all those who obey him the source of eternal salvation." – Hebrews 5:8-9.

---

[185] "to obtain information to be used against a person by trying to cause someone to make a mistake, 'to try to trap, to attempt to catch in a mistake.'" – Johannes P. Louw and Eugene Albert Nida, Greek-English Lexicon of the New Testament: Based on Semantic Domains (New York: United Bible Societies, 1996), 329.

Satan Released, Then Destroyed

Revelation 20:8-9 Updated American Standard Version (UASV)

⁸ and will come out to deceive the nations which are in the four corners of the earth, Gog and Magog, to gather them together for the war; the number of them is like the sand of the sea. ⁹ And they went up on the broad plain of the earth and surrounded the fortified camp of the holy ones and the beloved city, and fire came down from heaven and devoured them.

Satan is released after the thousand-year reign of Christ. Will he be successful at misleading perfect humanity yet again? He deceives "the nations which are in the four corners of the earth, Gog and Magog, to gather them together for the war." We might be baffled at who would join Satan again, after the thousands of years under his rule, followed by a thousand years of his being abyssed and humanity being under the kingdom of God. This is evidence of just how crafty and persuasive he is. He was able to mislead the perfect man Adam, as well as millions of angels, even after they saw what happened to humans after Adam was expelled up unto the flood. (2 Peter 2:4; Jude 6) Therefore, nothing should surprise us.

The expression "four corners of the earth" does not literally mean the humans are divided amongst themselves again. It just means that those siding with Satan will separate themselves from those siding with God. Here we have one last great battle between the forces of evil and the people of God. Gog is found in chapters 38 and 39 of Ezekiel and is there applied to the leader of a storm like, multinational assault against the people of God. Magog was a land or region "in the remote parts of the north." (Eze 38:2-4, 8, 9, 13-16; 39:1-3, 6) John is using "Gog's evil forces to represent all who oppose God in the final battle in the end times under the leadership of Satan." (Knight 2003, 181)

Those who join Satan will be like "the number of them is like the sand of the sea." These are ones who are affected by Satan's schemes, his deception. The above way of expressing it is simply to say that the number will be substantial, at least large enough that they "can surrounded the fortified camp of the holy ones and the beloved city."

"The beloved city" is the New Jerusalem, which a heavenly city, a symbolic city, as the dimensions and splendor of New Jerusalem could not be a literal city here on earth. The New Jerusalem are those made of the elect, chosen ones, who are part of the first resurrection, who as a bride of Christ, joined him on his throne in this symbolic city. (Rev. 21:2) It is the "new heavens" that will rule over the "new earth," which is made up of those great multitude of Christians who survived Armageddon, those resurrected at the beginning of the millennium, and those born during the millennium. John tells us that he "saw the holy city, new Jerusalem, coming down out of heaven from God, prepared as a bride adorned for her husband." (21:2) The New Jerusalem being Christ and his kingdom heirs coming down out of heaven is their directing their attention to the holy ones here on earth coming under attack. Thomas writes, "Fire from heaven as an instrument of divine punishment is well-known (cf. Gen. 19:24; Lev. 10:2; Ezek. 38:22; 39:6; 2 Kings 1:10, 12; Luke 9:54).[186] It is a fitting climax to this last battle with Satan and his armies. The brief κατέφαγεν αὐτούς (*katephagen autous*, 'devoured them') summarizes the fate of the rebels."[187]

The Lake of Fire and Sulfur

Revelation 20:10 Updated American Standard Version (UASV)

¹⁰ And the devil who deceived them was thrown into the lake of fire and brimstone, where the beast and the false prophet are also; and they will be tormented (Gr, *basanos*) day and night forever and ever.

We will deal with the lake of fire more extensively below. For now, the **lake of** fire is a symbolic place that "burns with fire and sulfur," also described as "the second death." Unrepentant sinners, the Devil, and even death and the Grave (or, Hades) are thrown into it. The inclusion of a spirit creature and also of death and Hades, all of which cannot be affected by fire, indicates that this lake is a symbol, not of everlasting torment, but of everlasting destruction. (Rev. 19:20; 20:14, 15; 21:8) See the footnote below.[188]

The Greek word used here for "torment," *basanizo*, primarily means "to test by rubbing on the touchstone" (basanos, "a touchstone"), then, "to question by applying torture."[189] The Bible is our case law (law established on the basis of previous verdicts), which will serve as a touchstone[190] (a standard by which something is judged) that humans were never designed to walk on their own, but to live under the sovereignty of their Creator. The issues raised by Satan will have been settled by humanities walking through thousands of years of an object

---

[186] Ibid.; Johnson, "Revelation," 12:588.
[187] Robert L. Thomas, *Revelation 8-22: An Exegetical Commentary* (Chicago: Moody Publishers, 1995), 425–426.
[188] Hellfire - Eternal Torment? http://www.christianpublishers.org/hellfire-eternal-torment Hellfire - Is It Just? http://www.christianpublishers.org/hellfire-is-it-just
[189] W. E. Vine, Merrill F. Unger, and William White Jr., Vine's Complete Expository Dictionary of Old and New Testament Words (Nashville, TN: T. Nelson, 1996), 176.
[190] A touchstone is a hard black stone formerly used to test the purity of gold and silver according to the color of the streak left when the metal was rubbed against it.

lesson, for which the Bible is the case law, the touchstone, which will be around forever, as a reminder of the issues raised and settled.

The Dead Judged before the White Throne

Revelation 20:11 Updated American Standard Version (UASV)

¹¹ Then I saw a great white throne and him who sat upon it, from whose presence earth and heaven fled away, and no place was found for them.

This judgment seat belongs to "God, the judge of all." (Heb. 12:23) The Father by way of the Son and his joint heirs in heaven will be judging humankind throughout the millennium. How is it that the "earth and heaven fled away"? What we have here is judgment being executed on Satan's earth and heaven.

Revelation 20:12 Updated American Standard Version (UASV)

¹² And I saw the dead, the great and the small, standing before the throne, and scrolls were opened; and another scroll was opened, which is the book of life; and the dead were judged from the things which were written in the scrolls, according to their deeds.

"The great and the small" encompasses the famous, well-known, important, prominent as well as the **less** famous, well-known, prestigious, prominent ones of humans that have lived and died since Adam was expelled from the Garden of Eden. On this, John wrote some two years after penning Revelation, "And he has given him authority to execute judgment because Son of Man he is. Do not marvel at this, because an hour is coming when all who are in the memorial tombs will hear his voice and come out, those who have done good things to a resurrection of life, and those who have practiced evil things to the resurrection of judgment." (John 5:27-29) The apostle Paul wrote, "That there is going to be a resurrection of both the righteous and the unrighteous." (Ac 24:15, LEB) Yes, millions will receive a resurrection at the beginning of the millennium, probably gradually, so as not overwhelm the great multitude who survived Armageddon.

"Book" is used figuratively several times in the Scriptures, as in the expressions "your [God's] book" (Ex 32:32), "book of remembrance" (Mal 3:16), and **book of life** (Php 4:3; Re 3:5; 20:15). It seems that all of these references are the same thing. In other words, they are a figurative book of remembrance that is used to reward **"the great and the small"** with eternal life (in heaven or on earth), if their name is written on it. If a person's name is written in the book of life, this does not mean that they were predestined to eternal life, nor that once there, it is guaranteed to remain. Continued obedience and a righteous standing before God are what leads to it remaining there. "Jehovah said to Moses, Whosoever has sinned against me, him will I blot out of my book." (Ex 32:32-33) This shows that a person's name can be written in, and it can be 'blotted out,' as well as rewritten in if he repented of his former course. – Revelation 3:5

In this section of Revelation, 20:11-15, we are dealing with the millennial reign, and it shows that the book of life is opened to receive additional names. This is because there is "a resurrection of both **the righteous** and **the unrighteous**." (Ac 24:15) The righteous are those that have a righteous standing before God, which would include the elect, the chosen ones, who received the first resurrection. In addition, the righteous would also include the great multitude, who survives the great war of Armageddon. The names of these righteous ones are already in the book of life prior to, but it is the unrighteous who are resurrected after Armageddon that is now being added to the book of life, as long as they are obedient and garner a righteous standing before God. Who are the unrighteous? These are ones that never had an opportunity to hear the good news, so as to act on upon it. The faithful ones who are resurrected, like Abraham, Moses, David, Elijah, John the Baptist, and millions of others, will also have their name already written in the book of life.

The elect, i.e., the chosen ones, who are serving with Christ as kings, priests and judges have their names *permanently* retained in "**the book of life**" (after they have faithfully died and are resurrected), as they were 'faithful until death, and God gave them the crown of life.' (John 2:10) John went on to write, "The **one who conquers** will be clothed thus in white garments, and I **will never blot his name out of the book of life**. I will confess his name before my Father and before his angels." (Rev. 3:5, ESV) For the **unrighteous**, which are resurrected and do not have their name in the book of life, if they are faithful and choose the sovereignty of God in the test of Satan at the end of the millennium, they will be written in the book of life. (Rev 20:7-8) Jesus said, "Those who have done good to the resurrection of **life**, and those who have done evil to the resurrection of **judgment**." (John 5:29, ESV) Here "life" and "judgment" are being contrasted with each other, showing that those resurrected ones "who have done evil" **after being instructed** in the inspired Scriptures and scrolls are judged to be undeserving of life. This is not talking about the wicked that dies before Armageddon, i.e., those that heard the biblical truth, yet continued to live in sin. This would be any who turned aside from pure worship at any time during the thousand-year reign of Christ or those who reject the sovereignty of God when Satan is let loose for a little while at the end of the millennium. Their names will be blotted out of the book of life.

Revelation 20:13 Updated American Standard Version (UASV)

¹³ And the sea gave up the dead which were in it, and death and Hades gave up the dead which were in them; and they were judged, every one of them according to their deeds.

Hades. Everyone knows that Hades was "the underground abode of the dead in Greek mythology."[191] However, as far as early Christianity, the Greek translation of the Old Testament, the Septuagint, uses the word Hades 73 times, employing it 60 times to translate the Hebrew word Sheol. Luke at Acts 2:27 write, "For you will not abandon my soul to Hades, or let your Holy One see corruption." Luke was quoting Psalm 16:10, which reads, "For you will not abandon my soul to Sheol, or let your holy one see corruption." Notice that Luke used Hades in place of Sheol. Therefore, Hades is the Greek equivalent of Sheol, as far as Christians and the Greek New Testament is concerned. In other words, Hades is also the abode of the dead in early Christian thought. Some translations choose to use a transliteration, Hades, as opposed to the English hell, ASV, AT, RSV, ESV, LEB, HCSB, and NASB.

The fire and burning within Scripture are merely representing annihilation or eternal destruction. Therefore, there is no eternal torment in Sheol (gravedom), Hades (the equivalent of Sheol) hell (English translation), Gehenna (symbol of destruction), or the lake of fire (symbol of destruction). What about the parable of the sheep (righteous) and the goats (wicked), which has the goats, or the wicked going away into eternal punishment?

Matthew 25:46 Updated American Standard Version (UASV)

⁴⁶ And these will go away into eternal punishment [*Kolasin*],[192] but the righteous into eternal life."

Kolasin "akin to *kolazoo*"[193] "This means 'to cut short,' 'to lop,' 'to trim,' and figuratively a. 'to impede,' 'restrain,' and b. 'to punish,' and in the passive 'to suffer loss.'"[194] The first part of the sentence is only in harmony with the second part of the sentence, if the eternal punishment is eternal death. The wicked receive eternal death and the righteous eternal life. We might at that Matthews Gospel was primarily for the Jewish Christians, and under the Mosaic Law, God would punish those

---

[191] http://biblia.com/books/mwdict11/word/hades
[192] That is eternal cutting off, from life. Lit., "lopping off; pruning."
[193] W. E. Vine, Merrill F. Unger, and William White Jr., Vine's Complete Expository Dictionary of Old and New Testament Words (Nashville, TN: T. Nelson, 1996), 498.
[194] Gerhard Kittel, Gerhard Friedrich, and Geoffrey William Bromiley, Theological Dictionary of the New Testament (Grand Rapids, MI: W.B. Eerdmans, 1985), 451.

who violated the law, saying they "shall be cut off [penalty of death] from Israel." (Ex 12:15; Lev 20:2-3) We need further to consider,

2 Thessalonians 1:8-9 Updated American Standard Version (UASV)

⁸ in flaming fire, inflicting vengeance on those who do not know God and on those who do not obey the gospel of our Lord Jesus. ⁹ These ones will pay the penalty of eternal destruction, from before the Lord[195] and from the glory of his strength,

Notice that Paul says too that the punishment for the wicked is "eternal destruction." Many times in talking with those that support the position of eternal torment in some hellfire, they will add a word to Matthew 25:46 in their paraphrase of the verse, 'eternal conscious punishment.' However, Jesus does not tell us what the eternal punishment is, just that it is a punishment, and it is eternal. Therefore, those who support eternal conscious fiery torment will read the verse to mean just that, while those, who hold the position of eternal destruction, will take Matthew 25:46 to mean that. Considering that Jesus does not define what the eternal punishment is, this verse is not a proof text for either side of the argument.

John writes, "They were judged, every one of them according to their deeds." Again, this is not talking about the wicked that dies before Armageddon, i.e., those that heard the biblical truth, yet continued to live in sin. This would be any who turned aside from pure worship at any time during the thousand-year reign of Christ or those who reject the sovereignty of God when Satan is let loose for a little while at the end of the millennium. Their names will be blotted out of the book of life.

The End of Death and Hades

Revelation 20:14-15 Updated American Standard Version (UASV)

¹⁴ Then death and Hades were thrown into the lake of fire. This is the second death, the lake of fire. ¹⁵ And if anyone was not found written in the book of life, he was thrown into the lake of fire.

Lake of Fire. A symbolic place that "burns with fire and sulfur," also described as "the second death." Unrepentant sinners, the Devil, and even death and the Grave (or, Hades) are thrown into it. The inclusion of a spirit creature and of death and Hades, not all of which can be affected by fire, indicates that this lake is a symbol, not of everlasting torment, but of everlasting destruction. – Revelation 19:20; 20:14, 15; 21:8.

---

[195] Lit *from before the face of the Lord*

At the end of the millennial judgment day, "death and Hades" are now able to be destroyed. Why was death and Hades not removed right after Armageddon? This is because some will be destroyed during the millennium and many will be destroyed after Satan is let loose for a little while.

1 Corinthians 15:23-28 Updated American Standard Version (UASV)

²³ But each in his own order: Christ the first fruits, afterward those who belong to the Christ at his coming,[196] ²⁴ then comes the end, when he hands over the kingdom to the God and Father, when he has abolished all rule and all authority and power. ²⁵ For he must reign until he has put all his enemies under his feet. ²⁶ The last enemy that will be abolished is death. ²⁷ For he put all things in subjection under his feet. But when he says "All things are put in subjection," it is evident that he is excepted who put all things in subjection to him. ²⁸ When all things are subjected to him, then the Son himself also will be subjected to the One who subjected all things to him, so that God may be all in all.

---

[196] Or *presence* (Gr *parousia*), which denotes both an "arrival" and a consequent "presence with."

CHAPTER 10 Correctly Understanding the Final Judgment

Satan Released, Then Destroyed

Revelation 20:7-9, 11-15 Updated American Standard Version (UASV)

⁷ When the thousand years are completed, Satan will be released from his prison, ⁸ and will come out to deceive the nations which are in the four corners of the earth, Gog and Magog, to gather them together for the war; the number of them is like the sand of the sea. ⁹ And they went up on the broad plain of the earth and surrounded the fortified camp of the holy ones and the beloved city, and fire came down from heaven and devoured them.

The Dead Judged

¹¹ Then I saw a great white throne and him who sat upon it, from whose presence earth and heaven fled away, and no place was found for them. ¹² And I saw the dead, the great and the small, standing before the throne, and scrolls were opened; and another scroll was opened, which is the book of life; and the dead were judged from the things which were written in the scrolls, according to their deeds. ¹³ And the sea gave up the dead which were in it, and death and Hades gave up the dead which were in them; and they were judged, every one of them according to their deeds. ¹⁴ Then death and Hades were thrown into the lake of fire. This is the second death, the lake of fire. ¹⁵ And if anyone was not found written in the book of life, he was thrown into the lake of fire.

The apostle John helps us to appreciate what takes place just before judgment day. He wrote, "Then I saw a great white throne and him who sat upon it, from whose presence earth and heaven fled away, ... And I saw the dead, the great and the small, standing before the throne, ... and the dead were judged from the things which were written in the scrolls, according to their deeds." (Rev. 20:11-12) Therefore, just before the thousand years of the Judgment Day begins, the heavens and earth will pass away. (1 John 2:17) This does not mean the literal earth, or the literal heavens.

Thus, unlike what most Bible scholars are suggesting, it is not **just** the resurrected dead that are judged on Judgment day, and Judgment Day is not a day of judgment, it is a thousand years long. Paul tells us that there is going to be "there is going to be a resurrection of both the righteous and the unrighteous." The righteous who survive Armageddon, are a great multitude of Christians. However, the righteous that were already dead will be resurrected in the beginning of that thousand-year reign of Christ. The unrighteous that never had an opportunity to hear and act on the good news, will be resurrected in the beginning of that thousand-year reign of Christ. All living on earth under the kingdom of God will be judge based on what they do throughout the millennial reign of Christ and after Satan is released for a little while at the end. In his vision, John saw how they are judged. "And I saw the dead, the great and the small, standing before the throne, and scrolls were opened; and another scroll was opened, which is the book of life; and the dead were judged from the things which were written in the scrolls, according to their deeds. And the sea gave up the dead which were in it, and death and Hades gave up the dead which were in them; and they were judged, every one of them according to their deeds." – Revelation 20:12-13

What are the "scrolls" from which the "living" and the "dead" will be judged? This will be a book or books that will be an addition to our present Holy Bible. The Bible was penned to get mankind from 1500 B.C.E. up unto Armageddon. Thereafter, more book(s) are to be penned to help us through the millennium. These new additions to the Bible will be inspired, and will give us God's will and purposes. It is based on the Holy Bible and these new books that mankind will be judged throughout the thousand year reign of Christ. Those who obey these books will receive the benefits of Jesus ransom sacrifice, growing into perfection through the millennium.

When the thousand years have ended, no one will be imperfect, nor need the ransom sacrifice of Christ any longer. Truly, Revelation 20:5a, the parenthetical talked about in the previous chapter, will be fulfilled. "(The rest of the dead [those besides the elect in heaven] did not come to life until the thousand years were completed.)" (20:5a) Once people are in the same condition that Adam and Eve were prior to the rebellion, what will happen?

After Judgment Day

Jesus has actually brought things full circle, so that God's original purpose has been fulfilled, the earth is fill with perfect humans, enjoying life, carrying our pure worship to their Creator, death had been brought to nothing, so Jesus hands the kingdom back over to the Father.

1 Corinthians 15:23-28 Updated American Standard Version (UASV)

23 But each in his own order: Christ the first fruits, afterward those who belong to the Christ at his coming,[197] 24 then comes the end, when he

---

[197] Or *presence* (Gr *parousia*), which denotes both an "arrival" and a consequent "presence with."

hands over the kingdom to the God and Father, when he has abolished all rule and all authority and power. **25** For he must reign until he has put all his enemies under his feet. **26** The last enemy that will be abolished is death. **27** For he put all things in subjection under his feet. But when he says "All things are put in subjection," it is evident that he is excepted who put all things in subjection to him. **28** When all things are subjected to him, then the Son himself also will be subjected to the One who subjected all things to him, so that God may be all in all.

How will God determine whose name are to go into **the book of life**? (Rev. 20:12, 15) It will be a test upon all perfect humans. Perfect Adam and Eve failed a test that was far less difficult. However, imperfect Job passed a test that was far more difficult than Adam and Eve. Many of the people alive at the end of the millennium will have never had their faith tested. The millions of unrighteous that were resurrected never knew God, nor had faith to be tested. Then, there will be millions born during the millennium. Life during the millennium will be easy because there is no Satan, all are devoted or become devoted to God in pure worship, perfection is being restored, and Satan and his demos are abyssed. Thus, we are looking at billions that will have to evidence their faith. Will Satan be able to do the same to them as he had done to Adam and Eve?

After the thousand-year reign of Christ, Satan and his demons are let loose from the abyss for a short period of time. What is the result? "The number of them [who side with Satan and reject God] is like the sand of the sea." (Rev. 20:8b) After the test, Satan, his demons and those who failed the test are destroyed, this is pictured by the symbolic **lake of fire**. This is the second death, eternal death, from which there is no resurrection, ever. (Rev. 20:7-10, 15) Those on earth, who passed the test, are in the book of life, having a righteous standing before God, and they will live forever here on earth, the paradise earth originally intended for Adam and Eve.

We have no reason to fear what lies ahead. The two great questions are; 'will we be there and how many people can we help to be there?' If we are going to be there, we must first survive "the day of judgment and destruction of ungodly men." (2 Pet. 3:7, NASB) This comes by way of the great tribulation and Armageddon. This takes place as "the Son of Man" and the elect who are in heaven, and all the angels with them separate us, "as the shepherd separates the sheep from the goats." – Matthew 25:31-46

CHAPTER 11 Correctly Understanding What Happens to the Unevangelized

"The righteous and the unrighteous." The apostle Paul said to a group of Jews who also entertained the hope of a resurrection that "there is going to be a resurrection of both the righteous and the unrighteous." – Ac 24:15, LEB

Fate of the unlearned

The **fate of the unlearned**, also known as the **destiny of the unevangelized**, is an eschatological question about the ultimate destiny of people who have not been exposed to a particular theology or doctrine and thus have no opportunity to embrace it. The question is whether those who never hear of requirements issued through divine revelations will be punished for failure to abide by those requirements.

It is sometimes addressed in combination with the similar question of the fate of the unbeliever. Differing faith traditions have different responses to the question; in Christianity the fate of the unlearned is related to the question of original sin. As some suggest that rigid readings of religious texts require harsh punishment for those who have never heard of that religion, it is sometimes raised as an argument against the existence of God, and is generally accepted to be an extension or subsection of the problem of evil.[198]

The "unrighteous" that Paul spoke of are persons, who are have died prior to Armageddon and have not had an opportunity to hear the good news of the kingdom, meaning they had no opportunity to accept it or reject it. While we have spoken of these ones prior to this chapter, the following comment is first mention here. God knows who would have accepted the good news had they heard and who would have rejected it. Thus, we can extrapolate that the unrighteous, i.e., unevangelized or unlearned that are resurrected will likely be those that God knew would have accepted it.

These unrighteous ones are not being resurrected to face an immediate adverse judgement, to then be sent off to some eternal pit of fire. No, rather, they are entering into a judgment period of a thousand years, where they have an opportunity to act on the Word of God as well as the new book(s) that will be penned. It is at the end of that judgment period when they will be judged, not on their previous life, but on what they did during the millennium. (John 5:29)

---

[198] Fate of the unlearned - Wikipedia, the free encyclopedia, https://en.wikipedia.org/wiki/Fate_of_the_unlearned (accessed March 14, 2016).

CHAPTER 12 Correctly Understanding the Book of Life and Whose Names Are Written in the Book of Life?

Book of Life: (Gr. *biblos tēs zōēs*) In biblical times, cities had a register of names for the citizens living there. (See Ps. 69:28; Isa. 4:3) God, figuratively speaking, has been writing names in the "book of life" "from the foundation of the world." (Rev. 17:8) Jesus Christ talked about Abel as living "from the foundation of the world," this would suggest that we are talking about the world of ransomable humankind after the fall. (Lu 11:48-51) Clearly, Abel was the first person to have his name written in the "book of life." The individuals who have their names written in the "book of Life" do not mean they are predestined to eternal life. This is evident from the fact that they can be 'blotted out' of the "book of life." (Ex 32:32-33; Rev. 3:5) Jesus ransom sacrifice alone gets one written in the "book of life," if they accept the Son of God. However, it is remaining faith to God that keeps them from being 'blotted' out of the "book of life." (Phil. 2:12; Heb. 10:26-27; Jam. 2:14-26) It is only by remaining faithful until the end that one can be retained permanently in the "book of life."–Matthew 214:13; Philippians 4:3; Revelation 20:15.

Bibliography

Akin, Daniel L. *The New American Commentary: 1, 2, 3 John.* Nashville, TN: Broadman & Holman , 2001.

Akin, Daniel L., David P. Nelson, and Jr. Peter R. Schemm. *A Theology for the Church.* Nashville: B & H Publishing, 2007.

Alden, Robert L. *Job, The New American Commentary, vol. 11 .* Nashville: Broadman & Holman Publishers, 2001.

Alleman, H. C., and E. E. Flack. *Old Testament Commentary.* Philadelphia: Fortress Press, 1954.

Anders, Max. *Holman New Testament Commentary: vol. 8, Galatians-Colossians .* Nashville, TN: Broadman & Holman Publishers, 1999.

—. *Holman Old Testament Commentary - Proverbs .* Nashville: B&H Publishing, 2005.

Anders, Max, and Doug McIntosh. *Holman Old Testament Commentary - Deuteronomy (pp. 359-360). .* Nashville: B&H Publishing, 2009.

Anders, Max, and Trent Butler. *Holman Old Testament Commentary: Isaiah.* Nashiville, TN: B&H Publishing, 2002.

Andrews, Edward D. *AN INTRODUCTION TO BIBLE DIFFICULTIES So-Called Errors and Contradictions.* Cambridge: Christian Publishing House, 2011.

—. *An Introduction to Bible Difficulties: So-called Errors and Contradictions.* Cambridge, OH: Christian Publlishing House, 2012.

—. *BIBLE DIFFICULTIES: Debunking the Documentary Hypothesis.* Cambridge: Christian Publishing House, 2011.

—. *BOOKS OF 2 JOHN 3 JOHN and JUDE CPH New Testament Commentary.* Cambridge: Christian Publishing House, 2013.

Archer, Gleason L. *A Survey of Old Testament Introduction.* Chicago: Moody, 1994.

—. *Encyclopedia of Bible Difficulties.* Grand Rapids: Zondervan, 1982.

Arndt, William, Frederick W. Danker, and Walter Bauer. *A Greek-English Lexicon of the New Testament and Other Early Christian Literature. 3rd ed. .* Chicago: University of Chicago Press, 2000.

Arnold, Clinton E. *Zondervan Illustrated Bible Backgrounds Commentary Volume 2: John, Acts. .* Grand Rapids, MI: Zondervan, 2002.

—. *Zondervan Illustrated Bible Backgrounds Commentary Volume 3: Romans to Philemon.* Grand Rapids: Zondervan, 2002.

—. *Zondervan Illustrated Bible Backgrounds Commentary Volume 4: Hebrews to Revelation.* Grand Rapids, MI: Zondervan, 2002.

—. *Zondervan Illustrated Bible Backgrounds Commentary: Matthew, Mark, Luke, vol. 1.* Grand Rapids, MI: Zondervan, 2002.

Balz, Horst, and Gerhard Schneider. *Exegetical Dictionary of the New Testament.* Edinburgh: T & T Clark Ltd, 1978.

Barclay, William. *New Testament Words.* Louisville: Westminster Press, 1974.

Barker, Kenneth L., and Waylon Bailey. *The New American Commentary: vol. 20, Micah, Nahum, Habakkuk, Zephaniah.* Nashville, TN: Broadman & Holman Publishers, 2001.

Bercot, David W. *A Dictionary of Early Christian Beliefs.* Peabody: Hendrickson, 1998.

Blomberg, Craig. *The New American Commentary: Matthew.* Nashville, TN : Broadman & Holman Publishers, 2001.

—. *The New American Commentary: Matthew.* Nashville, TN: Broadman & Holman Publishers, 1992.

Boa, Kenneth, and Kruidenier. *Holman New Testament Commentary: Romans.* Nashville: Broadman & Holman, 2000.

Boles, Kenneth L. *The College Press NIV commentary: Galatians & Ephesians.* Joplin, MO: College Press, 1993.

Borchert, Gerald L. *The New American Commentary: John 1-11 .* Nashville, TN: Broadman & Holman Publishers, 2001.

Borchert, Gerald L. *The New American Commentary vol. 25B, John 12–21.* Nashville: Broadman & Holman Publishers, 2002.

Boyd, Gregory A, and Paul R Eddy. *Across the Spectrum [Secon Edition].* Grand Rapids: Baker Academic, 2002, 2009.

Brand, Chad, Charles Draper, and England Archie. *Holman Illustrated Bible Dictionary: Revised, Updated and Expanded.* Nashville, TN: Holman, 2003.

Bratcher, Robert G., and Howard Hatton. *A Handbook on the Revelation to John.* New York: United Bible Societies, 1993.

Bromiley, Geoffrey W. *The International Standard Bible Encyclopedia (Vol. 1-4)*. Grand Rapids, MI: William B. Eerdmans Publishing Co., 1986.

Bromiley, Geoffrey W., and Gerhard Friedrich. *Theological Dictionary of the New Testament*, ed. Gerhard Kittel, vol. 4. Grand Rapids, MI: Eerdmans, 1964-.

Brotzman, Ellis R. *Old Testament Textual Criticism*. Grand Rapids: Baker Academic, 1994.

Bullinger, Ethelbert William. *Figures of Speech Used in the Bible*. London; New York: E. & J. B. Young & Co., 1898.

Buter, Trent C. *Holman New Testament Commentary: Luke*. Nashville, TN: Broadman & Holman Publishers, 2000.

—. *Holman New Testament Commentary: Luke*. Nashville, TN: Broadman & Holman Publishers, 2000.

Caba, Tedl et al.,. *The Apologetics Study Bible: Real Questions, Straight Answers, Stronger Faith*. Nashville: Holman Bible Publishers, 2007.

Cole, R. Dennis. *THE NEW AMERICAN COMMENTARY: Volume 3b Numbers*. Nashville: Broadman & Holman Publishers, 2000.

Collins, John. *Genesis 1-4: A Linguistic, Literary, and Theological Commentary*. Philipsburg: P&R, 2006.

Cooper, Lamar Eugene. *The New American Commentary, Ezekiel, vol. 17*. Nashville, TN: Broadman & Holman Publishers, 1994.

Cornwall, Judson, and Stelman Smith. *The Exhaustive Dictionary of Bible Names*. Gainsville: Bridge-Logos, 1998.

Davis, Christopher A. *THE COLLEGE PRESS NIV COMMENTARY: Revelation*. Joplin: College Press Publishing Co., 2000.

Davis, John J. *Paradise to Prison: Studies in Genesis*. Salem: Sheffield, 1975.

Easley, Kendell H. *Holman New Testament Commentary, vol. 12, Revelation*. (Nashville, TN: Broadman & Holman Publishers, 1998.

Elliott, Charles. *Delineation Of Roman Catholicism: Drawn From The Authentic And Acknowledged Standards Of the Church Of Rome, Volume II*. New York: George Lane, 1941.

Elwell, Walter A. *Baker Encyclopedia of the Bible*. Grand Rapids: Baker Book House, 1988.

—. *Evangelical Dictionary of Theology (Second Edition)*. Grand Rapids: Baker Academic, 2001.

Elwell, Walter A, and Philip Wesley Comfort. *Tyndale Bible Dictionary.* Wheaton, Ill: Tyndale House Publishers, 2001.

Enns, Paul P. *The Moody Handbook of Theology.* Chicago: Moody Press, 1997.

Erickson, Millard J. "Biblical Inerrancy: the last twenty-five years." *Journal of the Evangelical Theological Society*, 1982: 387-394.

—. *Introducing Christian Doctrine.* Grand Rapids: Baker Book House, 1992.

Erickson, Millard J. *The Concise Dictionary of Christian Theology.* Wheaton: Crossway Books, 2001.

Erickson, Milliard J. *Christian Theology (Third Edition).* Grand Rapids, MI: Baker Academic, 2013.

—. *Christian Theology.* Grand Rapids, MI: Baker Academic, 1998.

Ferguson, Everett. *Baptism in the Early Church: History, Theology, and Liturgy in the First Five Centuries.* Grand Rapids, MI: Eerdmans, 2009.

Friberg, Timothy, Barbara Friberg, and Neva F. Miller. *Analytical Lexicon of the Greek New Testament.* Grand Rapids: Baker Books, 2000.

—. *Analytical Lexicon of the Greek New Testament, Baker's Greek New Testament Library.* Grand Rapids, MI: Baker Books, 2000.

Friedman, Richard Elliot. *Who Wrote The Bible.* San Francisco: Harper Collins, 1997.

Friedman, Richard Elliott. *The Bible With Sources Revealed.* Northampton: Harper Collins, 2005.

Gangel, Kenneth O. *Holman New Testament Commentary: Acts.* Nashville, TN: Broadman & Holman Publishers, 1998.

Gangel, Kenneth O. *Holman New Testament Commentary, vol. 4, John.* Nashville, TN: Broadman & Holman Publishers, 2000.

—. *Holman Old Testament Commentary: Daniel.* Nashville: Broadman & Holman Publishers, 2001.

Garrett, Duane. *Rethinking Genesis: The Sources and Authorship of the First Book of the Pentateuch.* Grand Rapids: Baker Books, 1991.

Geisler, Norman L. *Systematic Theology in One Volume.* Minneapolis, MN: Bethany House, 2011.

Geisler, Norman L., and Thomas Howe. *The Big Book of Bible Difficulties.* Grand Rapids: Baker Books, 1992.

George, Timothy. *The New American Commentary: Galatians* . Nashville, TN: Broadman & Holman Publishers, 2001.

Green, Joel B, Scot McKnight, and Howard Marshall. *Dictionary of Jesus and the Gospels.* Downers Grove, IL: InterVarsity Press, 1992.

Grudem, Wayne. *Making Sense of the Bible: One of Seven Parts from Grudem's Systematic Theology (Making Sense of Series).* Grand Rapids: Zondervan, 2011.

Gruden, Wayne. *Are Miraculous Gifts for Today?: 4 Views (Counterpoints: Bible and Theology).* Grand Rapids: Zondervan, 2011.

Gunkel, Hermann. *The Stories of Genesis.* Translated by John J. Scullion. Edited by William R. Scott. Berkeley: BIBAL, 1994.

Harris, Robert Laird, Gleason Leonard Archer, and Bruce K Waltke. *Theological Wordbook of the Old Testament.* Chicago: Moody Press, 1999, c1980.

Harrison, R. K. *Introduction to the Old Testament.* Massachusetts: Hendrickson, 2004.

Hastings, James, John A Selbie, and John C Lambert. A *Dictionary of Christ and the Gospels.* New York, NY: Charles Scribner's Sons, 1907.

Hill, Jonathan. *Zondervan Handbook to the History of Christianity.* Oxford: Lion, 2006.

Hindson, Ed, and Ergun Caner. *The Popular Encyclopedia of Apologetics: Surveying the Evidence for the Truth of Christianity.* Eugene: Harvest House, 2008.

Hoerth, Alfred. *Archaeology and the Old Testament.* Grand Rapids: Baker, 1998.

Holden, Andrew. *Jehovah's Witnesses: Portrait of a Contemporary Religious Movement.* London: Routledge, 2002.

Holmes, Michael W. *The Apostolic Fathers: Greek Texts and English Translations.* Grand Rapids: Baker Academics, 2007.

House, Paul R., and Eric Mitchell. *Old Testament Survey (2nd Edition).* Nashville, TN: B&H Publishing Group, 2007.

Kaiser Jr., Walter C. *The Old Testament Documents: Are They Reliable & Relevant?* Downer Groves: InterVarsity Press, 2001.

Kass, Leon R. *The Beginning of Wisdom: Reading Genesis.* New York: Free Press, 2003.

Keener, Craig S. *The IVP Bible Background Commentary: New Testament.* Downer Groves, IL: InterVarsity Press, 1993.

Keil, Carl Friedrich, and Franz Delitzsch. *Commentary on the Old Testament.* Peabody, MA: Hendrickson, 1996.

Kenneth, Boa., and Kruidenier. *Holman New Testament Commentary: Romans, Vol. 6.* Nashville, TN: Broadman & Holman, 2000.

Kissling, Paul J. *The College Press NIV commentary: Genesis.* Joplin, MO: College Press Pub. Co., 2004.

Kitchen, K A. *On the Reliability of the Old Testament.* Grand Rapids: Eerdmans, 2003.

—. *The Ancient Orient and the Old Testament.* Chicago: Tyndale Press, 1966.

Kitchen, K. A. *Ancient Orient and Old Testament.* Downers Grove, IL: InterVarsity Press, 1975.

Kittel, Gerhard, Gerhard Friedrich, and Geoffrey William Bromiley. *Theological Dictionary of the New Testament.* Grand Rapids: Eerdmans, 1995, c1985.

Knight, George W. *The Layman's Bible Handbook.* Uhrichsville: Barbour Publishing, 2003.

—. *The Pastoral Epistles: A Commentary on the Greek Text, New International Greek Testament Commentary.* Grand Rapids, MI; Carlisle, England: W.B. Eerdmans; Paternoster Press, 1992.

Koehler, Ludwig. "Problem in the Study in the Language of the Old Testament." *Journal of Semitic Studies*, 1956: 3-24.

Koehler, Ludwig, Walter Baumgartner, M E J Richardson, and Johann Jakob Stamm. *The Hebrew and Aramaic Lexicon of the Old Testament.* Leiden; New York: E. J. Brill, 1999.

Lange, J. P. *Commentary of the Holy Scriptures: Revelation.* New York: Scribner's, 1872.

Language, John Peter. *A Commentary on the Holy Scriptures: Genesis.* Bellingham: Logos Research Systems, 1939, 2008.

Larson, Knute. *Holman New Testament Commentary, vol. 9, I & II Thessalonians, I & II Timothy, Titus, Philemon.* Nashville, TN: Broadman & Holman Publishers, 2000.

Lasor, William Sanford, David Allan Hubbard, and Frederic Williams Bush. *The Message, Form, and Background of the Old Testament: Old Testament Survey (2nd ed.)*. Grand Rapids: Wm. B. Eerdmans, 1996.

Lea, Thomas D. *Holman New Testament Commentary: Vol. 10, Hebrews, James*. Nashville, TN: Broadman & Holman Publishers, 1999.

Lea, Thomas D., and Hayne P. Griffin. *The New American Commentary, vol. 34, 1, 2 Timothy, Titus*. Nashville: Broadman & Holman Publishers, 1992.

Longman III, Tremper. *How to Read Genesis*. Downers Groves, IL: Intervarsity Press, 2005.

Longman, Tremper III, and Raymond B Dillard. *An Introduction to the Old Testament*. Grand Rapids: Zondervan, 2006.

Mangano, Mark. *Esther & Daniel, The College Press NIV Commentary*. Joplin: College Press Publishers, 2001.

Martin, D Michael. *The New American Commentary 33 1, 2 Thessalonians* . Nashville, TN: Broadman & Holman, 2001, c1995 .

Martin, Glen S. *Holman Old Testament Commentary: Numbers*. Nashville: Broadman & Holman Publishers, 2002.

Mathews, K. A. *The New American Commentary vol. 1A, Genesis 1-11:26* . Nashville: Broadman & Holman Publishers, 2001.

Matthews, K. A. *The New American Commentary Vol. 1B, Genesis 11:27-50:26*. Nashville: Broadman and Holman Publishers, 2001.

McMinn, Mark R. *Psychology, Theology, and Spirituality in Christian Counseling (AACC Library)*. Carol Stream, IL: Tyndale House Publishers, 2010.

McReynolds, Paul R. *Word Study: Greek-English*. Carol Stream: Tyndale House Publishers, 1999.

Melick, Richard R. *The New American Commentary: vol. 32, Philippians, Colissians, Philemon*. Nashville, TN : Broadman & Holman Publishers, 2001.

Miller, Stephen R. *THE NEW AMERICAN COMMENTARY Volume 18 Daniel*. Nashville: Broadman & Holman Publishers, 1994.

Mirriam-Webster, Inc. *Mirriam-Webster's Collegiate Dictionary. Eleventh Edition*. Springfield: Mirriam-Webster, Inc., 2003.

Morris, Henry M. *The Genesis Record: A Scientific and Devotional Commentary on the Book of the Beginnings.* Grand Rapids: Baker Books, 2007, 1976.

Morris, Leon. *Tyndale New Testament Commentaries: Revelation.* Grand Rapids: William Eerdmans Publishing Company, 1987.

Mounce, Robert. *Robert Mounce, The New International Commentary of the New Testament: The Book of Revelation.* Grand Rapids: William Eerdmans Publishing Company, 1977.

Mounce, William D. *Mounce's Complete Expository Dictionary of Old & New Testament Words.* Grand Rapids, MI: Zondervan, 2006.

Mounce, William D. *Basics of Biblical Greek Grammar.* Grand Rapids: Zonervan, 2009.

Myers, Allen C. *The Eerdmans Bible Dictionary .* Grand Rapids, Mich: Eerdmans, 1987.

Osborne, Grant R. *BAKER EXEGETICAL COMMENTARY ON THE NEW TESTAMET: REVELATION.* Grand Rapids, MI: Baker Academic, 2002.

Oswalt, John N. *The NIV Application Commentary: Isaiah.* Grand Rapids, MI: Zondervan, 2003.

Polhill, John B. *The New American Commentary 26: Acts.* Nashville: Broadman & Holman Publishers, 2001.

Pratt Jr, Richard L. *Holman New Testament Commentary: I & II Corinthians, vol. 7.* Nashville: Broadman & Holman Publishers, 2000.

Pratt Jr, Richard L. *I & II Corinthians, vol. 7, Holman New Testament Commentary .* Nashville, TN: , 2000: Broadman & Holman Publishers, 2000.

Ramsey, Boniface (Editor). *Manichean Debate (Works of Saint Augustine).* New City Press: Hyde Park, 2006.

Reyburn, William David, and Euan Mc G. Fry. *A Handbook on Genesis (UBS Handbook Series).* New York: United Bible Societies, 1997.

Roberts, Alexander, James Donaldson, and A. Cleveland Coxe. *THE ANTE-NICENE FATHERS 1: The Apostolic Fathers with Justin Martyr and Irenaeus.* Buffalo: The Christian Literature Company, 1885.

Robertson, A.T. *Word Pictures in the New Testament.* Oak Harbor, MI: Logos Research Systems, 1933, 1997.

Robertson, Paul E. "Theology of the Healthy Church." *The Theological Educator: A Journal of Theology and Ministry*, Spring 1998: 45-52.

Rooker, Mark. *Holman Old Testament Commentary: Ezekiel.* Nashville: Broadman & Holman Publishers, 2005.

Schaeffer, Francis A. *Genesis in Space and Time: The Flow of Biblical History.* Downers Groves: Intervarsity Press, 1972.

Smith, Gary. *The New American Commentary: Isaiah 1-39, Vol. 15a.* Nashville, TN: B & H Publishing Group, 2007.

—. *The New American Commentary: Isaiah 40-66, Vol. 15b.* Nashville, TN: B&H Publishing, 2009.

Society, Watchtower Bible & Tract. "Greater Blessings Through the New Covenant." *Watchtower*, 1998: 2/1 17.

Society, Watchtower Bible & Tract. "Investigative Judgment"—A Bible-Based Doctrine?" *Watchtower*, 1997: 7/15 29.

Society, Watchtower Bible & TRact. "Jehovah Unsheathes His Sword!" *Watchtower*, 88: 9/15 19-20.

Society, Watchtower Bible & Tract. "Kingdom—Superior in Every Way." *Watchtower*, 2006: 7/15 6-7.

—. *Mankind's Search for God.* New York: Watchtower Bible & Tract Society, 2006.

—. *New World Translation.* New York: Watchtower Bible & Tract Society, 2013.

—. *Pay Attention to Daniel's Prophesy.* New York: Watchtower Bible & Tract Society, 2006.

Society, Watchtower Bible & Tract. "THE WATCHTOWER Announcing Jehovah's Kingdom." *Watchtower*, 2006: 6-7.

Society, Watchtower Bible & Tract. "THE WATCHTOWER Announcing Jehovah's Kingdom." *Watchtower*, 1894: 1677.

—. *What Does the Bible Really Teach.* New York: Watchtower Bible & Tract Society, 2009.

Speiser, E. A. *Genesis Anchor Bible 1.* Garden City: Doubleday, 1964.

Stein, Robert H. *A Basic Guide to Interpreting the Bible: Playing by the Rules.* Grand Rapids: Baker Books, 1994.

—. *The New American Commentary: Luke.* Nashville, TN: Broadman & Holman , 2001, c1992.

Swanson, James. *A Dictionary of Biblical Languages - Greek.* Washington: Logos Research Systems, 1997.

Swindoll, Charles R., and Roy B. Zuck. *Understanding Christian Theology.* Nashville, TN: Thomas Nelson Publishers, 2003.

Terry, Milton S. *Biblical Hermeneutics: A Treatise on the Interpretation of the Old and New Testaments.* Grand Rapids: Zondervan, 1883.

Thomas, Robert L. *New American Standard Hebrew-Aramaic and Greek Dictionaries: Updated Edition.* Anaheim: Foundation Publications, Inc., 1998, 1981.

—. *Revelation 1-7: An Exegetical Commentary .* Chicago, IL: Moody Publishers, 1992.

—. *Revelation 8-22: An Exegetical Commentary .* Chicago, IL: Moody Publishers, 1995.

Torrey, Reuben A., and Edward D. Andrews. *DIFFICULTIES IN THE BIBLE Alleged Errors and Contradictions: Updated and Expanded Edition.* Cambridge: Christian Publishing House, 2012.

Towns, Elmer L. *Concise Bible Dictrines: Clear, Simple, and Easy-to-Understand Explanations of Bible Doctrines.* Chattanooga: AMG Publishers, 2006.

—. *Theology for Today.* Belmont: Wadsworth Group, 2002.

Vincent, Marvin. *Word Studies in the New Testament.* Bellingham: Logos Research Systems, 2002.

Vine, W E. *Vine's Expository Dictionary of Old and New Testament Words.* Nashville: Thomas Nelson, 1996.

Vine, W. E., Merrill F. Unger, and William White. *Vine's Complete Expository Dictionary of Old and New Testament Words.* Nashville, TN: Thomas Nelson, Inc., 1996.

Walls, David, and Max Anders. *Holman New Testament Commentary: I & II Peter, I, II & III John, Jude.* Nashville: Broadman & Holman Publishers, 1996.

Walton, John H. *Zondervan Illustrated Bible Backgrounds Commentary (Old Testament) Volume 1: Genesis, Exodus, Leviticus, Numbers, Deuteronomy.* Grand Rapids, MI: Zondervan, 2009.

—. *Ancient Near Eastern Thought and the Old Testament.* Grand Rapids: Baker Academic, 2006.

—. *Zondervan Illustrated Bible Backgrounds Commentary (Old Testament) Volume 3: 1 & 2 Kings, 1 & 2 Chronicles, Ezra, Nehemiah, Esthe.* Grand Rapids, MI: Zondervan, 2009.

—. *Zondervan Illustrated Bible Backgrounds Commentary (Old Testament) Volume 5: The Minor Prophets, Job, Psalms, Proverbs, Ecclesiastes, Song of Songs.* Grand Rapids, M: Zondervan, 2009.

Walton, John H. *THE NIV APPLICATION COMMENTARY Genesis.* Grand Rapids: Zondervan, 2001.

Walton, John H., Victor H. Matthews, and Mark W Chavalas. *The IVP Bible Background Commentary: Old Testament.* Downers Grove: IVP Academic, 2000.

Walvoord, John F. *Daniel: The Key to Prophetic Revelation.* Chicago, IL: Moody Publishers, 1971, reprint 1989.

Walvoord, John. *The Revelation of Jesus Christ.* Chicago: Moody Press, 1996.

Watson, Richard. *A Biblical and Theological Dictionary: Explanatory of the History, Manners and Customs of the Jews.* New York: Waugh and T. Mason, 1832.

Weatherly, Jon A. *THE COLLEGE PRESS NIV COMMENTARY: 1 & 2 Thessalonians.* Joplin: College Press Publishing Company, 1996.

Weber, Stuart K. *Holman New Testament Commentary, vol. 1, Matthew.* Nashville, TN: Broadman & Holman Publishers, 2000.

Whiston, William. *The Works of Josephus.* Peabody, MA: Hendrickson, 1987.

Wood, D R W. *New Bible Dictionary (Third Edition).* Downers Grove: InterVarsity Press, 1996.

Wuest, Kenneth S. *Wuest's Word Studies from the Greek New Testament: For the English Reader.* Grand Rapids: Eerdmans, 1997, c1984.

Zodhiates, Spiros. *The Complete Word Study Dictionary: New Testament.* Chattanooga: AMG Publishers, 2000, c1992, c1993.

Zuck, Roy B. *Basic Bible Interpretation: A Prafctical Guide to Discovering Biblical Truth.* Colorado Springs: David C. Cook, 1991.